Counselling Male Sexual O

Counselling Male Sexual Offenders: A Strengths-Focused Approach informs readers how to utilize an easily accessible, integrative, strengths-focused counselling approach with men who pose a sexual risk. There is currently a scarcity of published material which teaches people in a practical way how to conduct one-to-one counselling with different sorts of male sex offenders. However, as the number of internet offenders increases exponentially and more historic abuse cases emerge, understanding and treating the phenomenon of sex offending can play a significant role in preventing sexual crime and reducing harm to victims.

In addition to being a 'how to do' book, in *Counselling Male Sexual Offenders* the author explores at depth the inner processes of counsellors working with this client group. It presents treatment formats and exercises for engaging individuals who deny and minimize harmful sexual behaviour. With illustrative case studies of various types of sex offenders – as well as statements from sex offenders and probation officers themselves – this text provides one of the most comprehensive insights available into the authentic experience of treating this population.

Counselling Male Sexual Offenders will be of value to counsellors and psychotherapists, alongside other practitioners such as psychologists, social workers, probation officers, and support workers.

Andrew Smith is a therapist, trainer, and expert witness, working in private practice. www.andrewhowardsmith.uk

Counselling Male
Sexual Offenders

A Strengths-Focused Approach

Andrew Smith

Routledge
Taylor & Francis Group

LONDON AND NEW YORK

First published 2018
by Routledge
2 Park Square, Milton Park, Abingdon, Oxon OX14 4RN

and by Routledge
711 Third Avenue, New York, NY 10017

Routledge is an imprint of the Taylor & Francis Group, an informa business

© 2018 Andrew Smith

The right of Andrew Smith to be identified as author of this work has been asserted by him in accordance with sections 77 and 78 of the Copyright, Designs and Patents Act 1988.

British Library Cataloguing-in-Publication Data
A catalogue record for this book is available from the British Library

Library of Congress Cataloging-in-Publication Data
A catalog record for this book has been requested

ISBN: 978-1-138-06285-6 (hbk)
ISBN: 978-1-138-06765-3 (pbk)
ISBN: 978-1-315-16141-9 (ebk)

Typeset in Times New Roman
by Apex CoVantage, LLC

MIX
Paper from responsible sources
FSC C013985
www.fsc.org

Printed in the United Kingdom
by Henry Ling Limited

Contents

Acknowledgements

Knowledge and experience is, for me, primarily relational. Hence, I would like to thank all the colleagues I have worked and trained with over the years, especially colleagues at the Lucy Faithfull Foundation, from whom I have learnt so much. I would also like to pass on my appreciation to the movers and shakers at StopSO (Specialist Treatment Organization for the Prevention of Sexual Offending), for developing the means by which increasing numbers of people with sexual offending problems in the UK can access counselling outside of the criminal justice system. Whenever I conduct a training event for StopSO I am always inspired by the counsellors and therapists attending the course. Once again, I would like to express gratitude to the sexual offenders and probation officers who agreed to talk to me when I completed my doctoral research a number of years ago, as their narratives form an important aspect of the book. The clients I see, both as a therapist and a risk assessor, continue to be my primary source of learning. Lastly, I would like to thank my wife, Ruth, for her sagacity, patience, and editorial input.

Introduction

This book is about providing strengths-focused counselling to males convicted, accused or at risk of sexual offending. The approach can be traced back to positive psychology (Seligman, 2002), and various therapeutic variants will be subsequently discussed. My own definition is:

> Ways of working with individuals within their own motivational frame of reference to bring about desired change, which focuses upon resources and strengths, rather than deficits and weaknesses.
>
> (Smith, 2009: 6)

The reader will quickly notice, however, that I am not a purist strengths-focused counsellor in that I borrow from other models. In my view, counselling is more of an art than a science. I simply endeavour to take what seems to be the next best step, whilst always striving for critical, reflective awareness of why I am doing one thing and not another in the here-and-now of the therapeutic moment.

Hence, one intention in writing this book is to delve backstage into the counselling process, in order to convey the challenges, anxieties, and felt experience of working in this emotive area. The focus is not just on 'what to do', as if working with people can ever be reduced to the level of a car manual, but to illustrate the complexities involved in 'doing it'. Counselling, in my experience, rarely conforms to a neat pattern. In reality, counselling is different with each person, with each stage overlapping the next, being revisited and taking differing lengths of time. Invariably, this depends on the motivation of the client, the style of and approach used by the counsellor, and the organizational restraints in which the encounter takes place. The terms 'counsellor' and 'counselling' will mostly be adopted in this book, but 'therapist' and 'therapy' will also be used, as well as practitioner, as the professional terms overlap.

This book will not present a strengths-focused way of working as a panacea that can 'cure' or completely obviate the risk of sexual offending. To do so would be to fall into a seductive fiction: an archetypal narrative of the hero (the therapist) coming to the rescue and providing a fairy tale ending through her own special powers (the favoured counselling method). If only life were that simple! How can one approach ever claim to consistently solve any problem a client may have, when the main ingredient in the therapeutic recipe is the client's motivation and capacity to change, together with the quality of the relational alliance?

I attended a training day on sexual addictions a number of years ago, where the speaker talked about the difficulties most people have in giving up their sexual compulsions. Somebody from the audience asked, 'Why bother giving them therapy then?' The speaker replied, 'Community'. I believe there is significant scope for people who have offended sexually to change. As I explain more fully further on, many individuals who have committed a sexual offence are not addicted to sexually abusing others, in the classic sense of addiction, their offending having occurred within a particular context, with a particular victim, at a particular time in their life. I have attempted to work therapeutically with people with all sorts of human problems, including sexual offending difficulties, and with some of them it would be difficult to evidence obvious change. Most of these individuals still valued coming to see me. Why? I think the answer, to echo the earlier speaker, is related to the human need for community. To experience, for a short time, another human being non-judgementally and non-collusively coming alongside us and witnessing the stories we tell about our lives; this, in itself, is a fundamentally humanizing process. It is not only humanizing for the client, I believe, but ultimately also for the society which supports such a non-utilitarian, relational activity with the damaged, demonized, and difficult.

This is not just a 'how to do it' textbook, although the book does suggest a structure and the content of a typical counselling process that can be used with clients with sexual offending problems. The book presents narratives of counselling encounters with different clients who have offended sexually in different ways. The clients who appear in the fictional case studies have committed various sexual offences including hands-on abuse of male and female children and teenagers, sexual assaults on adults, internet offending, indecent exposure, and voyeurism. All are fictitious but more real than true, as it were, based on composites of therapeutic experiences I have had with individuals over the years and lessons learnt from them that continue to inform my practice. There is evidence that female abuse of children has been on the increase for some years, is particularly under-reported (Davin, 1999) and that the traumatic impact on victims of abuse by women is often minimized. However, the bulk of my experience of working with sexual abusers has been with men, so the case studies I have used all feature males.

I have chosen not to use authentic case studies for two practical reasons. Firstly, I wish to protect the identities of the people with whom I have worked, as they must continue to live in a society where the stigma of sexual offending is perhaps greater than that attached to any other human misdeed. Secondly, I did not ask the permission of individuals to write about our experiences of working together, because I did not have this book in mind at the time.

The book does include qualitative data gathered when I interviewed 15 individuals who had sexually offended and 15 probation officers working in this area, for my doctoral thesis (Smith, 2009). At the time, these respondents gave me permission to cite their views and statements concerning rehabilitation in future publications. I have included these data, as they illustrate many issues and challenges similar to those faced by counsellors and therapists working with this client group.

I now have my own private counselling and training practice but have also worked as a probation officer. For the last 14 years I have worked as an expert witness in the family courts, mainly for the Lucy Faithfull Foundation, a national voluntary organization in the UK, specializing in working with persons who have committed sexual offences and their partners. In addition I train counsellors and therapists for StopSO (Specialist Treatment Organization for the Prevention of Sexual Offending). These experiences all inform the content of the text.

My hope in writing this book is that it will inform counsellors and other practitioners working in this field of what seems to work best, at least for me, with this profoundly stigmatized client group. I also hope to provide some understanding of the people behind the stereotype that sees all sex offenders as unredeemable monsters and beasts, who will inevitably continue to offend.

Counsellors can share this widely held scepticism about the possibility of change. Many are put off by the particular folklore that has developed around sex offenders as universally and pathologically prone to manipulation, together with the erroneous belief that 'once a sex offender, always a sex offender'. In fact, significant numbers of sex offenders are assessed as posing a low risk of reoffending, and the conviction rate for many sex offenders is relatively low (Harris and Hanson, 2004). At the same time, it is important to take into account that the conviction rate, as for many other offences, is significantly lower than the actual prevalence of crimes committed. It should always be remembered that sexual offending is a so-called dark figure crime, with much of it never being detected.

Many clients with sexual offending problems who seek counselling will have committed sexual crime on the internet. For some such individuals, viewing indecent images will develop or consolidate distorted thinking, and make crossing over to hands-on abuse more likely. For many other individuals, who live generally pro-social lives and have little additional dysfunction in their background, the rate of reoffending and crossing over from viewing to hands-on abuse is relatively low (Seto and Eke, 2005). This contradicts the lazy assumption that all people who commit sexual offences are high risk, when many such individuals are able to go on to live law-abiding lives, and form non-abusive sexual relationships with appropriately aged, adult partners.

There are individuals who are at such risk of sexual offending that they should never be allowed to live with children, who remain unmotivated or unable to change, and who will have a life-long attraction to sex with minors or harming adults for sexual gratification. For these individuals, management of their risk through long-term restrictions on their conduct, and police monitoring, is the only viable way of lowering the risk to children and the general public. But even for these persons, counselling – if they are motivated to seek it – can be of use. It can help them to adapt to the limitations put on their life, and manage the reality that they cannot exercise their sexual inclinations because to do so would seriously harm others.

As is explained later on in the book, to provide counselling to this client group is to work with shame, either due to sexual offences committed or because of the socially unacceptable sexual fantasies going on in a client's head. There are numerous debates about whether paedophilic attraction to children is related to nature (Feierman, 1990) or predominantly to nurture (Marshall et al., 1993), but I find that clients experience it as helpful and shame reducing when I offer them a simple metaphoric explanation of human sexual arousal. I hope the following description will also be of benefit to the reader.

I explain to clients that everyone has an arousal pattern that they are either born with and/or develop through significant experiences which can render certain forms erotic: high-heeled shoes; hairy chests; extremes of masculinity or femininity; different body shapes etc. For some, body shapes and looks connected to childhood are eroticized. I ask clients to imagine the arousal template like an artist's paint palette. If one is heterosexual there will only be blue paint on the palette. If one is homosexual there will be green paint. If one is bisexual there will be a mixture of blue and green paint. If one is asexual there might be little or no paint on the palette at all. If one is attracted to pre-pubescent children only, who have not developed secondary adult sexual characteristics such as curves, breasts, pubic hair, and the general look of being an adult, then there might be only purple paint on the palette.

Nevertheless, sexuality is complex. Some individuals might have only 20% of purple paint (paedophilic arousal to children), with the other 80% consisting of blue or green paint (arousal to peer adults). In the general run of things the individual might focus on the 80%, forming sexual relationships with peer-age partners and controlling the latent 20%. However, if a certain child the person finds particularly attractive comes into his orbit and the opportunity presents itself to have sexual contact with that child (either in real life or on the internet), especially if the individual is in a negative or uninhibited mood state, then abuse can be the consequence.

I also point out that from the perspective of evolutionary psychology, many men can be seen to be hard wired to become sexually interested in females as soon as they reach puberty and become potentially fertile (Franklin, 2010). This is likely one reason why so many teenage girls are sexually abused. It probably also explains the market for schoolgirl erotica, why sexualized pop stars look increasingly younger, and why many idealized images of female sexuality (e.g. Marilyn Monroe and the Barbie doll) mimic the look of childlike innocence. Most men realize that teenage girls and younger females on the brink of or entering puberty are legally and psychologically children and are not sufficiently mature to make informed decisions about having sex. However, some men – perhaps immature themselves or lacking moral consideration – give in to latent instincts and take what they want, objectifying the child as a sexual object or holding distorted thinking that the child is somehow a peer. For some clients, counselling can be a means of adjusting their moral compass in those respects.

Chapter 1 in the book explores shame, sexual offending, and the moral panic about sexual abuse, which will inevitably impact on the counsellor as well as the client. How clients experience lifestyle transformation including identity change, facilitated through the therapeutic process, is explored. This chapter will be more heavily loaded with qualitative data than subsequent chapters.

Chapters 2 and 3 deal with the initial stage of counselling, focusing on contracting and goal-setting with clients. Risk management, disclosure, working with other agencies, and the legal and ethical position with regard to confidentiality will be discussed, as well as working within the client's motivational frame of reference. These two chapters feature a fictitious adult male client, 'Marcus', who has been arrested for viewing indecent images of underage, teenage girls on the internet, and who also has a record of general offending and anti-social behaviour.

Having explored issues related to the initial stage of counselling, in Chapters 4, 5, and 6 I examine life story issues, with each chapter presenting a different adult client who has offended as an adolescent. Chapter 4 features 'Thomas', a single man in his 20s who comes for counselling, having previously committed an incest offence as an adolescent against his younger sister. He is now worried about his internet pornography use. This chapter also picks up on the themes of attachment and trauma in the client's background, which can be factors in the development of common entrenched, sometimes subconscious, ways of viewing the world, often found in the narratives of men who sexually abuse. The themes of patriarchy and power are explored in Chapter 5, which presents 'Jay', a male in his 20s who is suspected of perpetrating domestic abuse on his wife within an arranged marriage. He has a background of serious sexual assaults on teenage girls and the attempted rape of a woman. His latest offence is the online grooming of two teenage girls. Chapter 5 also introduces three profiles of sexual offenders I use in order to provide the reader with increased understanding of the different ways sexual crime can occur. It is hoped that these two chapters will provide insight into how sexual offending pathways can emerge in various ways, early in life.

Life story work continues into Chapter 6 with a discussion about providing counselling to individuals who have been victims of sexual abuse, but who then go on to offend themselves. The case study features 'Martin', a 32-year-old client with borderline intellectual difficulties, who has spent his entire adult life in institutional care, and who comes to counselling after disclosing he was sexually abused by his father as part of a sexual abuse ring.

While most counsellors will be familiar with life story work in one way or another, Chapter 7 deals with an area that is more familiar to probation officers and forensic psychologists: offence-focused work. This work involves the counsellor exploring with the client, the circumstances, thoughts, feelings, and actions, before, during, and after the offence: the purpose being to help raise the individual's awareness of risk triggers, so the client can better manage such triggers in the future. This process also assists in developing more understanding of the harm caused to victims by sexual abuse. The case study in this chapter returns to the previous protagonist, Martin, providing insight into how to work with both victim and offending issues with the same client.

Chapter 8 explores psycho-educational means by which a counsellor can raise a client's awareness of offence-related issues, with this approach often proving particularly effective with mandated clients in denial of their offending, who nevertheless need to demonstrate to child protection professionals that their risk can be managed. How to incorporate case studies into counselling practice is also discussed. In this chapter 40-year-old 'Michael' is introduced. He grooms a vulnerable mother, Janet, in order to abuse her daughter.

Chapter 9 discusses ways of encouraging clients to develop victim empathy, revisiting related themes discussed previously. It is posited that an increase in victim empathy is more likely to be in evidence towards the latter stages of the therapeutic process, after the client's self-awareness and appreciation of the perspectives of others has hopefully been increased. The reader is re-familiarized with Michael, who comes to counselling 15 years after committing an offence against Janet's daughter, having served a prison sentence. He says that he is now at the stage to look at the harm caused to his victim.

How to assist clients to manage troublesome sexual fantasies is discussed in Chapter 10. The case study features 'Brian', a 58-year-old businessman convicted of indecent exposure in relation to teenage schoolgirls, who is significantly defended against talking about his sexual fantasies. This chapter also explores the issue of whether or not sexual offenders can be viewed as being sexually addicted.

Finally, Chapter 11 demonstrates how to incorporate the accumulated gains from the counselling process into a final New Life Safety Plan. Ongoing, longer-term therapy is also discussed and how the evolving here-and-now life experiences of the client, or whatever material the client brings to counselling, can be used to consolidate and increase previous therapeutic gains. Two final case studies feature in this chapter. The first involves a retired family man, 'Sandy', who has lived an apparently upstanding life, but has now been convicted of voyeuristic offending against females. Whereas this client has a future within a family setting, as he is considered a low risk, the second case study is about a high-risk paedophilic offender. 'George' has a significant history of predatory sexual offending against boys and will never be allowed to live in a family setting where there are children, but he wants to enhance his life in the community, nevertheless.

The structure of the book presents a general framework for providing counselling to individuals who have sexually offended in different ways and who are at varying risk of doing so again. Hopefully, it will provide ideas and tools for working with this marginalized client group, contributing to the protection of children and adults from sexual crime.

References

Davin, P.A. (1999) 'Secrets revealed: A study of female sex offenders', in P.A. Davin, J.C.R. Hislop and T. Dunbar (eds.) *Female sexual abusers: Three views*. Brandon, VT: Safer Society Press, pp. 1–134.

Feierman, J. (ed.) (1990) *Pedophilia: Biosocial dimensions*. New York: Springer-Verlag.

Franklin, K. (2010) 'Hebephilia: Quintessence of diagnostic pretextuality', *Behavioral Sciences and the Law*, 28 (6): pp. 751–768.

Harris, A.J.R. and Hanson, R.K. (2004) *Sex offender recidivism: A simple question* (User Report 2004–03). Ottawa: Public Safety Canada. Available from: www.static99.org/pdf docs/harrisandhanson2004simpleq.pdf [22 Aug 2016].

Marshall, W.L., Hudson, S.M. and Hodkinson, S. (1993) 'The importance of attachment bonds in the development of juvenile sex offending', in H.E. Barbaree, W.L. Marshall and S.M. Hudson (eds.) *The juvenile sex offender*. New York: Guilford Press, pp. 164–181.

Seligman, M.E.P. (2002) 'Positive psychology, positive prevention and positive therapy', in C.R. Snyder and S.J. Lopez (eds.) *Handbook of positive psychology*. New York: Oxford University Press, pp. 3–12.

Seto, M.C. and Eke, A.W. (2005) 'The criminal histories and later offending of child pornography offenders', *Sexual Abuse: A Journal of Research and Treatment*, 17 (2): pp. 201–210.

Smith, A. (2009) *Sex offenders and the probation officers who supervise them: How relevant are strengths-based approaches?* Doctoral thesis for Cardiff University School of Social Sciences. Available from: http://orca.cf.ac.uk/55909/ [31 May 2017].

Chapter 1

Shame, identity, and lifestyle transitions

Introduction

One of the major challenges of counselling people with sexual offending problems is responding helpfully to the high level of shame they often present with; working with people who have offended sexually is to work with shame. This chapter explores some ideas as to why there is such preoccupation with demonizing sex offenders in contemporary society, at least in the UK, and the emotional toll this can exact from counsellors working with this most marginalized of client groups. The costs, benefits, and drawbacks of facilitating individuals to engage at depth with the details of their offending, and with the harm caused to others, will be examined. How offenders can transform their perception of themselves and their place in the world is discussed, as well as the challenges faced by counsellors and clients alike in trying to realize such profound change.

Sexual offending – the ultimate taboo

Anthropologist Douglas (2002 [1966]) states that 'no other social pressures are potentially so explosive as those which constrain sexual relations' (p. 194). The instinctive reaction of repellence to such abuse is also compounded by the fear and risk issues which preoccupy contemporary society, at least in the UK and USA, particular with regard to sexual risk to children.

Childhood has been a site of moral panic over the last 30 years in the UK. Child rearing has become increasingly separated from marriage. Families have become more fluid, with couples no longer expecting lifelong commitment from each other. The hope that was previously invested in marriage and the family is now focused more on the child (Parton, 2006). Rather than being secondary to that of the marriage or partnership relationship, the parent–child relationship increasingly takes the position of prime importance. Whilst the emotional stock of the child has arguably increased, so too, at the same time, has the level of perceived threat to children. Childhood has always been a site of fear and fantasy but, more recently, anxiety has increased as traditional concepts of the meaning of childhood have become eroded (Buckingham, 2000). Populist media can be seen as increasingly promoting sexualized images of youth: whether displaying adult women dressed as schoolgirls or portraying ever-younger youth role models, such as pop stars, in a sexual light (Jackson and Scott, 1999). At the same time, anxieties about the sexual targeting of children and young people are shifted onto the figure of the paedophile.

Thompson (1990, 1996) illustrated how the mass, and now 24-hour, media dumb down, using stories of sex, crime, and scandals to appeal to the popular market. The media communicate, in simplistic and sensational ways, what is 'good' and what is 'bad'. Within this paradigm, there is no figure, perhaps, who inhabits the space of the 'bad' quite as firmly as the sex offender, becoming perhaps the most salient contemporary 'Folk Devil', a term coined by Cohen (1972) in relation to 'moral panics' about anti-social gangs.

Living in a postmodern world, with few points of absolute reference, can produce a displacement and projection of anxiety and an increased desire for security (Holloway and Jefferson, 1997). Such insecurity can create a need for seemingly clear-cut certainties, providing the basis for projection of uncomfortable and insecure parts of self onto demonized others (Young, 1999). This projection process can be seen powerfully at work with individuals who commit sexual offences; 'I may be many things but at least I'm not like that.'

Over the last 25 years, there has been a mass media–fuelled social and political preoccupation with risk (Ericson and Haggerty, 1997; Horlick-Jones, 2002; Giddens, 1992; Parton et al., 1997): a pervading, defensive, late modern preoccupation with preventing the worst and with protection from harm (Parton and O'Byrne, 2000). Contemporary social conditions, at least in the developed world, have created a society in which individuals are significantly less likely to suffer harm than their ancestors. This has created a greater expectation of protection and safety (including safety from sexual crime) and a concomitantly greater public outcry when this is not delivered (Ferguson, 2004).

The emotional challenge for counsellors when working with sexual offending

Sex offending, especially against children, generates instinctive revulsion and is an area of great social concern. As human beings and members of society, counsellors will be impacted by such issues. My research with probation officers points to some of the challenges of working as a change agent in this emotive area, challenges which are also likely to be experienced by counsellors. Negativity can be pronounced when victims are particularly young.

> *Yeah, some of the victims, they are so vulnerable and young. Obviously some of them are babies and that, you know. . . . Yeah, it is horrible.*
> (Probation Officer 11)

Antipathy can also be pronounced when victims are similar ages to workers' own children.

> *[T]alking about infant children, that, you know, I find that particularly difficult. I used to find it difficult when the ages of the victims were similar to the ages of my children.*
>
> (Probation Officer 16)

Probation Officer 12 also articulated how working with sex offenders made her more aware of potential danger to her own children.

> *I think on a personal level, I'm a 30-year-old mother of two girls. I've got a 10-year-old daughter and a 9-months-old baby. . . . It makes me more aware of the risk to my own children. . . . I read a horrific offence on a child my daughter's age . . . and when I was pregnant I dropped all other sex offender cases because of the nature of the files, and the content of the files. . . . There are certain things you have to do to protect myself. Don't have my children (photographs) all over my desk and stuff.*
>
> (Probation Officer 12)

Most of the probation officers I interviewed expressed strong feelings of antipathy to sex offenders that was not felt about other sorts of criminals.

Denial and lack of victim empathy

As noted later denial and minimization of sexual offending are no longer viewed as straightforward risk factors, with regard to the risk of reoffending (Hanson, 1997), as these states are in many cases, although not all, induced by shame and fear of the consequences of being labelled a sex offender, rather than simply by callousness. However, when individuals were seen to be in denial of their crimes, this produced increased negativity in the probation officers interviewed, with officers being worried about being taken in, or groomed, and losing sight of the person's crimes. Similar issues are likely to pertain to counsellors working with this client group.

> *Well, I mean some of them obviously deny everything, which is really difficult to work with and you've got others who try to manipulate you as well, which I find extremely difficult to work with. So obviously that's what they're used to doing, so they do try to manipulate you as well.*
>
> (Probation Officer 8)

> *I think it's on the detail that people try to wriggle away, or minimize their offending, so I suppose it's about being able to be dispassionate so you know that any revulsion you might feel, you've got to get beyond that.*
>
> (Probation Officer 5)

I just thought he was an absolute disgrace because of how he minimized things.
(Probation Officer 12)

I have to be careful that I'm not being groomed.
(Probation Officer 3)

The challenges clients face in engaging with shameful acts

Practitioners working with people who have sexually offended will soon realize that much of the work involves helping clients to overcome shame which usually presents, in part, as denial and minimization. Among my research sample, many of the men I interviewed about their rehabilitation reported that talking about the details of their offending and the harm caused to victims was the most difficult aspect of treatment.

It's the hardest. It was painful. It was massively painful. . . . Sometimes I would drive home, and I had to sometimes stop in the lay-by for 20 minutes to collect my thoughts.
(Offender 5)

You sit back and think 'Phew!' All of the sudden you go from just being well, ah well, get over it, to being . . . saying to yourself, 'you horrible, evil, vindictive bastard!'
(Offender 9)

Offender 8, an ex-psychiatrist, commented in a similar vein:

I think the self-esteem during the actual therapeutic process was still fairly low; the whole sense of devastation, shame, having – you know, particularly for a person from my background and opportunities and kind of professional standing – having acted in this appalling way, was very difficult.
(Offender 8)

However, many offenders said that this most difficult aspect of treatment (engaging with the details of their sexual offending and the harm caused to victims) was also the most valuable.

I was put into a situation on the programme; what it must have been like being in her (the rape victim's) shoes, and that brought home how much I destroyed somebody's life and family, and also my family and friends as well. I feel that was the biggest step I made. The biggest thing as well to go through; it was enormous and I feel that that helped me so much.
(Offender 3)

Yes, yes, OK, it (the group work programme) goes deep into offending, and one of the things, the sort of, now I don't want to use the word 'turning point,' but it's the only thing that comes to mind, but something that really opened the door, opened my mind, was the victim empathy part of the course. When you sat there, and what effect this has, or you have . . . I had to write a letter (letter of apology to victim taking responsibility for the abuse, that is never sent). . . . That is seriously hard to do. But when you sit in the room, there is a group of eight guys there and two facilitators, and you're talking about the empathy side of it, and I think that really put it home to me, well hang on, the damage I caused here.

(Offender 6)

The goal of developing victim empathy and empathy for others, generally, has been a staple of most treatment programmes (Brown, 2005), even though absence of victim empathy is not cited as a risk factor. Leaving this anomaly aside, a number of criminological theorists have noted that shame can be a barrier to rehabilitation. Roys (1997) found sexual offenders who felt shame tended to have a focus on self rather than on the welfare of others. Hanson (1997) similarly found that encouraging sex offenders to identify with the suffering of victims could provoke a shame reaction, resulting in an increase in self-defensive victim blaming and cognitive distortion. Bumby (2000) also found that shame impedes sex offenders' emotional recognition and perspective taking with regard to victims. Tangney and Dearing (2002) argue that shame is about identity and results in blame shifting whilst guilt is linked to behaviour more liable to 'facilitate feelings of other orientated empathy' (p. 110). Gilbert (1999), however, makes the sobering point that individuals who do not acknowledge that illegal sexual activity is morally wrong, may not be affected by either shame or guilt.

Ahmed et al. (2001), writing with Braithwaite about integrative shaming in relation to drunk driving and bullying, explores how shame management can occur if an institutional space can be made for it. Counselling, I would contend, can become this institutional space, where the therapist can lead the client nonjudgementally to the darkest place (engaging with the harm caused by his sexual offending), supported by unconditional regard within the therapeutic relationship, and then out from this darkest place into social reintegration. Goode (2009) argues that support for paedophiles may make it less likely that such individuals will turn to other paedophiles for succour. This is important as involvement in such underground communities will likely consolidate distorted thinking and permission giving beliefs that it is legitimate to have sex with children.

From a social constructionist perspective (Milner and O'Byrne, 2002), the concepts of shame and guilt can be viewed as socially constructed grand narratives, situated arbitrarily within differing professional discourses. Nevertheless, a therapeutic journey from shame to guilt can provide a framework for therapists to assist clients with sexual offending to develop an increased general appreciation of the suffering caused to others, in addition to increased awareness of risk triggers, all acting as protective factors against further offending.

In my experience, many clients will not be at a motivational stage to publicly admit to sexual offending and, consequently, to engage with the harm done to others. If this is the case, one of the key messages of this book is the importance of the counsellor working with, not against, the motivation of the client. If a client will not go to this darkest place, as it were, then there are still many constructive ways of working with denial and minimization from a strengths-focused perspective, which will be illustrated throughout this book.

Developing a pro-social identity and finding reasons not to offend

Irrespective of whether or not clients are in denial and are able to express empathy for victims, helping them to develop a pro-social identity in place of a shame-saturated one is one way the counsellor can help individuals desist from sexual offending. Individuals desist from offending by constructing a narratives of their lives in which they, the central character, have a 'core self' that is essentially 'good' or has been 'good', or is in the process of becoming 'good' (Maruna, 2001: 88). Within this strengths-based paradigm, it is important to invite clients to believe in such transforming stories, encouraging them to earth emerging new identities in constructive lifestyles. By contrast, concentrating only on their deficits and problems can counterproductively result in loss of self-esteem, which can itself trigger reoffending (Ward and Maruna, 2007).

Farrall's (2002) desistance research describes how individuals who achieve a real change of identity and social purpose, leading to reduction in crime, commonly do so through the accumulation of pro-social rather than deviant social capital (i.e. good family relationships and a satisfying occupation), which they come to fear losing through reoffending. With regard to sexual offending, Ward and Stewart (2003a and b) have developed, in parallel, a strengths-based 'Good Lives' model, whereby it is posited that individuals desist from sexual crime if they can find satisfaction and meaning in pro-social ways. The following are some examples of individuals talking about valued aspects of their lives which they do not want to lose.

Mostly, friends and family, and girlfriend, and thinking about the future. I mean, I've got so much to lose. Yeah, so it's working towards that; something that I don't want taken away from me.

(Offender 2)

My family stuck with me, even though my offences were connected to the family. . . . As I say I got responsibilities, and that is another thing that goes against anybody, stopping them reoffending, being responsible to someone, and thinking, you know, well these people are good. They are looking after you, and don't you dare let them down.

(Offender 1)

Other men talked about a fundamental shift in identity and values taking place through a therapeutic process, which they said was crucial in their rehabilitation. Two individuals describe global shifts in how they now perceive prospective sexual partners.

> *Also women; it has given me a bigger perspective of women as well. I respect them so much more now than I did do. I didn't have that respect in the past . . . relationships breaking down and things like that, I wasn't really bothered, you know. . . . My family, my victim, my friends, the probation officer; it made me realize that life is not about me; it's about other people around me and that's how I felt.*
>
> (Offender 3)

> *I don't see them [young boys] as sexual targets, if you like. I'm happy with the sex life that I have with my partner, with the life beyond sex I have. I don't want to jeopardize that at all. But even if I didn't have that, I think I would have come to a point where I didn't see them as . . . it's kind of like that I'm bisexual and accept that. Like I say I think that Matt Damon [the actor] is nice. I still see people who I think are attractive, but I don't feel I want to go beyond that. It's almost as if you can look, but you can't touch. I don't think I'll ever, ever get rid of the attraction or the thought of it. But I don't want to. The fact that it would be destructive to me, destructive to the person, destructive to my family.*
>
> (Offender 5)

The following individuals reflected remorsefully on being self-orientated in the past in other ways too, apart from their sexual offending.

> *I told him (probation officer) lots of things about the thieving I done, and how I used to treat other people, people who were really good to me, and how I treated them really bad.*
>
> (Offender 1)

> *I was a very selfish person; didn't think about anybody else; didn't want to know about anybody. All I talked about was myself, you know. My family, you know, didn't have contact with my family. I was working 70 hours per week, you know.*
>
> (Offender 3)

> *I had always felt I was concerned about other people, but because I stopped worrying about things that could happen to me, I then became much more focused on 'well, how are you?' I became a much more interested person to other people. . . . I had become a more caring, more attentive, and more relaxed person.*
>
> (Offender 13)

Offender 10, who was 60 years old at the time of interview, had committed two offences of rape, serving a 20-year prison sentence. He described his previous offending history.

> *I've got a serious criminal history; I've been involved in attempted murder, shootings and all that sort of stuff.*
>
> (Offender 10)

The same individual talked of a gradual but fundamental change of values and identity.

> *I'm a Buddhist. I've got a degree [a Social Sciences degree, gained in prison]. But then I started looking into the Arts, and that opened a whole different world to me. I just wasn't interested before . . . I only cared about myself. I failed to really appreciate or realize how selfish I was, or have any aware-ness at all about the people I hurt, her family, her friends. It affects people's lives. Obviously affected mine, and my family, and what they have had to endure. But that [realization] doesn't happen overnight.*
>
> (Offender 10)

Similarly, Offender 5 described fundamental shifts in the way he experiences life and perceives himself.

> *I realize that there's such a lot of things in life that you can do and be involved in that aren't motivated by sex, and I think that for a large part of my life, if I couldn't see any sexual outlet at the end of something . . . I would engineer one . . . because that was the icing on the cake, if you like, I would still do things, but I would feel I missed out on something. Maybe as a natural age-ing process, as I've got older, you don't think so much about sex. . . . My 40th birthday was the first time that I actually felt as if I was older.*
>
> (Offender 5)

Offender 10 proceeded to illustrate the extent to which he had changed as a per-son, by describing a previously close relationship with a woman, which had ended not very long before our interview. He explained how the break-up of relation-ships with women had been a risk trigger for him in the past, leading to serious offending. In this most recent break-up, however, he had been able to sensitively support his partner, with whom he had been having a much-valued relationship, when she chose to return to her husband. According to the offender, the woman had felt guilty when her husband had been seriously injured in an accident, and this is why she had gone back to him. What seems apparent in the following account is the difference between the respondent's current pro-social perspective and his previous anti-social viewpoint.

> *I felt a certain compassion for this guy . . . because of the way I would've reacted years ago . . . 'Fuck him, bollocks to him' . . . you know, all that sort*

of stuff. . . . I would have had some seriously hostile feelings toward that. I would have fucked them up, one way or the other, being spiteful, vindictive, and stuff like that. I wouldn't have seen it from any other person's point of view except my own.

(Offender 10)

Charles Taylor (1989: 47) posits that human beings make sense of their lives through narratives, the stories we tell about ourselves. Taylor suggests that self-identity is formed in terms of how we orientate ourselves to what we perceive as 'the good', the preferred values around which identity is constructed.

Hence, for an unredeemed individual who has committed sexual offences, or is perhaps still doing so, the 'good' could be developing the street-wise guile to deceive a probation officer (or a counsellor) about the true state of their lives. Offender 10 comments upon such a situation.

I think I put this front on, this model parolee, and I led a secret life. I would come in and everything would be fine and rosy, but my life would be in fucking chaos.

(Offender 10)

The same individual talked about coming to view himself differently.

Grendon [a therapeutic prison regime] was the main thing for me. I saw myself differently, my offence differently.

(Offender 10)

Offender 10 described a Gestalt-type moment, in which his sense of the 'good' changed. He now constructs his previous deceptive 'Jack the Lad' type behaviour in terms of the 'bad', in terms of psychopathology, and no longer wants to be associated with this.

But I have empathy with things now, where I didn't before. I'm . . . I knew about this psychopath, and all this . . . but in actual fact it was me, if you don't give a toss about people.

(Offender 10)

The challenges of rebuilding life and identity

Having discussed the therapeutic benefits of profound life and identity change, it is important not to be overly idealistic. The difficulties for a person who has committed a sexual offence in escaping his demonized status to live a constructive, pro-social life should not be underestimated.

Hudson (2005) utilizes the concepts of stigma (Goffman, 1990 [1963]) and 'master status' (Becker, 1997: 32), to explain how the socially constructed stigma surrounding sexual offending can become internalized, forming an intrinsic part of the way sex offenders perceive themselves. Being a sex offender becomes the 'master status' for that individual, the most salient part of identity. Ward (2007: 187) also refers to individuals who have committed sexual offences as perceived 'bearers of risk'. Such labelling was apparent in the way respondents in my study talked about themselves.

> *I am very aware that I am a typecast person, if you like. It does make you more . . . I think it makes you more aware of yourself and you are that typecast.*
>
> (Offender 6)

The following respondents amplified the point.

> *People thinking 'there is a bloody paedophile walking down the street here', and it is that type of thing, because, again, the media coverage is so great today.*
>
> (Offender 6)

> *Yeah, I can't get rid of it. It's no good people keep on saying, 'don't keep beating yourself up about it. You're not a bad person.' That's alright for that moment, and you go away and it all comes bloody back again. I see people in the street, and say, what the hell was wrong with me? I could be like that. Look what you've done, you know. It's like, it's part of your punishment, that's the way I look at it. It will be with me until I die, I suppose.*
>
> (Offender 1)

Apart from identity issues, there are also significant limitations put on the lives of those who have offended sexually, preventing them from being integrated back into the community and living a pro-social life. Like many general offenders, individuals who are convicted of a sexual offence often automatically lose rented accommodation when they go into prison.

> *When I went inside, I lost everything. I lost all my belongings, all my records, my video, my TV, everything. . . . I had to re-buy everything. . . . I'm quite happy where I am now, because it's a quiet area. I don't see anyone. I don't really bother with anyone. . . . I lost everyone . . . mainly friends.*
>
> (Offender 14)

Other individuals move because they fear reprisals in their local area.

> *When I was inside, I made the decision, it was best if I moved from the area, so that if anyone did know me, that have got any sort of grievance against you.*
>
> (Offender 11)

Even when respondents were in their own homes, some feared for their safety.

When something comes on TV, they [the offender's family] are not worried about it. I am, because I think it's going to come back on us all again, you know, like having my name out on a website or whatever. I've spoken to the police about that, because I did tell them if that happened, I am going to have to move away from my wife, because I don't want that address on the website. I said I don't care where I end up, as long as you know where I am, as long as my wife knows where I am. I said I can't put her in the firing line, you know what I mean, because some terrible things can bloody happen.

(Offender 1)

Reading about myself in the paper, it gave me great anxiety, obviously, because people know who I am, and even my address where I was staying was in the paper.

(Offender 12)

It was evident from many of the respondents' accounts that achieving the goal of community integration is particularly difficult if you have committed a sexual offence.

The first few weeks after, when I came out of prison, I was scared, I came up here, and went, had a walk through the shopping centre. I felt scared.

(Offender 6)

There is always that looking over my shoulder, and I could bump into someone. . . . I moved away, and it's a real weight off my shoulders.

(Offender 13)

For some, the price of safety, or feeling safe, appeared to be isolation and a significant loss of quality of life and community ties.

I did have loads of friends out there, and I let everybody down, really. They [relationships] have been shattered really, quite a lot shattered.

(Offender 11)

Of the 15 individuals I interviewed who had committed sexual offences, one had retired and five respondents had not been in employment for many years. The respondents who had not worked for a number of years appeared to be particularly disadvantaged. Offender 12, for instance, stated that he had no thoughts of gaining paid employment, and described the following prohibiting issues.

Alcohol issue, mental health issues; I'm on a lot of medication at the moment which, shall we say, is keeping me on the straight and narrow.

(Offender 12)

Offender 9 seemed similarly disadvantaged.

> *Everything has been offered to me. But I'm on incapacity benefit, so work isn't an option for the foreseeable future. . . . I'm one of those who like my own space, my flat is my own, you know, my family's fine, but I don't have visitors, I don't want visitors.*
>
> (Offender 9)

Even for the less-disadvantaged respondents, finding employment was a significant challenge. Offender 6 was in a semi-skilled technical job before committing his sexual offence.

> *Yes, I lost my job. I was in quite a good job beforehand. I worked as an inspection engineer. I was earning 30 grand a year, and I had been working for them 17 years. I can understand it. They cut and run and I cannot blame them and I don't blame them. I don't hold a grudge.*
>
> (Offender 6)

He described the challenges of trying to find employment once he left prison.

> *I went to several agencies, and all the agencies – if you have got a criminal record . . . So you got to disclose. You know you got a legal duty to disclose, and once you disclose that, you never hear another word from them.*
>
> (Offender 6)

Only one of the respondents had remained in the same employment after being convicted of a sexual offence, and he talked about his experience of dealing with this situation in work.

> *One said it directly to my face, and I appreciated him for that. He was the only person – this was at work – who openly said 'I don't want you to talk to me.' The other one was a female . . . she made snide comments, you know. But I got that stopped at work because obviously there is a discrimination act and that, so they pulled her in and said look, do it again, and if she done it again, right, next time we sack you. . . . You just hid somewhere and cried. I guess that's all you could do.*
>
> (Offender 4)

Various offenders illustrated how the social stigma and disapproval created by committing a sexual offence impacts on close friendships and family relationships.

> *Other people, you've been friends for 20 years, and boom, they don't want to know you because you've done that, because they don't know the details of the case. They just think that you're on that register [Sex Offender Register].*
>
> (Offender 7)

My Mum and Dad are fine, but I got three brothers; it's trying to build up relationships back with them. I'm talking to two of the brothers; one I'm not talking with. . . . Like, you can feel the atmosphere, that there is still something there, do you know what I mean?

(Offender 11)

My sister and brother-in-law have stood by me, thick and thin. But this last offence, even they didn't want to know me. My sister has only really recently started to talk to me on the telephone. It's a question of healing time really.

(Offender 12)

Not all individuals who have committed a sex offence are rejected by their families. However, respondents described how social services' child protection concerns about risk often prevented them from living within the family again, or having unsupervised contact with children, a separation that endures (necessarily so in many cases, due to the risk posed to children) after the criminal sentence has ended.

My wife, it's very up and down because Sharon [pseudonym] has been under a lot of stress and pressure, because a] what I have done and b] she has had a partner for 30 years who she has known and trusted, and I've committed a cardinal sin, haven't I [sexual abuse of own daughter]? The worst sin in their eyes you can possibly admit. We do have some contact but it's very limited.

(Offender 6)

I found out my daughter was hit by a bus. So the first thing you know, she could be in hospital; can I see her there? No you're not allowed. You'll be in prison if you do. And that hits you as a bullet.

(Offender 4)

It is clear from the previous accounts that, having been convicted of a sexual offence, an individual faces severe challenges in maintaining existing relationships. Individuals also face severe challenges in developing a new relationship with a partner, as Offender 10 outlines.

Obviously, it wouldn't be right to get into a relationship, and let it develop actually, and then declare 'well listen love, I'm a convicted rapist.' I didn't want to do that at all, that was in my thinking. So after some time, I had to tell her. It wasn't easy, because you are vulnerable, you might lose her as a friend, or a future partner, whatever, and they could go and tell all sorts of people.

(Offender 10)

Offender 8 described the long-term practical difficulties of existing risk protocols, which stipulate that he should never have a child in the house.

Even if their [the offender's] kids are grown up, they are going to have grandchildren or even if they don't have children at all, they are going to have friends with children. Just imagine this scenario. Me and my partner are sitting one Sunday morning enjoying a cup of coffee, reading the newspapers. The doorbell rings. There's a mutual friend of ours, with a 10-year-old child. 'Oh, can I pop in for a cup of coffee?' 'No you can't.' 'Why, what's going on?' So immediately you've got a situation, whereby people start asking questions.

(Offender 8)

Offender 8 goes on to explain how emphasizing risk, without regard for the welfare of offenders, can counterproductively increase risk.

But just imagine somebody else who is a bit more sticky about their offending. They struggle for five years to find an adult relationship, and they have something like this SOPO [Sexual Offences Prevention Order], and they can't. They can easily, excuse my language, say 'fuck you' and just. . . . But what is so grossly irresponsible in these SOPOs is they fail to recognize that the people they are dealing with are human beings with needs, who need to form healthy, intimate relationships, and they don't realize that by doing this they are seriously impairing one's capacity to be rehabilitated.

(Offender 8)

Conclusion

Some individuals pose such a sexual risk that their lives in the community need to be constrained to protect the public and vulnerable children. However, the development of a 'master status' of 'sex offender', fuelled by the socially alienating processes described in this chapter, would seem inimical to the development of a shame-free, pro-social identity and lifestyle, which are protective factors with regard to reoffending. It is perhaps with the most alienated and isolated individuals, those with indelible self-hatred and/or those faced with severe constraints with respect to social reintegration and developing safe personal relationships, that counsellors can be of particular help. In addition to the more obvious rehabilitative aspect of therapy, counselling can offer human acceptance, communion, and understanding, helping such individuals learn how to self-soothe, thus reducing the risk of hopelessness triggering a sexual offence. The themes discussed in this chapter – the emotiveness of sexual crime, shame, denial and minimization, and identity transformation – will be revisited and expanded upon in the forthcoming chapters, as the process of conducting counselling with this particular client group unfolds.

References

Ahmed, E., Harris, N., Braithwaite, J. and Braithwaite, V. (2001) *Shame management through integration*. Cambridge: Cambridge University Press.

Becker, H.S. (1997) *Outsiders: Studies in the sociology of deviance*. New York: The Free Press. First published 1963.

Brown, S. (2005) *Treating sex offenders: An introduction to sex offender treatment programmes.* Devon: Willan.

Buckingham, D. (2000) *After the death of childhood: Growing up in the age of electronic media.* Cambridge: Polity Press.

Bumby, K.M. (2000) 'Empathy inhibition, intimacy deficits and attachment difficulties in sex offenders', in D.R. Laws, S.M. Hudson and T. Ward (eds.) *Remaking relapse prevention with sex offenders: A sourcebook.* Thousand Oaks, CA: Sage, pp. 143–166.

Cohen, S. (1972) *Folk devils and moral panics.* London: MacGibbon and Kee.

Douglas, M. (2002) *Purity and danger.* London: Routledge. First published in 1966, by Routledge and Kegan Paul.

Ericson, R.V. and Haggerty, K.D. (1997) *Policing the risk society.* Toronto: University of Toronto Press.

Farrall, S. (2002) *Rethinking what works with offenders: Probation, social context and desistance from crime.* Devon: Willan.

Ferguson, H. (2004) *Protecting children in time: Child abuse, child protection and the consequences of modernity.* Basingstoke: Palgrave Macmillan.

Giddens, A. (1992) *The transformation of intimacy: Sexuality, love and eroticism in modern societies.* Cambridge: Polity Press.

Gilbert, P. (1999) 'Shame and humiliation in the treatment of complex cases', in N. Tarrier, A. Wells and G. Haddock (eds.) *Treating complex cases: The cognitive behavioural therapy approach.* Chichester: Wiley-Blackwell, pp. 241–271.

Goffman, E. (1990) *Stigma: Notes on the management of spoiled identity.* Harmondsworth: Penguin. First published 1963.

Goode, S.D. (2009) *Understanding and addressing adult sexual attraction to children: A study of paedophiles in contemporary society.* New York: Routledge.

Hanson, R.K. (1997) 'Invoking sympathy: Assessment and treatment of empathy deficits among sex offenders', in B.K. Schwartz and H.R. Cellini (eds.) *The sex offender: New insights, treatment innovations and legal developments*, Vol. 2. Kingston, NJ: Civic Research Institute, pp. 1.1–1.9.

Holloway, W. and Jefferson, T. (1997) 'The risk society in the age of anxiety: Situating the fear of crime', *British Journal of Sociology*, 48 (2): pp. 255–266.

Horlick-Jones, T. (2002) 'The language and technologies of risk', in N. Gray, J. Laing and L. Noaks (eds.) *Criminal justice, mental health and the politics of risk.* London: Routledge, pp. 149–168.

Hudson, K. (2005) *Offending identities: Sex offenders' perspectives on their treatment and management.* Devon: Willan.

Jackson, S. and Scott, S. (1999) 'Risk anxiety and the social construction of childhood', in D. Lupton (ed.) *Risk and sociocultural theory: New directions and perspectives.* Cambridge: Polity Press, pp. 86–107.

Maruna, S. (2001) *Making good: How ex-convicts reform and rebuild their lives.* Washington, DC: American Psychological Association.

Milner, J. and O'Byrne, P. (2002) *Assessment in social work*, 2nd edition. Basingstoke: Palgrave Macmillan.

Parton, N. (2006) *Safeguarding childhood: Early intervention and surveillance in a late modern society.* Basingstoke and New York: Palgrave Macmillan.

Parton, N. and O' Byrne, P. (2000) *Constructive social work: Towards a new practice.* Basingstoke: Palgrave Macmillan.

Parton, N., Thorpe, D. and Wattam, C. (1997) *Child protection: Risk and the moral order*, 2nd edition. London: Palgrave Macmillan.

Roys, D.T. (1997) 'Empirical and theoretical considerations of empathy in sex offenders', *International Journal of Offender Therapy and Comparative Criminology*, 41 (1): pp. 53–64.

Tangney, J.P. and Dearing, R.L. (2002) *Shame and guilt*. New York: Guilford Press.

Taylor, C. (1989) *Sources of the self: The making of the modern identity*. Cambridge: Cambridge University Press.

Thompson, J.B. (1990) *Ideology and modern culture*. Cambridge: Polity Press.

Thompson, J.B. (1996) *The media and modernity: A social theory of the media*, 2nd edition. Cambridge: Polity Press.

Ward, T. (2007) 'On a clear day you can see forever: Integrating values and skills in sex offender treatment', *Journal of Sexual Aggression*, 13 (3): pp. 187–201.

Ward, T. and Maruna, S. (2007) *Rehabilitation: Beyond the risk paradigm*. London and New York: Routledge.

Ward, T. and Stewart, C.A. (2003a) 'The treatment of sex offenders: Risk management and good lives', *Professional Psychology: Research and Practice*, 34 (4): pp. 353–360.

Ward, T. and Stewart, C. (2003b) 'Good lives and the rehabilitation of sex offenders', in T. Ward, R. Laws and S.M. Hudson (eds.) *Sexual deviance: Issues and controversies*. London: Sage, pp. 21–44.

Young, J. (1999) *The exclusive society: Social exclusion, crime and difference in late modernity*. London: Sage.

Chapter 2

Initial stage of the counselling process

The counselling contract

Introduction

Any definition of the 'initial stage of counselling' is, of course, an arbitrary concept. With each client the process is different, and individual counsellors will conceptualize the therapeutic journey in varying ways. However, for illustrative and practical purposes, in this book the initial stage of counselling is defined as the first conversation with the client at the referral stage (whether by phone or email) and initial sessions following this, when the presenting problem is discussed, the counselling contract presented, and the goals of counselling agreed. This chapter will focus on negotiating the counselling contract. A case study, Marcus, will be introduced, so that theory can be applied to descriptive practice.

Working as a private counsellor

Practising as a private counsellor or therapist in the area of sexual offending presents challenges distinct from those of working for an organization. When employed as a practitioner in a child protection agency, for instance, there are clear organizational policies and procedures to follow. The worker is integrated within a multi-agency setting, working perhaps with social services, the probation service, and the family courts, where it is generally understood by all that information will be shared and the main purpose of any intervention is increased public protection.

As a private counsellor, it is the practitioner alone – albeit with the support of a supervisor – who makes decisions about boundaries, if and when to disclose information if a person is thought to be at risk, and whether or not to work with other agencies. In the UK, there is still no legal duty for a private counsellor or therapist to break client confidentiality and report that a child may be at risk of sexual harm. As stated in the Children's Commissioner's Inquiry Report (2015), this might change in the near future, if government proposals to make it a criminal offence to wilfully neglect those at risk and victims of child sexual abuse become law, and extend to private counsellors and therapists. However, for the moment, striking an ethical balance between maintaining confidentiality as part of the counsellor's professional duty of care to her/his client, and the wider responsibility all professionals have for child protection, enshrined in 'Working Together' (2015), can be approached on a case-to-case basis only (Bond et al., 2015).

Confidentiality

Turnell and Edwards (1999: 35), solution-focused practitioners working in the field of child protection, comment that child protection workers cannot successfully build partnerships with clients by trying to pretend that they are in an equal relationship with service recipients. In a similar vein, Trotter (2006: 67) outlines the importance of practitioners clarifying clear boundaries of 'social control and helping' early on in the relationship with involuntary clients.

These principles can also be applied to counsellors working in this area. Most clients with a sexual offending problem coming to see a counsellor are not involuntary, mandated clients. Nevertheless, some may be, or are under significant pressure from social workers or partners to address their offending behaviour or issues which might result in sexual offending. Power relations in the therapeutic relationship are fundamentally unequal, as the client is asking for help from the counsellor. However, even with mandated clients, it is still possible to develop co-operation, and as MacKinnon and James (1992) point out, with regard to intervening in domestic abuse.

> The exercise of coercion appears to be . . . leverage for change. Unless coercion is used in a considered, skilful fashion, however, it is likely to reinforce the very beliefs that allow an abusive parent to maintain violence.
>
> (MacKinnon and James, 1992: 175–176)

MacKinnon and James are referring to child protection social workers here, but the same points are relevant to counsellors working with clients at risk of sexual offending.

To reiterate, all counsellors need to comply with the confidentiality policy of the agencies that employ them. But independent counsellors and therapists, working with individuals who pose a sexual risk, are reliant on their own informed personal ethics, applied on a case-to-case basis, in the matter of confidentiality boundaries. In reality, private counsellors will place themselves on different points of an ethical spectrum, when it comes to confidentiality and disclosure. Some counsellors will be at one end of the spectrum, believing that the counselling profession is different from other statutory agencies, with responsibility for public protection and risk management. The special value of counselling, they argue, is that it offers a confidential space where clients can say what they like, without thoughts and behaviour being disclosed. This is the position adopted by the German Dunkelfeld project (NOTA, 2014), a preventative counselling service for individuals at risk of sex offending, whose proponents argue that unless confidentiality is guaranteed, individuals at risk of sexual offending will not come forward for help and this, in the end, leads to more children and adults being sexually abused. On the other end of the spectrum are those who argue that blanket confidentiality can never be provided, pointing out that currently counsellors have a legal duty to report, for instance, drug trafficking or an act of terrorism being planned. Moreover, many counsellors could simply not countenance knowing that a child is being or has been sexually abused without reporting this, whilst still working with the perpetrator of the abuse.

First contact with a client

The therapeutic process can be seen to begin from the first time a client contacts the counsellor: usually, in the case of private counsellors, by email or phone. It's always a tricky business to establish confidentiality boundaries at the beginning of the relationship, when there has not been time to communicate consistent unconditional regard. The very act of implying that a client could pose a risk can be interpreted as rejection. However, it is possible to communicate unconditional regard even when delivering a tough message. Regard is not so much a matter of the words used, as the inner attitude and value base of the practitioner. If a worker has a genuinely non-judgemental attitude and deep respect for the essential humanity of each individual, despite the harm he may have caused to others, this will be picked up by the client. Judgementalism will also be discerned, as illustrated by the following individual talking about his probation officer.

> *It was just the sort of abruptness, the way he was speaking to you, you can see in him that he didn't like sex offenders, you know. I mean he was professional with it.*

(Offender 11)

Research by Ambady et al. (2002) into doctor–client relationships demonstrates that, independent of the content of the conversation, the tone of voice of the practitioner – whether it is essentially dominant or supportive – has a profound effect on the goodwill that clients feel for doctors, even on whether or not they will sue doctors for medical errors. Similarly Mehrabian (1972) posits that 93% of our communication is non-verbal. The importance of underlying tone and attitude was commented on by Offender 6 in my research study:

> *You hear somebody's voice on the telephone, and you take a perception by the tone, by the way they use language, of how the person is.*

(Offender 6)

Wherever a private counsellor situates herself or himself on the spectrum with regard to confidentiality issues, when working with individuals who may pose a sexual risk to children or adults, it is necessary to clarify the boundaries of confidentiality as early as possible, so the client can make an informed choice about what to reveal. Most clients are grown-up enough to accept the need for limited confidentiality, and appreciate knowing where the boundaries are from the start.

In my experience it is rare for a client who is being investigated or going through criminal proceedings for a contact sexual offence to seek counselling. In most cases solicitors will forewarn their clients that they may disclose information to a counsellor that could be used in evidence against them, if the counsellor feels he must report an offence, or if the counsellor's notes are subpoenaed. Nevertheless, clients under investigation for contact offences may seek counselling. In such circumstances, clients are likely to be very guarded in what they say, potentially hindering the therapeutic process. My personal view is that to avoid such difficulties and being caught up in legal proceedings, it is usually better for counsellors to say they will offer counselling only when legal proceedings have concluded. It is important to point out, though, that many clients seeking counselling will have been arrested for non-contact internet offences, and are waiting to be charged and sentenced. The majority will plead guilty, as the evidence will be on their computer, and so the counsellor is unlikely to be caught up in evidential issues. Many of my counselling clients, for instance, are in this position.

Whatever the situation, agreeing to a contract at the beginning of counselling is vital. Below is the counselling contract that I use with clients with sexual offending issues. This is not meant to be prescriptive, but instead reflects my personal position at the time of writing this book. A copy of this contract is also available in Appendix 1. I will comment on specific points of the contract in the rest of this section.

Counselling contract

1   My aim, as your counsellor, is to be compassionate, respectful, and genuine, endeavouring to create the therapeutic conditions for you to achieve your goals.
2   If you require, I will confirm to a third party that you have attended counselling, stating duration and what themes have been explored. However, I cannot make any comments regarding risk issues.
3   Minimal notes will be taken to help me remember significant details and for us to reflect on progress. I will keep a copy of these notes in a locked cabinet.
4   No individual or professional body will have access to these notes, unless there is a court order subpoenaing the information in the event of a court case or official investigation.
5   It is regulatory practice that I undertake regular confidential supervision with an accredited supervisor. I may discuss aspects of your case, along with others, without reference to identifying details.

6   As a member of BACP (British Association for Counselling and Psychotherapy), I adhere to their Ethical Framework for Good Practice and am aware of my primary responsibility for maintaining confidentiality between myself and the client. However, this general rule of confidentiality can be broken in the following exceptional circumstances:

a   If you disclose information about a criminal offence or conduct that puts others or yourself at serious risk of harm. An attempt would be made to talk to you before disclosure if this does not further compromise anybody's personal safety.

b   If you are involved with social services, probation, the police or mental health professionals, I may ask your permission to liaise with them.

7   Before the start of the first session, two copies of this agreement need to be signed, to stipulate that this policy has been read and understood. Both parties will keep a copy.

Counsellor ....   Date ....

Client ....   Date ....

When I speak to a client for the first time, usually over the phone, if I sense the client may have been involved in abusive activity or may be about to unwittingly reveal something that might compromise him, I say, as early as possible, something like the following:

Before we discuss your situation in detail, I need to tell you something that I tell all the people I work with. If you say anything about an unreported crime having been committed, or I think that a child or other person is at serious risk of harm, I may have to report this. Are you OK with this before we proceed?

Most clients respond affirmatively and continue telling me about their problem. Often it has taken a lot of courage to contact me about a sexual offending issue, and they can be in a heightened state of anxiety. Therefore, they may not have internalized what I have said to them. For this reason, I ask if I can email or post a copy of the counselling contract, making sure to check whether the client is concerned about such a sensitive document being sent by email or through the post. I then ask the client to sign the contract at the start of the first session, making sure he understands the terms. I, personally, will not counsel a client unless he agrees to work to my counselling contact, as these are the terms with which I am comfortable when providing counselling to this particular client group. Other counsellors may take a different view, and be prepared to negotiate a different contract with each client.

Risk assessment issues

The counselling contract states:

2   If you require, I will confirm to a third party that you have attended counselling, stating duration and what themes have been explored. However, I cannot make any comments regarding risk issues.

I clarify from the beginning with clients that I will not provide a risk assessment report as a result of the counselling undertaken with me. Clients sometimes seek counselling to obtain a low risk assessment, rendering counselling a gateway for increased contact with children. This potentially puts children and others at risk. Hence, I clarify that any risk assessment should be completed by a specialist risk assessor, so that any rehabilitative gains can be independently assessed, rather than the counsellor assessing the fruits of her own labour. There is also a danger of the counsellor being inclined to provide an overly positive risk assessment, either overestimating the impact of the counselling or because the counsellor has come to value and have hope for the client. These are necessary therapeutic conditions, but can easily influence the counsellor to underestimate risk, despite best intentions to remain objective. There has been much research on 'confirmation bias' and risk, showing how we tend to select information to confirm our own prejudices (Gardner, 2009), including underestimating the risk posed by people to whom we are well disposed.

Providing a risk assessment might also mean that the counsellor becomes embroiled in family court proceedings, and may be asked to attend court as an expert witness. This can be a potentially bruising experience for the counsellor, if cross-examined by informed and adversarial barristers. More significant than a bruised ego is counsellors laying themselves open to unprofessional and potentially dangerous practice, if they do not have specialist experience of assessing the risk of sexual offending within a family and community context.

As a private counsellor, I am willing to provide a letter to a court, however, or other professional body, confirming the number of sessions a client has attended, explaining the general therapeutic issues covered, and commenting on whether there has been any general progress, although this falls short of making any statement about risk. An example letter can be found in Appendix 2.

As noted earlier, many clients coming for counselling with regard to sexual offending issues are men who have been arrested for internet offences. The Sentencing Council Guidelines (2013) for this offence state that mitigation is awarded if the person seeks rehabilitative help of his own accord. Some counsellors take exception to such self-interest being a significant motivation for attending counselling rather than, for instance, remorse. As a strengths-focused counsellor I am comfortable with working with whatever motivation the client brings to counselling. I take the view that most people who seek counselling want to promote their own self-interest, whether they desire to remain in a relationship, remain in employment, or remain happy for more of the time. Few clients in my experience choose to undergo counselling because they want to become more sensitive and loving human beings. However, if they do solve their problems and become more content and happy, or just more able to cope with day-to-day difficulties, this usually means that they cause less damage to themselves and to those around them. Moreover, clients usually bring a mix of motivations into the counselling room, regardless of the story clients may tell the counsellor and/or themselves about coming for help, and motivations shift and change throughout the therapeutic process – and, in actual fact, from moment to moment. As discussed in the introduction, many hold the mistaken view that if a person commits one sexual offence, that person will inevitably go on to commit further sexual offences. However, when people attend counselling in a crisis – and being arrested for a sexual offence or being worried about committing a sexual offence is certainly a crisis in most cases – the severe disruption can precipitate strong motivation for change. As one probation officer put it:

> *Personally speaking, I see more change with sex offenders than people who offend generally, much more than people who offend, of a physically violent nature. . . . I think people who have been caught committing sex offences are generally more compliant and more motivated to work and co-operate and change.*

(Probation Officer 6)

With regard to risk and sexual offending, counsellors do have to consider the level of risk a client might pose, for a number of reasons. I would suggest that what actually occurs is that counsellors start assessing risk from the first contact with a client, even if they would not call it risk assessment: calculating whether they are comfortable working with a client and whether they have the experience and competency to do so, or whether they need to refer the person to another professional or agency. Counsellors also make ongoing assessments of risk and need (whether explicitly or implicitly) in order to decide on the formulation of counselling: what to do, when and why. For instance, I am constantly collaboratively assessing with clients how the counselling is progressing and checking if what is happening in sessions is working for them, and if we need to carry on doing the same thing or need to try something different.

The counselling contract states (in Appendix 1):

6   As a member of BACP (British Association for Counselling and Psychotherapy), I adhere to their Ethical Framework for Good Practice and am aware of my primary responsibility for maintaining confidentiality between myself

and the client. However, this general rule of confidentiality can be broken in the following exceptional circumstances:

a   If you disclose information about a criminal offence or conduct that puts others or yourself at serious risk of harm. An attempt would be made to talk to you before disclosure if this does not further compromise any-body's personal safety.

Counsellors sometimes find themselves in the position of having to make an assessment about whether the person they are working with may pose a risk to others, as more information and knowledge of the client is gleaned through the developing therapeutic process. The following risk factor check list can help a therapist reflect, ideally with the input of a supervisor who has knowledge of sexual offending issues, upon whether the risk to a child is serious enough to war-rant disclosure to social services, the police, or some other agency (a copy can also be found in Appendix 3).

Risk factor check sheet (factors in bold should be especially considered)

- **Client has court appearances for sexual offences.**
- **Client has been accused of sexual offending more than once.**
- **Client has sexually offended against unrelated victim (did not know the victim 24 hours before the offence).**
- **Client has committed contact sexual offence against a pre-pubescent boy.**
- Client has an exclusive sexual preference for children.
- Client has a pattern of meeting social, emotional, and esteem needs predominantly through children rather than adults.
- Client is currently abnormally sexually preoccupied.
- Client has a strong sense of sexual entitlement.
- Client has a history of violence (including domestic abuse).
- Client believes that children enjoy sex and are sexually seductive.
- Client has a current pattern of grievance thinking.
- Client has a pattern of callousness.
- Client has a current pattern of lifestyle impulsiveness.
- Client has history of chaotic/shallow attachments.
- Client has dropped out of a prison or probation group work programme.
- Client has poor cognitive problem solving.
- Client has current substance misuse problems.

- **Client is in contact with children of the same age and sex that he has shown deviant interest in.**
- **Client is an intimidating presence in the home where the child at risk resides.**
- **The child at risk's parent/s does not recognize the risk posed by the client.**

The risk factor check list describes recognized risks that can be found in most sexual offending risk assessment tools (Craig et al., 2009). Assessing sexual risk is a complex business; 'risk is a hazard that is incompletely understood and whose occurrence can be forecast only with uncertainty' (Hart et al., 2003: 207). Ultimately, clinical experience and judgement are needed with regard to how much weight to put on each risk factor and how to contextualize risk. However, the check list provides counsellors with an idea about what risks to look out for. The factors in bold are particularly pertinent in deciding whether to disclose to the authorities or not, as they tend to denote high risk. If one does decide to disclose, following are some good practice guidelines, in terms of defensible decision making (a copy can be found in Appendix 4).

Guidelines: disclosing

- Decision was made on basis of confidentiality policy (better if written and signed)
- Client revealed criminal behaviour, or breaking child protection agreements
- Client began to have more intimate contact with children similar to the ages and sex he was aroused to
- Risk suddenly increased (see risk factors)
- Disclosure was discussed with supervisor
- Disclosure was discussed with client, and you tried to get him to report abuse himself, first (consider consequences of this in terms of risk of harm to self)

Following are good practice guidelines for when no disclosure about risk is made (a copy can be found in Appendix 5).

Guidelines: not disclosing

- Decision was made on basis of confidentiality policy (better if written and signed)
- Client did not reveal criminal behaviour, or breaking child protection agreements
- No indications emerged that client began to have more intimate contact with children similar to the ages and sex he was aroused to
- No evidence of increased risk (see risk factors)
- Decision not to disclose was discussed with supervisor

One note of additional caution, in relation to disclosure, is the practice of shifting or opting out of responsibility by referring the client to another counsellor, or ceasing the counselling and justifying this choice with the rationale that the client has such complex needs that he requires more specialist help. This may well be the case – but this passes on to the next counsellor the responsibility for disclosure and/or leaves a child or children at continued risk of abuse.

Working with other professionals

The counselling contract (available in Appendix 1) states:

6b   If you are involved with social services, probation, the police or mental health professionals, I may ask your permission to liaise with them.

Each counsellor has her or his own boundaries and comfort zone. As noted earlier, for many the essential value of counselling is that it sits outside of the multi-agency network, which is often focused on the risk the client may pose to others, rather than on the welfare of the client *per se*. I believe it is possible for a counsellor to maintain a client-centred approach and to liaise with other professionals. This is done by the counsellor clearly asserting to other workers and agencies that he will not disclose the details of what takes place in the counselling sessions but will provide a brief outline of therapeutic issues to be covered, and will disclose if he thinks a client poses a significant risk to a child or another adult, as stipulated in the counselling contract agreed with the client. In my experience, clients involved in the criminal justice or child protection systems are often keen for me to send their probation officer or social worker a brief outline of the counselling they are undertaking, as this indicates intent to change. Whether this is so or not, the bottom line for me is that I will not work with a client within a child protection context, unless he gives permission for me to contact any criminal justice or child protection professionals involved, such as the police, probation service or social services. I may decide there is no reason to do this, but I want to have that option. There are a number of reasons for this:

- To obtain other professionals' views of any risk or health and safety issues the counsellor should be aware of (e.g. for female counsellors, if there have been sexual assaults on women)
- To find out if there are any child protection agreements or statutory orders, so the counsellor will not be inadvertently encouraging or colluding with a client to behave in ways which might breach such agreements and orders (e.g. discussing how a client can rebuild a relationship with a child he is not allowed to see)
- To make splitting less likely (the client saying to other professionals, for instance, 'my counsellor doesn't think I'm a risk to children'; 'I'm doing work with my counsellor, who understands me, so I don't have to do work with you')

When a private counsellor or therapist informs a professional (such as a social worker or probation officer) that the client is receiving help, the reaction, in my experience, can be unpredictable. Some professionals may welcome the input. Others may view private counsellors working with people who have committed sexual offending as naïve and liable to be 'taken in' or manipulated by the client into believing that they have not offended or that they pose no risk. Often such attitudes can be based on unhelpful stereotypical views: all 'sex offenders' are highly manipulative and will inevitably offend, and all counsellors are wishy-washy, liberal do-gooders. If, after discussion, I think such prejudice is the basis for the objection, then I will continue the counselling regardless, as long as it does not seriously compromise the client's relationship with the statutory professional to the client's detriment, or increase risk to others. This can be decided only through negotiation with the client on a case-to-case basis.

Providing counselling to a client at risk of sexually abusing others is not always a straightforwardly benign activity, despite the best intentions of the counsellor. Clients can sometimes, consciously or unconsciously, use therapy as a sop to facilitate continued offending. Distorted thinking can run along the following lines: 'At least I'm trying to get help with my problems.' This can appease the conscience of the individual in the same way that working hard all week or doing some sort of good deed can seem like a justification for binge drinking at the weekend to a person with an alcohol problem. Hence, counsellors need to use clinical judgement, and reflect with their supervisors, to decide whether counselling is proving counterproductive and the best way to address this issue with the client. In some cases, cessation of counselling may be the most appropriate path.

If the client is subject to probation supervision and is engaged in a sex offender group work programme, the probation officer might consider that additional therapeutic input may undermine the effectiveness of the group work. Splitting can occur and if the client is resisting engaging fully with the group work programme, and using counselling as the justification, the probation officer may have a valid point. Group work programmes run by the probation service tend to be lengthy and in-depth, with members being challenged about their offending behaviour through observing the anti- and pro-social attitudes of individuals who have sexually offended. This can be a powerfully rehabilitative group experience, which one-to-one counselling cannot offer. Clients can find such group work challenging and may want to use one-to-one counselling as a way of opting out. Having pointed out these caveats about the danger of 'splitting', the latest research into group work treatment programmes run in prisons in England and Wales indicates a small increase in reoffending rates for those attending these programmes when compared with sex offenders in prison who did not receive this treatment (UK Ministry of Justice, 2017). The reasons for this are not clear, but it is speculated that group programmes may normalize offending behaviour and that the group work programmes do not offer individualized treatment. One-to-one counselling avoids any group normalizing effect, and does offer individualized treatment.

Where to see clients

When I work with individuals who have committed sexual offences, or are at risk of doing so, I do not see them at home. I know my neighbours, especially those with children, would be concerned about this. However, it does depend on where the counsellor lives, with regard to this particular issue. Some home situations may be safe and appropriate, others not – though I would advise that counsellors not use their home to see a client if the sexual offending involves stalking or harassment, or if the person has committed a sexual offence against an adult the same gender as the counsellor, and the counsellor will be alone in the house with the client. This last caution obviously also applies to any isolated counselling venue.

I would advise that the counselling premises are not used by children whilst the counselling is taking place. It is unlikely that a client would commit a sexual offence on his way to and from the therapy room, but most parents would not want their children attending a venue at the same time that, unbeknownst to them, people who pose a risk to children are turning up for counselling. On one hand, I believe this concern should be respected. On the other hand, this issue should be set in context. Sex offenders go to GP surgeries, dentists and other social settings all the time, where children are present.

Case study: Marcus

Marcus is 39. He went to private school but left with few qualifications because he could 'never get on with the teachers'. His parents are both retired lawyers who, he feels, are disappointed in him. His father has alcohol problems and has been violent to his mother. He presents as good looking for his age – obviously in the habit of working out – and is intelligent and witty. When he was 19, he was sentenced to a two-year community order for having sex with a 14-year-old girl. Apart from this, he has two convictions for being drunk and disorderly, three driving convictions, and an ABH (actual bodily harm) conviction, against an ex-partner. In the past he had successful businesses, but lost them, getting into large amounts of debt, having spent his money on flash cars, drink and cocaine. He jokes that he 'wasted the rest.' He says his substance misuse is now under control and he is making a decent living working for a firm, selling expensive sports cars. Marcus says he has had many sexual partners and relationships and used to go regularly to Thailand with a mate and have sex with prostitutes. He married in his 20s, having first met his wife when she was 14 and he was 18. The marriage ended bitterly when she accused him of domestic violence, which he denies. He no longer has any contact with his daughter from this relationship, saying that his ex-wife turned his daughter against him. He wants counselling because the police found indecent images of children on his computer, mostly teenage girls. He will plead guilty. His current partner, Jill, told him he had to get help (while he is waiting for the police to investigate the computer and charge him) for there to be any chance of the relationship continuing, although she doesn't think he would ever harm her daughters. His partner has two teenage daughters, aged 13 and 15, with whom, he says, he gets on very well. Marcus maintains that he has never viewed his stepdaughters sexually and that, in his case, there is a big gap between fantasy and reality. Social services have required him to move out of the family home, and he is now back living with his parents. He is allowed contact with his partner's daughters only once a fortnight, at a contact centre. They express a strong wish to see him. This arrangement will be in place until it is known whether the police will press charges or not. Marcus has been told that this may take anything from three to 12 months. At the start of the counselling the counsellor is unaware of these child protection stipulations.

Setting boundaries and establishing rapport

Marcus talked rapidly on the phone, with brittle self-confidence. He fairly straightforwardly outlined the basics of his predicament in the initial phone call to the counsellor and then the above details about his life over the subsequent two face-to-face sessions. When he first contacted by phone, the counsellor sensed his underlying anxiety; she knew that for most people it is a brave step to tell a stranger that you need help with a sexual offending problem. From false jollity, Marcus suddenly seemed on the verge of tears, saying 'I don't know what I would do if I couldn't live with Jill and the girls again.' The counsellor was aware of the high suicide rate amongst internet offenders. Many have never committed a previous crime (although this was not so in Marcus's case). Many have responsible jobs and families. The prospect of losing all this, the stigma of being labelled a 'sex offender', and the fear of going to prison is too threatening and distressing for some and can result in suicide.

The counsellor felt her own anxiety levels rise when Marcus added, 'It would be the end of me if Jill and the girls left me.' But the counsellor felt mixed. Although she understood the risk of suicide, she was still irritated with Marcus. She felt he was trying to emotionally manipulate her, and possibly Jill and his stepdaughters too, by constructing himself as the victim of events. The counsellor took some deep breaths, endeavouring to accept her anxiety and conflicted feelings, whilst trying not to give them undue importance. She reminded herself that, for her, anxiety was an old friend who no longer called around so often but, when it did visit, often had something useful to tell her. Now anxiety was telling her that she should address the risk of suicide in a strengths-focused way.

The counsellor empathized with Marcus – saying that it sounded as if he had been through a really rough time – and asked how he had got through it so far. Marcus said he had been telling himself that everything is going to be alright and was managing to keep busy. He then told her, in a dismissive tone, not to worry as he was too much of a coward to 'top' himself. The counsellor felt that Marcus had read her thoughts, and she registered feeling undermined by this.

If the discussion had gone differently and the counsellor had had more serious concerns about suicide, she might have had a fuller discussion with him. As it was, she merely affirmed Marcus for making the efforts and made a mental note to explore more thoroughly with him how these strategies were working if and when they next met. She then tried to help him identify any further overlooked resources he could use to cope with his situation.

The counsellor then told Marcus that she wanted to say a bit about confidentiality, before they went any further. She informed him that she sends all her clients a counselling contract (Appendix 1) to sign before meeting up in person for the first session. Before this, she explained to Marcus that he needed to be aware that anything he said to her in this first conversation was confidential, apart from if she thought a child or an adult was at serious risk of harm or a significant new crime had been committed. She might then feel she would have to report this to the authorities. She inquired what Marcus thought about this. He replied 'no problem, fine', before resuming his narrative. The counsellor was not convinced he had given much thought to what she had said, but she had made her position clear, and she decided that to labour the point at this early stage would undermine rapport.

They proceeded to arrange the first appointment. The counsellor asked if it was OK for her to send the counselling contract by email or through the post, so

Marcus could sign it at the beginning of the first session. Marcus said he would prefer the contract to be emailed, in case somebody else opened the letter.

At the start of the first session, Marcus said that he had forgotten to bring the counselling contract along with him. The counsellor had anticipated this and, as with all first sessions with clients, she had brought spare copies of the contract. She handed Marcus a copy to read through. Once she had checked that he understood and agreed to the terms, they signed and dated it, with each retaining a copy.

At the end of the first session, Marcus reiterated how much he missed Jill and his stepdaughters. He casually mentioned that he had suggested, when having a meal with Jill and his stepdaughters the previous evening, that 'after this is all over' maybe they could move to another part of the country to make a fresh start of things. By the time Marcus had said this, he had already explained that he had been arrested for viewing abusive child images (mainly of teenage girls) and how he had been 'in trouble' in the past, when he was 'young and immature'. He added that he had nothing to hide, and was 'an open book'.

The counsellor had concerns, as many factors in Marcus's life corresponded to the risk factor check list (Appendix 3). She suspected, given that Marcus's stepdaughters were a similar age to many of the teenage girls in the child abuse images, which he admitted to looking at, that social services may well have put some restrictions around his contact with his stepdaughters. The counsellor decided she needed to check this out. At the end of the first session she reminded Marcus that, as per the contract, she would be contacting his arresting officer and the social worker to inform them that counselling was occurring, and to obtain their view of circumstances. Marcus looked a bit sheepish, but said that was fine, as he'd 'got nothing to hide'.

Immediately after the first session, the counsellor contacted Marcus's arresting officer and the case social worker. She always felt uncomfortable about doing this, as the reception to such a contact can prove unpredictable. Reactions might include:

- Disinterest
- Suspicion
- A flat refusal to discuss the case
- Openness, and positivity that somebody is conducting work with the client.

Depending on the response, the counsellor sometimes experienced herself as feeling stupid, humiliated, or conversely affirmed and respected. She reminded herself that being attached to such feelings and thoughts is to give way too much significance to an arbitrary storyline about her, based on unreliable perceptions of what others might be thinking. She reflected that it is always tempting to not make the calls, telling herself that private counsellors do not have to bother with such things. She ended up making the call.

She started with the arresting police officer, saying something like:

This is a courtesy call to say I'm a counsellor who has started working with Marcus Bellingham. He has given me his permission to contact you. I was just wondering if there are any safeguarding issues or health and safety concerns I should be aware of.

The police officer in this instance did not seem particularly interested, but said he would make a note that Marcus was receiving counselling and thanked her for contacting him.

Next she phoned the social worker and said something similar, also inquiring if there were any contact restrictions between Marcus and his stepdaughters of which she should be aware. The social worker said she would be happy to provide this information, but that she would need to get Marcus to confirm that he had no objection to her disclosing these data. In the counsellor's experience, some social workers are happy to reveal this sort of information without seeking the client's permission, on the basis that child protection trumps personal privacy. Others are not. The counsellor reminded herself that inconsistency is part of life. She suggested to the social worker that in addition to her contacting Marcus, she would send the social worker a copy of the counselling contract. The social worker seemed suitably impressed and said she would be in touch.

The counsellor felt comforted by the tenor of the phone call; she was not being neurotically risk averse or simply covering her own back. Then the main anxiety raised its head. Marcus had told her about having dinner with his partner and stepdaughters a few nights previously. What would she do if it turned out that Marcus was not allowed to see his stepdaughters, outside of the contact centre? It transpired that this, indeed, was the case.

The social worker informed her that Marcus was allowed to have contact with his stepdaughters at a contact centre only because she and her line manager deemed that the mother, Jill – although feeling very angry and betrayed by Marcus's behaviour on the internet – did not think he posed a risk to her daughters. Therefore, Jill was not considered currently able to protect her daughters from any sexual risk posed by Marcus.

The first thing the counsellor did was to talk the situation over with her supervisor. They looked at the list of risk factors (Appendix 3) and a number of factors seemed to apply:

- Client has court appearances for sexual offences.
- Client has been accused of sexual offending more than once.
- Client has a history of violence (including domestic abuse).
- Client has a history of chaotic/shallow attachments.
- Client is in contact with children of the same age and sex that he has shown deviant interest in.
- The parent of the child at risk does not recognize risk posed by client.

The counsellor and supervisor were particularly concerned about the last two contextual risk factors. Consequently, they decided it would be best for her to have a discussion with Marcus, to give him the opportunity to inform social services, himself, that he had breached the child protection agreement. The supervisor and counsellor agreed that it would be best if this discussion took place over the phone. Their thinking was that if the counsellor were to tell Marcus that she would have to report the breach if he did not report it himself, he might be very angry. He had a history of violence. He had a lot to lose. The counsellor could not easily call for help from the therapy room she used. The phone conversation with Marcus proceeded as follows:

Counsellor:　Marcus, I'm afraid that I've got a difficult issue to discuss with you. You mentioned in the last session that you had dinner with your partner and stepdaughters. I understand from the social worker that this is against the child protection agreement.

Marcus:　Oh, it was only a one-off. Nothing could have happened with Jill being there, for goodness sake!

The counsellor felt somewhat conflicted. Marcus had clearly broken the child protection agreement, but part of her thought that social services were overreacting. She could understand them insisting that Marcus did not live with the girls as, if he did, it would be inevitable that there would be times when he would be alone with them. However, his stepdaughters had never accused him of any mistreatment, although victims of sexual abuse often remain silent. Wasn't Marcus right? Even if his partner did not believe he would harm the girls, it would be very unlikely that anything would happen with them all sitting around a table, eating a meal together. It crossed her mind that if she had not contacted the social worker, then social services would have not known anything about the breach. She would not have to be going through this difficult conversation now and perhaps risk losing a chance to help a client, and much needed income, if Marcus were to feel betrayed or lose faith in her, and put an end to the counselling.

The counsellor was sufficiently self-aware to know that even if there was some credibility to these arguments, she also had a bias against rules and authority, stemming from having authoritative parents. This bias could impact on her judgement in this situation, especially when she considered that a risk-averse bureaucracy was probably using a sledge hammer to crack a nut. She reminded herself that her stable value base was such that she was not comfortable working with a client, possibly posing a serious sexual risk to teenage girls, without liaising with other child protection professionals. Ultimately, not to ensure the breach was reported would be to collude with her client. If Marcus had breached this boundary so soon after being arrested, what other boundaries might he go on to breach?

Counsellor:　Marcus, I understand your point. But I can't continue to work with someone when I know they've recently breached a child protection agreement. Can we talk about the pros and cons of you informing the social worker that you have breached the agreement?

Marcus:　Look, you don't know them. If I tell them, they might stop me seeing the girls altogether or even take the girls into care or something. I won't do it again. I promise you.

It was tempting to leave the matter to rest in the light of Marcus's promise not to do it again. She could console herself in having raised the matter with her client. After all, this challenge would probably contribute to a change of behaviour in Marcus, with him realizing that he had to comply with all child protection agreements in the future. She would have modelled a positive use of accountability. The counsellor decided she was kidding herself. How would she know if Marcus would make good on his promise? And he would certainly be more guarded about telling her anything in the future that might compromise him. If he were to offend against his stepdaughters, or even had already offended against them, and this came to light, and she had kept a breach of a child protection agreement to herself, this would likely undermine her professional credibility. More significantly, she would have failed to act in a way that could have possibly protected children from abuse.

Counsellor: OK, those things you said could possibly occur, but what would happen if social services found out in the future that you had breached the agreement, and you hadn't told them anything about it?

Marcus: Well that would be it. End of sports. Probably I wouldn't be allowed to see the girls, unless I battled for them through court. But social services don't need to know, do they?

Once again, the counsellor felt her insides churn.

Counsellor: Marcus, I want to work with you to help you get your life back on track, but it's past the point where social services can remain ignorant of the breach, because I have a professional duty to report it, if you don't. It would be much better if you did it. If you like, we can discuss a form of words you could use, and if you reported it, this might establish more trust between you and social services. Also, if you do report it, I will back you all the way and would be prepared to contact the social worker and say this has been a valuable learning experience for you, as you now realize the serious consequences of breaking child protection agreements in the future.

Marcus reluctantly accepted that, given the choices on offer, his best option was to inform the social worker. The social worker was under no illusion that Marcus would have done this of his own accord, without pressure from the counsellor. Marcus received a warning that if there were any more breaches of agreements then all contact with his stepdaughters would be suspended.

The social worker seemed swayed by the counsellor's argument that part of the therapeutic work with Marcus was helping him to be less impulsive, to develop more consequential thinking, and for him to experience a transparent therapeutic relationship with firm boundaries, modelling a way for Marcus to relate with more honesty in his relationships and life in general. Sexual offending, including looking at abusive images of children and young people on the internet, always involves secrecy and deception. It is less likely to occur if a person is in the habit of relating transparently with others, and if being deceptive comes to seem incompatible with a desired self-image.

Conclusion

What is evident from the case study is that the therapeutic process begins from the moment a client contacts the counsellor. The contracting and setting of boundaries at the beginning of the counselling process is not merely 'stuff to get through' before the 'real' therapy begins. This negotiation process is an intrinsic part and parcel of the counselling, as is each encounter with a client, whether it is a phone call, email, or saying hello and goodbye to each other. All can be seen as therapeutic encounters, valuable human interactions, even the difficult ones such as that in the case study, in which positive interpersonal learning can take place. Below are some useful tips related to the content and themes of this chapter:

*   Obtain a general outline of the problem.
*   In the initial referral conversation, verbally state the terms of your confidentiality policy, if necessary.
*   Send your counselling contract to the client to read, before signing it at the start of the first session. Ask the client how he wants this sent.
*   Ask the client if he has ever been arrested or if there are any allegations or convictions, with regard to sexual or violent offending.
*   Ask whether any other professionals are involved in the client's life.
*   Clarify that you will not provide a risk assessment report.
*   Clarify that you want to liaise with other agencies and the terms of this, if this is the case.
*   Enquire if there is any risk of self-harm or suicide.
*   Use discretion to contact other professionals for information about risk, health, and safety issues, and the terms of any court orders or child protection agreements.
*   Set boundaries with other professionals, with regard to what you will and will not disclose.

References

Ambady, N., LaPlante, D., Nguyen, T., Rosenthal, R., Chaumeton, N. and Levinson, W. (2002) 'Surgeon's tone of voice: A clue to malpractice history', *Surgery*, 132 (1): pp. 5–9.

Bond, T., Brewer, W. and Mitchels, B. (2015) *Breaches in confidentiality*: G2 information sheet. Available from: http://personacounselling.com/BACP%20Information%20 Sheet%20%20-%20Breaches%20in%20Confidentiality.pdf [20 August 2016].

Children's Commissioner's Inquiry Report. (2015), *Protecting children from harm: A critical assessment of child sexual abuse in the family network in England and priorities for action*. Available from: www.childrenscommissioner.gov.uk/learn-more/child-sexual-exploitation-abuse/protecting-children-harm [18 December 2015].

Craig, L.A., Beech, A.R. and Harkins, L. (2009) 'The predictive accuracy of risk factors and frameworks', in A.R. Beech, L.A. Craig and K.D. Browne (eds.) *Assessment and treatment of sex offenders: A handbook*. Chichester: Wiley-Blackwell, pp. 53–76.

Gardner, D. (2009) *Risk: The science and politics of fear*. Canada: Virgin Books.

Hart, S.D., Kropp, P.R., Laws, R., Klaver, J., Logan, C. and Watt, K.A. (2003) *The risk for sexual violence protocol (RSVP)*. Burnaby: Mental Health, Law and Policy Institute, Simon Fraser University.

MacKinnon, L. and James, K. (1992) 'Working with 'the Welfare' in child-at-risk cases', *Australian and New Zealand Journal of Family Therapy*, 13 (1): pp. 1–15.

Mehrabian, A. (1972) *Nonverbal communication*. Chicago: Aldine-Atherton.

NOTA. (2014) *NOTA Conference 2013 at Cardiff: Further coverage*. Available from: www.nota.co.uk/media/1015/72notanewsapril2014.pdf [March 2015].

Sentencing Council. (2013) *The sexual offences definitive guidelines*, pp. 75–80. Available from: www.sentencingcouncil.org.uk/publications/item/sexual-offences-definitive-guideline/ [24 August 2016].

Trotter, C. (2006) *Working with involuntary clients: A guide to practice*, 2nd edition: London: Sage.

Turnell, A. and Edwards, S. (1999) *Signs of safety: A solution and safety oriented approach to child protection casework*. New York: Norton.

UK Ministry of Justice (2017) Impact evaluation of the prison-based Core Sex Offender Treatment Programme. Available from: www.gov.uk/government/publications/impact-evaluation-of-the-prison-based-core-sex-offender-treatment-programme [14 August 2017]

Working together to safeguard children: A guide to inter-agency working to safeguard and promote the welfare of children. (2015) HM Department for Education: Office of the Children's Commissioner. Available from: www.gov.uk/government/uploads/system/uploads/attachment_data/file/419595/Working_Together_to_Safeguard_Children.pdf [25 August 2016].

Chapter 3

Goal-setting

Introduction

A strengths-focused approach to counselling highlights the need to work within a client's motivational frame of reference. Increasingly, as a counsellor, I find that sessions go well when I put big ideas about what the client needs to do out of my head, and concentrate on where the client is in the present moment, what the client is motivated to think about, and the next small constructive step forward which seems to be achievable for the client. This chapter will discuss how to be person-centred in these respects, whilst stimulating the client in challenging but not too threatening ways, to consider goals which are personally meaningful. Finally, the Marcus case study from Chapter 2 will be revisited, as the therapeutic process with him develops from contracting to goal-setting.

Working with the client's motivations within the therapeutic relationship

In the 1980s and 1990s, treatment with individuals who had sexually offended, almost exclusively taking place within the criminal justice system in England and Wales, often consisted of confrontational interviewing. The person was asked, or pressurized, to describe his sexual offence in detail. The account was then systematically questioned, with perceived cognitive distortions, denials, and minimizations highlighted. This approach often led to the 'confrontation-denial trap' (Miller and Rollnick, 1991), a dynamic in which the more the worker confronts, the more the client retreats into counterproductive resistance, leaving the practitioner feeling frustrated and deskilled. For these reasons, Motivational Interviewing (Miller and Rollnick, 1991), which was first used with people addicted to substances, gradually replaced the confrontational approach. Motivational interviewing became the interactional method of choice in the UK prison and probation services when working with all offenders, including sex offenders (Chapman and Hough, 1998).

Motivational interviewing was informed by the human potential movement, which became particularly influential in the 1960s and 1970s through the writings of key figures such as Abraham Maslow and Carl Rogers. Key to this movement was the importance of the therapeutic relationship and being client-centred, as opposed to the importance previously placed on the analytical ability of the therapist. The therapeutic philosophy and method was encapsulated in Carl Rogers' core conditions for therapeutic change: unconditional regard, empathy, and genuineness (Rogers, 1957, 1961).

Strengths-based proponents point to the repeated finding that the quality of the relationship between individual and practitioner is a crucial factor in facilitating positive change with all client groups (Paul and Charura, 2014). A substantial body of research evidence suggests that the characteristics of the therapist constitute one of the most important factors facilitating positive client outcomes (Luborsky et al., 1985). Hubble et al. (1999) also cite the importance of the therapeutic alliance, regardless of the technique or model used. The particular therapeutic model used has been seen to account for less than 15% of variance in treatment outcomes, with the quality of the therapeutic relationship being the main variable (Lambert, 1992).

Lengthy cognitive-behavioural group work programmes with sexual offenders (on average between 50 to 180 hours, depending on the perceived risk of the offender), run by the prison and probation services, have traditionally been the main treatment method for persons who have committed sex offences in the UK. It has been found that a primary element in promoting long-term change is group cohesiveness and offenders engaging in the group process, factors encouraged by group work facilitators displaying positive regard, respect, and non-judgementalism (Beech and Fordham, 1997). Variance in treatment gains in perspective taking and victim empathy, as a result of group work programmes, has been shown to be related to the interpersonal style of the group facilitators (Mulloy et al., 1999). A review of desirable therapist characteristics for working with this client group cites factors such as warmth, empathetic ability, emotional expressiveness, and confidence (Marshall et al., 2003). Mann et al. (2002) found that the therapist's ability to display positive regard and an open, inquiring mind is important for effective therapy with people who have sexually offended. Generally, rehabilitative effectiveness with people who have committed sexual offending is strongly linked to the practitioner's therapeutic ability (Sandhu and Rose, 2012).

In many ways, Motivational Interviewing and Solution-Focused Therapy (Steve de Shazer, 1985, 1994) can be seen as being strengths-focused in that both models emphasize working in a client-centred way, with the practitioner avoiding confrontation, emphasizing client choice, identifying resources and strengths, looking for small steps of change, and underlining that the client is the expert on his own life, rather than privileging the expert interpretations of the therapist. The Solution-Focused Therapy approach has been used with people who have sexually offended, or are suspected of having done so, in a child protection context by Turnell and Edwards (1999) in their Signs of Safety approach. Jenkins (1990) also adopts a solution-focused approach, alongside narrative therapeutic ideas, in his work with men who have committed violent and sexual crimes: inviting them to take responsibility for their offending. Essex et al. (1996) and Turnell and Essex (2006), have also adopted the Solution-Focused Therapy approach with families struggling to manage the risk of sexual abuse. With the exception of these examples, in the UK Solution-Focused Therapy has traditionally not been widely used in a rehabilitative context with people who have committed sexual crime, although it has been used in most other settings (O'Connell, 1998).

Solution-focused therapy places significant emphasis on how words are used and is concerned with how language has been colonized by powerful and professional elites. De Jong and Berg (2002) outline how traditional therapeutic approaches have tended to be based on scientific and medical models, which began to achieve impressive success in the late 19th century, in approaching previously untreatable diseases. The success was based on the scientific method of analyzing and diagnosing the problem before administering treatment. This view of an objective reality, knowable through reason, can be seen as an inherent part of a modernist world view (Milner and O'Byrne, 2002).

O'Connell (1998) goes on to describe how, in the subsequent social constructionist, postmodern view, there is no such thing as objective reality outside that created by social forces and language – the stories and narratives we use to describe experience. Thus, categories which are considered real, such as various diagnoses of mental disorders (and in the world of sexual offending treatment, tropes such as denial, distorted thinking, and empathy deficits), can be seen as dominant discourses of the powerful, constructed through language.

Solution-focused practitioners reject the modernist-influenced view that a problem has to be understood, with much time invested in collecting information about the difficulty in order to categorize it, before effective solutions can be found. De Jong and Berg (2002) make the solution-focused argument that a lot of time is wasted on gathering and recording information about problems, with helping professionals' credentials being based on their perceived ability to understand the problem and to prescribe a remedy.

Rappaport (1981) points out that the human problems people bring to therapeutic practitioners are not puzzles to be solved. Jenkins (1990) illustrates how this view of abuse as a puzzle can be shared by practitioner and client alike. People who have sexually offended often present as being preoccupied with the question of why they have behaved in harmful and self-destructive ways, a question that is almost impossible to answer with any certainty. The premise behind such a question seems to be a belief that if one knows why, one can stop the problematic behaviour. Jenkins, like other solution-focused practitioners, makes the point that such cause and effect rarely obtains when dealing with the complexities of the relational and social world, unlike in the medical model; a doctor needs to know, for instance, if she or he is dealing with a bacterial infection or a virus in order to know whether or not to prescribe antibiotics. The world of human motivations and relations is more complex and shifting, with few straightforward causes of multifactorial human problems. I personally find that although it is perhaps a universal human need to understand events and our own behaviour, the 'why' question can be a blind alley or an introspective smoke screen, allowing the client to avoid taking active responsibility for changing and managing abusive behaviour. In my experience, most clients do have a need for explanations, although my emphasis is not on whether or not these explanations are 'true' but on co-constructing with the client narratives which facilitate rather than hinder pro-social behaviour.

In my research into which factors lead to successful rehabilitation of men who have sexually offended, the importance of the quality of the therapeutic relationship was evident. The following men are talking about their relationship with probation officers, but the insights are pertinent to other practitioners working with this client group, including counsellors.

When I come and see him (my probation officer) it's never felt that it's been a chore or anything like that. It's been a pleasure.

(Offender 4)

I actually missed coming in and just having that 10-minute chat to someone who is objective and is away from your personal life.

(Offender 6)

In the study, the men who had offended also described the importance of the communication of regard, empathy, and genuineness. In relation to the quality of regard, Offender 4 stated that when his probation officer first met him, she probably thought, 'Oh God! I've got another case here, another pervert.' Since she had got to know him better, he considered that his probation officer had come to view him with positive regard, in the following way.

Now, a man's done an error in his life, and he's tried to make things right as best he can . . . but he's going to try and do what he can.

(Offender 4)

Offender 13 described not only his probation officer's sincerity but her empathic ability to perceive his state of mind.

She's sincere; it hasn't taken her long to suss me out, she knows just by the way I talk. If I start to get anxious, if I got this problem, maybe that is like a warning to her. It's how I'm adapting, and how I'm behaving as a result of these triggers, these problems. If I start getting some CD [cognition distortions] problems, she can see that, it's a slight warning sign for me, not everything is going as well as it was last week.

(Offender 13)

Bottoms (2001) described how clients can choose to adhere to boundaries through 'normative compliance' based upon moral obligation rather than 'instrumental compliance' based upon deterrents and incentives. This was apparent in the accounts of some of the men who cited not wanting to lose the respect of or to let down the probation officer as factors, among others, preventing them from reoffending.

> *I feel it would be letting him [the offender's probation officer] down, if I reoffended. He's like the main person I can visualize, also can inspire me to not reoffend. He's put faith in me.*

(Offender 2)

> *That's another thing. I never wanted to reoffend since 25 years, but even if that feeling did come back, I would pull myself up. 'Look what these people have done for you. You can't let them down.' Speak to (my probation officer) about it. That's what I would do if I had any problems like that. I'd get on the phone to my probation officer.*

(Offender 1)

As noted in Chapter 1, philosopher Charles Taylor (1989) posits that identity is related to how human beings orient themselves to what they perceive to be good. Taylor also makes the point that the self is constructed only through language, in relation to others: 'I am a self only in relation to certain interlocutors: in one way in relation to those conversational partners who were essential to my achieving self-definition' (Taylor, 1989: 36). Counsellors are such conversational partners.

The strengths-focused approach will now be applied to practice, using the same case study which featured in Chapter 2. The initial stage of counselling is illustrated again as the exploration of client motivation and goal-setting is conducted by the counsellor. Marcus's circumstances are repeated to remind the reader of the details of the case.

Case study: Marcus

Marcus is 39. He went to private school but left with few qualifications because he could 'never get on with the teachers'. His parents are both retired lawyers who, he feels, are disappointed in him. His father has alcohol problems and has been violent to his mother. He presents as good looking for his age – obviously in the habit of working out – and is intelligent and witty. When he was 19, he was sentenced to a two-year community order for having underage sex with a 14-year-old girl. Apart from this, he has two convictions for being drunk and disorderly, three driving convictions, and an ABH (actual bodily harm) conviction, against an ex-partner. In the past he had successful businesses, but lost them, getting into large amounts of debt, having spent his money on flash cars, drink and cocaine. He jokes that he 'wasted the rest.' He says his substance misuse is now under control and not a problem, and he is making a decent living working for a firm, selling expensive sports cars. Marcus says he has had many sexual partners and relationships and used to go regularly to Thailand with a mate and have sex with prostitutes. He married in his 20s, meeting his wife when she was 14 and he was eighteen. The marriage ended bitterly when she accused him of domestic violence, which he denies. He no longer has any contact with his daughter from this relationship, saying that his ex-wife turned his daughter against him. He wants therapy because the police found indecent images of children on his computer, mostly teenage girls. He intends to plead guilty. His current partner, Jill, told him he had to get help (while he is waiting for the police to investigate the computer and charge him) for there to be any chance of the relationship continuing, although she doesn't think he would ever harm her daughters. His partner has two teenage daughters, aged 13 and 15, with whom, he says, he gets on with very well. Marcus maintains that he has never viewed his stepdaughters sexually and that, in his case, there is a big gap between fantasy and reality. Social services have required him to move out of the family home, and he is now back living with his parents. He is only allowed contact with his partner's daughters once a fortnight, at a contact centre. They express a strong wish to see him. This arrangement will be in place until it is known whether the police will press charges or not. Marcus has been told that this may take anything from three to 12 months. At the start of the counselling the counsellor is unaware of these contact stipulations.

Establishing motivation

The counsellor began trying to obtain an idea of what motivated Marcus to come to counselling by asking the simple question, 'What brings you here today?' Marcus replied that he had been stupid and wanted to turn his life around. This reply gave the counsellor the opportunity to ask the following future-orientated, strengths-focused question.

Counsellor: OK, say that you managed to change your life around in a year's time. What would your life be like?

Marcus: What do you mean?

Counsellor: Well, if 'you turned your life around', as you say, what would be different from how your life is now?

The counsellor repeated the same words, 'turn your life around', that Marcus had used. From a strengths-focused perspective, adapting to the same expressive mode as the client, without this being too obvious and patronizing, builds rapport and can contribute to mutual understanding. Marcus replied to the counsellor's question in the following way.

Marcus: I'd be at home with my wife and family.
Counsellor: That's obviously important for you. What needs to happen to bring that about?
Marcus: Well, it's out of my hands, isn't it? That bitch the social worker says I can't go home until I'm charged and sentenced and if after this, after fucking months, I'm assessed as being a risk to kids, I'm done for.

The sudden use of the swear word 'fucking' and particularly the word 'bitch', expressed with such resentment and supressed anger, took the counsellor back for a few seconds. Sexual offending involves the sexual objectification of women, men, and children. The objectification of women often takes an unpleasant and aggressive form. Some practitioners may choose to challenge language such as 'bitch', believing that not to do so would be to collude with sexist language and a pro-offending attitude. This counsellor took a different view. From her work with other clients she knew that they will frequently express views with which she may disagree, which she may find objectionable, and which reflect anti-social and sexist attitudes. As a female counsellor, with feminist sympathies, she experienced herself feeling angry with her client for disparaging a woman in this way, and with the chauvinism it represented. However, rather than challenging him head on, for the time being the counsellor bracketed the anti-social utterances and affirmed the pro-social ones, in order to encourage the latter. The counsellor would challenge the use of aggressive and objectifying language at a later stage, through planned psycho-educational work, consisting of raising the client's awareness of the harmful impact of such language (examples of this sort of psycho-educational work, challenging sexism, are presented in Chapter 5).

To directly confront the client about such language in the early stages of counselling, when this kind of talk may be part of the discourse of the cultural groups in which the client socializes and relates, would perhaps counterproductively lead to resistance, rendering the possibility of lasting change more unlikely. The client also needs to feel free to have a space to express his most negative thoughts and feelings, without being judgementally jumped on.

It could be argued that individuals who have sexually offended only have themselves to blame for the situation they are in, and in all likelihood they have caused much harm to victims and distress to loved ones. Nevertheless, it is usually the case that they also suffer and need a therapeutic space where this suffering can be expressed and acknowledged. It is also important for counsellors to be aware of the profound impact committing a sexual offence can have on an individual's family life. The following statements provide a flavour of the unenviable predicaments of men who have committed sexual offences, and are worth considering before returning to the Marcus case study, and the process of goal-setting.

Offender 8 in my research study, an ex-psychiatrist, had committed a sexual offence against an adolescent girl outside of the family. As a result of his actions, he was not allowed to live with his previous wife and children. In the interview, he talked about the psychological effects of such permanent estrangement.

Normally speaking a person would be separated from the family indefinitely. I think the risk is when you do that, you continue and freeze the trauma. There's no possibility of healing and rapprochement.

(Offender 8)

He also described an incident which exemplifies the social consequences of being viewed as a risk to children. The account is cited at length because it provides a relatively rare insight into this, often hidden, social phenomenon.

And also I am not allowed to ever set foot on the premises of a school now. I've never hung around school. I don't know where that came from . . . my children have moved elsewhere, because my ex-wife has re-married, and it's probably not relevant. Should, say, that my children want me to see them perform in a school play, I can't, and that seems totally unnecessary. . . . There was a situation fairly recently, my sister, she's a very keen viola player. She was performing in a Mozart symphony. She invited us to go. We thought 'great, lovely', so mother and I set off, and as we were approaching this place . . . Well, where exactly is it being held? Oh it's at a girls' school. I said 'Mummy, I can't go.' Even though it was school holiday time and it was Sunday evening, no children around at all, but I couldn't go. I had to drop her off, and of course I was in a distracted state, got a speeding ticket. I didn't clock the sign saying it had changed from 40 to 30, and I then had a few days of thinking, 'Oh my God I've committed another offence; I'm going to be sent back to prison.' I told my probation officer. She said 'don't worry about this.' But that's an example of the mindless, indiscriminate sort of conditions restrictions.

(Offender 8)

Whether or not it is reasonable for the state to put restrictions and sometimes total bans on contact between parents who have sexually offended and their children (and in my view this is often necessary), the reality is that clients often come to counselling resentful and angry about such curtailment of freedom. It is important to engage with these difficulties, without allowing them to dominate the therapeutic process.

With regard to Marcus's aggressive use of the word 'bitch', the counsellor did not challenge this head on, but responded as follows:

Counsellor: That must be very tough, feeling that the situation is out of your hands. Tell me, with regard to that word 'risk' you used, where would you place yourself on a scale of 0 to 10, if 0 equalled no risk and 10 equalled high risk, with regard to you sexually abusing your stepdaughters?

In that intervention, the counsellor began with an empathic comment about the toughness of the client's situation. Counselling can be viewed as being a bit like banking. The more you invest in terms of empathy and affirmation, the more you can withdraw in terms of addressing psychologically threatening matters, such as sexual offending. While it is important for a counsellor to endeavour to be as unconditionally regarding as she can, it is also important to name core issues – such as sexual crime and sexual risk – early on in the counselling process and to communicate from the beginning that you are not going to dance around difficult subjects. Most clients will be embarrassed, guilty, or ashamed in relation to sexual offending, but will also be relieved that they have found a counsellor who can talk about it and the risk they pose in a straightforward way.

Having empathized with the client, the scaling question used by the counsellor is meant to quantify the complex matter of risk, in order to make risk easier to talk about. The scaling question also provides an insight into the client's perspective on risk issues. Marcus put himself at 0, saying he presented no sexual risk to his stepdaughters. The counsellor considered this an unrealistic self-assessment. She could easily have pointed this out to Marcus (and it was tempting to do so), presenting him with the facts that he had been looking at illegal sexual images of girls the same age as his stepdaughters, in the past he had received a two-year community order for having underage sex with a 14-year-old girl, and he had met his previous wife when she was 14. All this suggested that he had a significant sexual interest in teenage girls below the legal age of consent. But to confront him in this way would probably have been to provoke argument: the counsellor arguing that he surely poses some sexual risk to his stepdaughters, the client arguing that he doesn't.

The counsellor considered that a more profitable path was to ask Marcus where he thought his partner would put him on the scale. Often, clients are wrapped up in their own pain. This type of scaling question encourages clients to consider the perspective of others – a consciousness-raising experience. Marcus's silence and body language suggested that he found the question painful to contemplate. He replied, 'Jill knows I wouldn't ever harm her daughters.' The counsellor asked him to scale Jill's level of concern anyway. Marcus placed Jill at 2 on the scale. This was significant. It was the first acknowledgement from him that there was some sexual risk with regard to his stepdaughters to be considered.

The counsellor then asked him where he thought the social worker would place him on the scale. He replied, 'She would probably put me at 8.' The counsellor commented that, as Marcus had already implied, the social worker had a lot of power and that it was she and probably her superiors who would have a very significant say in whether or not he could eventually go back home to live with the family. She then asked how low the social worker would need to score him for him to be allowed to return to his family. Marcus estimated that she would have to see him as being around 2. The counsellor inquired how he could convince the social worker that he was such a low risk. Marcus replied, 'Haven't a fucking clue'.

Providing clients with information to make informed choices

Inevitably, clients who have sexually offended will want to be considered a lower risk than they are currently considered to be. However, they have usually not been told by professionals what exactly needs to happen, or what they must do, to obtain a lower risk categorization. Often professionals are uncertain about this as well. Providing people with such information (not advice) with which to make informed choices is consistent with a strengths-focused approach. Hence, I frequently provide clients with an outline of what people generally have to do to receive a reduced risk categorization, or to make sexual offending less likely. I take care to stress that there can be no guarantees that future risk assessors will make an assessment of decreased risk by virtue of the client having undergone counselling, but counselling offers the possibility for this. I reiterate (as discussed in Chapter 2) that it will be somebody else – a social worker or specialist risk assessor – who will decide if the counselling has been effective in terms of reducing risk. I then provide clients with the following information sheet, consisting of indications of reduced risk (a copy of which is in Appendix 6).

Indications of reduced risk

- The longer there is an absence of sexual reoffending or allegations of sexual abuse, the less child protection professionals will worry about the risk of reoffending.
- Whilst you do not have to admit to sexual offending or say you pose a risk, genuinely acknowledging that others have legitimate concerns which need to be addressed, is necessary.
- Rather than being preoccupied with why life is not as you would want it, focus on everything you can do to change the situation.
- Understand the factors (including your life history) which resulted in your current situation.

- Understand the thoughts, behaviour, and situations to avoid in order to make future sexual offending and allegations less likely.
- Understand the impact and consequences of sexual offending on victims and loved ones.
- Establish a satisfying, safe life, where you don't have to resort to destructive behaviour to meet needs and desires.
- If you remain with a partner, develop a relationship in which you are open and transparent and accountable about your behaviour.
- If social services require your partner to monitor your risk, with regard to children, do everything you can to make this as easy as possible for her.
- Negotiate a New Life Safety Plan, consisting of *Signs of Safety* that you are living a constructive and safe life, *Signs of Risk* that you may be going down a pathway which could cause harm to others or yourself, and agreeing upon *Responses to Emerging Signs of Risk* which could be implemented if things start to go wrong.
- Agree that this New Life Safety Plan can be shared with significant others, freely making yourself accountable so you can be supported in living an offence-free life.

Clients can be provided with this information sheet to read in the initial stage of counselling, or the contents can be discussed without reference to the sheet. I discuss each point, asking whether or not it is relevant. I then ask what indications of risk the client would be prepared to work on, checking if there are any additional issues they would like to explore.

Some clients will deny sexual offending, maintaining that there has been a miscarriage of justice and they are a victim of false allegations. Sometimes no offence has been committed, but there are concerns on the part of the clients themselves (or somebody else) related to sexually harmful behaviour. In both instances, most aspects of the programme of therapeutic work described earlier can be completed.

In my experience, most clients coming to counselling in relation to sexual offending are in a state of crisis in their lives and will be motivated to do whatever they can, short perhaps of actually admitting to sexual abuse or saying the words, 'Yes I pose a sexual risk.' Clients are often relieved that they can complete constructive, focused work on sexual offending issues, whilst being able to keep face and not admitting to a highly stigmatized identity as a dangerous sex offender or predatory paedophile.

Increasing motivation

If a client has low motivation, he will not be keen to engage at significant depth with the points discussed earlier. When this happens, we discuss the counselling goals we can work towards, whether this is anxiety or depression management, or coping with the distress of the situation. Other clients will be stuck in the place of wanting circumstances and other people to change, but being unwilling or unable to take responsibility themselves. This was initially the case with Marcus, having read the indication of reduced risk sheet.

Marcus: I don't see how any of this really applies to me.

Again, the counsellor did not directly challenge Marcus on his view of matters, but obtained his permission to conduct an exercise with him. She placed two chairs to the side of them. (When this is not possible, the client can be asked to imagine two chairs.) The counsellor then asked Marcus to imagine that two guys are sitting in the chairs. Each of them has been charged and has admitted looking at abusive images of teenage girls on the internet. She then handed Marcus the following sheet to read (a copy can be found in Appendix 7).

Person A completely denies risk, and sees no need to undertake protective work	Person B denies, or accepts risk to some extent, but either way recognizes the concerns of others, and is willing to undertake protective work
Does not take on the concerns of others	Is willing to focus on the concerns of others
Focuses on how allegations are false, exaggerated, or how there has been a miscarriage of justice	Decides to learn all about how different sexual abuse occurs so he can make sure he does not put himself into situations where children may be at risk or another allegation could be made against him
Thinks that by repeating that there is no risk, this is enough	Is willing to discuss how safe boundaries can be maintained in the home
	Is prepared to make himself accountable to loved ones
Makes it difficult for others, including loved ones, to talk about concerns by becoming angry, upset, or showing by tone of voice, body language and facial expression that people should not mention the subject	Is realistic about the difficulties of being challenged and monitored by a loved one and being thought of as a possible risk to children
	Accepts that a loved one might have to report him if serious risk emerges, and encourages the loved one that this would be the right thing to do
Not being open, or only giving people scraps of information about the abuse or alleged abuse	Is willing to work with professionals and child protection agreements

After Marcus had finished reading this, the counsellor explained that individuals convicted or accused of sexual offending tend to take one of the two above pathways. She asked Marcus to put himself into the shoes of a social worker or other professional with a responsibility for protecting children. She then asked him which person out of the two would be most likely to persuade the professional that he was safe to be with children. Marcus replied soberly, 'Person B'.

This exercise can be very effective in providing the client with the objective space to better appreciate the concerns of others and how he may be perceived by professionals. It also provides a concrete picture to the client of how a motivated and an unmotivated client commonly presents.

The counsellor asked Marcus which pathway he was on. Marcus recognized that he was on the first pathway, like Person A. The counsellor asked which pathway he wanted to be on in the future. Marcus replied that he had better get on the second pathway of Person B, if he had any chance of wanting to be reunited with his family.

Rather than just affirm the client that he has chosen a more constructive path, reverse psychology can be employed in order for the client to make a more informed choice about embarking on this second path. With this in mind, the counsellor explained to Marcus that the second pathway is an emotional juggling act. He must accept that loved ones may have concerns about him posing a risk and this is likely to engender feelings of loss of self-esteem and resentment. At the same time, he needs to maintain a loving and respectful relationship with his partner. This can be a tough ask. The counsellor then explored with Marcus the pros and cons of taking the second pathway, and how he might manage the emotional juggling act.

At the end of this process, the counsellor suggested a broad outline of the content of counselling (that can be used with most clients with sexual offending problems), which could possibly help Marcus reach his goal of being reunited with his family, whilst reiterating that there can be no guarantees:

- Agree upon initial evolving goals of counselling
- Agree upon an initial, evolving New Life Safety Plan
- Explore early life experience
- Explore later experiences
- Understand sexual abuse, who commits it and where it often occurs
- Understand why and how people commit sexual abuse
- Consequences and impact of sexual abuse
- Sexual fantasy management
- Agree on an end-of-counselling New Life Safety Plan
- Maintain a New Life Safety Plan.

Duration of counselling

I inform clients that the programme of counselling can take anything from around 12 one-hour sessions over three months to 24 one-hour sessions over six months.

I can also see some clients for ongoing sessions for up to one or two years, or longer. In this longer-term engagement the client uses counselling to assist in applying the new ways of thinking and being (discovered through counselling) to the ongoing ups and downs of life over a protracted period. Some clients can also come back to counselling for a top-up from time to time, or to cope with a particular situation or explore a pertinent issue arising in their life.

I am personally comfortable with allowing the client to dictate how long counselling will last. Life is endlessly complex and changeable, and I tend not to look too much further than the present session with the client, attempting to facilitate small steps of positive change or helping the client to better manage his experience, whilst having an overarching process in mind, to which I try not to be too attached.

New Life Safety Plan

In the initial stage of counselling, a 'New Life Safety Plan' can be established if this seems appropriate with a client. Traditionally, when working with people who have committed sexual offending, the therapy or rehabilitation is concluded with a 'Relapse Prevention Plan' or 'Risk Management Plan' at the end of the intervention. An advantage of establishing such a plan at the beginning of counselling (what I call a 'New Safety Life Plan') is that it can then be used as an ongoing working document that can evolve as the counselling proceeds and therapeutic goals change and evolve, rather than ending up with a document that may look impressive, but is put away in a drawer somewhere after the end of the intervention.

As I discuss further in the final chapter, such plans in themselves are, in my view, sometimes not worth the paper they are written on, if the client has not bought into them and if they reflect the 'good sense' of the practitioner rather than accurately reflecting the genuine needs and desires of the client. It is not so much the words on the page that are important but the quality of the collaborative negotiation process between client and practitioner that has informed the plan and raised the client's consciousness.

If a New Life Safety Plan is agreed in the initial stages of counselling, it can become a truly useful and living document, referred to regularly in sessions, an aid to checking progress, keeping client and counsellor focused on pertinent issues and reflecting the shifting circumstances of the client. Another advantage of introducing a plan early on is that it can help manage any immediate risks of the client harming others or harming themselves.

In my view, such plans are often too complicated, with clients having difficulty in remembering all the constituent parts. Hence, my New Life Safety Plan has only three sections:

- Signs of a positive and safer life
- Signs of risk
- Responses to signs of risk

An example copy of a final New Life Safety Plan can be found in Appendix 8 and a blank copy for use can be found in Appendix 9. The example is an ideal type, meant to illustrate the scope of what can be potentially put into a plan. In reality, the plans I use are simpler and more focused. The main principles, apart from the plan being client-centred, is prioritizing the most important Signs of Safety and Signs of Risk first, and for the plan to be preferably shared with significant others such as partners and child protection workers, in order to contribute to transparency and accountability.

Having extolled the virtue of such plans, I find that they are only constructive to use with certain clients, who appreciate the order and structure. Other clients (and counsellors) have little interest in plans, viewing counselling as a more organic process with therapeutic gains being internalized through osmosis. If this is so, I am just as happy to work without one. In the case of Marcus, he and the counsellor came up with the following initial plan, which would have been subsequently developed and amended as the counselling progressed.

New Life Safety Plan

Signs of a positive and safer life

- Complying with all child protection agreements
- Keeping in mind that suicide would cause more pain for loved ones than the stigma of a living loved one having committed a sexual offence
- Drinking moderately
- Telling the truth
- Continuing to come to counselling
- Keeping fit
- Reading positive-thinking books

Signs of risk

- A developing pattern of the above being compromised or broken
- Looking at online pornography which, in the past, led to searching for abusive images of teenage girls
- Prolonged thoughts about ways to commit suicide
- Feeling there is no hope
- Staying in the house
- Becoming verbally abusive

Responses to signs of risk

- Inform counsellor or social worker of any breaches of child protection agreements

---

- Ring Samaritans
- Discuss taking anti-depressants with the GP
- Talk to the counsellor about feelings of hopelessness and going to prison
- Read the first section of a favourite self-help book
- Remember that this crisis point could lead to a more fulfilling life
- Play favourite inspiring music

Strengths-focused questions

A general danger of using strengths-focused questions is being strengths-forced rather than strengths-focused, becoming relentlessly positive (and irritating), insisting on concentrating only on the positive. Often, when this occurs, the counsellor is either inexperienced or neglecting the 'core conditions', of which empathy is a very important one. Some counsellors who favour the strengths-based approach may fear being engulfed by the emotional pain of others. They may want to flee into rational problem solving and may be unable to just be there, holding a client (metaphorically) in their pain, which is sometimes the only response required.

Following are some examples of strengths-focused questions which can be used by the counsellor to help set goals in a collaborative fashion. Many of these will be used in the different case studies, in subsequent chapters. When using such questions, it is important to remain congruent as a counsellor. A client can usually detect when a practitioner is being phoney and is using an intervention or asking questions in a style that does not seem to sit comfortably with the counsellor's character. The result can be 'therapy-speak' in which authentic interaction is lost. Readers should use only those questions with which they are comfortable and should feel free to adapt the wording of the questions to whichever form seems useful. Clinical judgement is always necessary when considering the appropriateness of any of the following questions:

- On a scale from 0–10, if 0 is no risk at all to children, and 10 is very high risk, where would you put yourself on this scale?
- Can you say why you put yourself at this point on the scale?
- Where would you put yourself on the scale before you committed your first offence? What has happened to move you on the scale?
- Where do you think other professionals or family members would put you on this scale? (Think, in turn, of significant professionals and personal others.) Why would they think that?
- Where do you think that you need to be on the scale for people to think you are safe to live in the community? (Think, in turn, of various significant professional and significant others.)
- What do you think needs to happen in order for you to reach this point on the scale of being safe enough?

- What do other people think must happen before you are considered safe to be in the community?
- Imagine you have been living in the community safely for two years and you are living an offence-free, satisfying life. What sort of life would you be living?

  - How would you be thinking about your offending?
  - Who would you be seeing and not seeing?
  - How would you be managing your relationships?
  - Take me through an average day; how would you be spending your time?
  - How could others tell that you were not at risk of reoffending?

- If you felt like offending, what would you say to yourself to manage this urge?
- If you felt like offending, what action would you take to manage this urge?

Other general tips for interacting in a strengths-focused way are:

- Avoid directly confronting distortions, minimizations, and denial.
- Roll with the resistance.
- Keep on asking for practical details and examples.
- Utilize the language of the client where appropriate.
- Don't ask more than three questions in a row.
- Punctuate questions with reflective listening, empathic responses, clarifying, and summarizing.
- Pay genuine compliments.
- Affirm strengths.
- Nurture any small sign of resource or positive change.
- Keep on asking clarifying questions to ground generalization and abstract concepts. For example, Tell me more, what would that look like in real life? Can you say anything else? If that was happening, how would you be feeling, thinking, and acting?

Conclusion

The earlier examples of goal-setting give a flavour of my take on applying a strengths-focused approach to this therapeutic task: providing counselling to clients who have sexually offended, or who are at risk of doing so. The key elements are working within the client's motivational reference on a therapeutic moment-by-moment basis, picking up when a client is showing resistance, and being able to respond with the appropriate intervention. This may be an empathic response, leaving room for silent reflection in order for the client to experience the emotion of the moment, or accepting the resistance and trying a different tack. However, by the end of the initial counselling period (discussed in this chapter and the last) four therapeutic tasks should be ideally achieved:

- Some degree of rapport established;
- A counselling contract, including terms of confidentiality, agreed upon;
- The presenting problem explored, particularly from the client's point of view; and
- The initial evolving goals of counselling established.

References

Beech, A.R. and Fordham, A.S. (1997) 'Therapeutic climate of sexual offender treatment programs', *Sexual Abuse: A Journal of Research and Treatment*, 9 (3): pp. 219–237.

Bottoms, A.E. (2001) 'Compliance and community penalties', in A.E. Bottoms, L. Gelsthorpe and S. Rex (eds.) *Community penalties: Change and challenges*, Cambridge Criminal Justice Series. Devon: Willan Publishing, pp. 87–116.

Chapman, T. and Hough, M. (1998) *Evidence based practice: A guide to effective practice*. London: Home Office Publication Unit.

de Jong, P. and Berg, I. (2002) *Interviewing for solutions*, 2nd edition. Pacific Grove, CA: Brooks Cole.

de Shazer, S. (1985) *Keys to solution in brief therapy*. New York: Norton.

de Shazer, S. (1994) *Words were originally magic*. New York: Norton.

Essex, S., Gumbleton, J. and Luger, C. (1996) 'Resolutions: Working with families where responsibility for abuse is denied', *Child Abuse Review*, 5 (3): pp. 191–201.

Hubble, M., Duncan, B. and Miller, S. (1999) *The heart and soul of change: What works in therapy*. Washington, DC: APA Press.

Jenkins, A. (1990) *Invitations to responsibility: The therapeutic engagement of men who are violent and abusive*. Adelaide: Dulwich Centre Publications.

Lambert, M.J. (1992) 'Psychotherapy outcome research: Implications for integrative and eclectic therapists', in J.C. Norcross and M.R. Goldfried (eds.) *Handbook of psychotherapy integration*. New York: Basic Books, pp. 94–129.

Luborsky, L., McLellan, A.T., Woody, G.E., O'Brien, C.P. and Auerbach, A. (1985) 'Therapist success and its determinants', *Archive of General Psychiatry*, 42 (6): pp. 602–611.

Mann, R., Ginsburg, J.I.D. and Weekes, J.R. (2002) 'Motivational interviewing with offenders', in M. McMurran (ed.) *Motivating offenders to change: A guide to enhancing engagement in therapy*. Chichester: Wiley-Blackwell, pp. 87–102.

Marshall, W.L., Fernandez, Y.M., Serran, G.A., Mulloy, R., Thornton, D., Mann, R.E. and Anderson, D. (2003) 'Process variables in the treatment of sexual offenders: A review of the relevant literature', *Aggression and Violent Behavior: A Review Journal*, 8 (2): pp. 205–234.

Miller, W.R. and Rollnick, S. (1991) *Motivational interviewing: Helping people change*. New York: Guilford Press.

Milner, J. and O'Byrne, P. (2002) *Assessment in social work*, 2nd edition. Basingstoke: Palgrave Macmillan.

Mulloy, R., Serran, G. and Marshall, W.L. (1999) 'Group therapy processes with sex offenders', Paper Presented at the Canadian Psychological Association Annual Convention, Halifax, NS, June 1999.

O'Connell, B. (1998) *Solution-focused therapy*. London, Thousand Oaks, CA and New Delhi: Sage.

Paul, S. and Charura, D. (2014) 'The therapeutic relationship in counselling and psychotherapy', in S. Paul and D. Charura (eds.) *The therapeutic relationship handbook: Theory and practice*. Maidenhead: Open University Press, pp. 3–17.

Rappaport, J. (1981) 'In praise of paradox: A social policy of empowerment over prevention', *American Journal of Community Psychology*, 9 (1): pp. 1–25. Available from: http://grow.ie/wp-content/uploads/2012/03/In-Praise-of-Paradox-A-Social-Policy-of-Empowerment-Over-Prevention-.pdf [24 August 2016].

Rogers, C.R. (1957) 'The necessary and sufficient conditions of therapeutic personality change', *Journal of Consulting Psychology*, 21: pp. 95–103. Available from: https://app.shoreline.edu/dchris/psych236/Documents/Rogers.pdf [24 August 2016].

Rogers, C.R. (1961) *On becoming a person*. Boston: Houghton Mifflin.

Sandhu, D.K. and Rose, J. (2012) 'How do therapists contribute to therapeutic change in sex offender treatment? An integration of the literature', *Journal of Sexual Aggression*, 18 (3): pp. 269–283.

Taylor, C. (1989) *Sources of the self: The making of the modern identity*. Cambridge: Cambridge University Press.

Turnell, A. and Edwards, S. (1999) *Signs of safety: A solution and safety oriented approach to child protection casework*. New York: Norton.

Turnell, A. and Essex, S. (2006) *Working with 'denied' child abuse: The resolutions approach*. Maidenhead: Open University Press.

Chapter 4

Life story themes

Introduction

Following the initial stage of counselling, covered in the previous two chapters, in which the counselling contract and initial therapeutic goals are established, the counsellor can then begin to explore the client's history. The chapter starts by presenting a strengths-focused perspective on exploring a client's past, before examining how poor attachment and trauma issues can be seen in the early lives of many individuals who have sexually offended. Such deficits, and related dysfunctional circumstances, can lead to the development of distorted ways of looking at the world, sex and, children: acting as permission-giving beliefs, with regard to sex offending. The fictional case study presented in this chapter features an adolescent, 'Thomas', and illustrates how incest can occur in a family situation.

Strengths-focused perspective on life story work

The danger of life story work is that focusing on the problematic past can counterproductively consolidate narratives of shame and failure. However, it is also important to avoid becoming strengths-forced and, in doing so, fail to acknowledge pain in an individual's life, collude with the person in avoiding unpleasant realities, and miss the opportunity of accompanying the client through his past, which can lead to many therapeutic and rehabilitative gains.

From a strengths-focused perspective, the value of a person reflecting on the past is primarily to be found in the exploration of often-overlooked resources. Life story work can focus on exceptions to problems, illuminating and honouring times of coping, pro-social behaviour, and success, whilst extracting constructive learning from negatives. Reviewing previous experiences can also be a means of facilitating the client to develop insight about how the past affects the future in terms of psychodynamic patterns, scripts, and risk triggers. As the client stands back from his experience, putting his life history into a larger context, insight can occur, providing a welcome sense of meaning to otherwise inscrutable events and behaviour. As stated in the introduction, I am not a strengths-focused purist, but believe that it is important for most people – perhaps for all of us – to make constructive sense of the ways we feel, think, and act and the events which occur in our lives.

The therapeutic relationship itself can also be a focus for life story patterns which can re-emerge through the dynamics between counsellor and client. If such dynamics are sensitively and non-judgementally explored, this can lead to fresh learning and new ways of being. With regard to attachment issues (discussed later in this chapter), the counsellor can provide a limited but significant re-parenting and re-socializing experience for the client, with notions and methods of increased emotional regulation and pro-social thinking being downloaded via this therapeutic re-parenting link. Below, a probation officer describes how her relationship with a sex offender altered his view of women.

> *Now his thing is that he doesn't trust women at all, and he'd said to me a few weeks ago, that's beginning to change. I'm beginning to trust you, and I thought, well, you know, I worked hard.*

(Probation Officer 4)

Traditionally, most counsellors explore a client's past through a particular mode of conversation or therapeutic discourse, relying on an exchange of words, often with the client doing most of the talking. Some counsellors use additional pictorial life story representations, rather than just listening and talking, to assist reflection, making use of various illustrative life-line patterns. Other counsellors and therapists use art (Edwards, 2014) or drama therapy exercises (Jennings, 1992) to help clients process the past in constructive ways, the aim being for the client to engage on a feeling, experiential level, not just a cognitive one. A wide range of exercises for people who have committed offences, which can also be used with clients who have sexual offending problems, has been helpfully described and catalogued by Baim and Guthrie (2014).

Most counsellors reading this book will be trained and experienced in facilitating clients to reflect on experiences of childhood, adolescence, and later life, and will have developed their own approaches to conducting life story work. These methods are perfectly transferable to working with people who have sexually offended, as long as the counsellor is clear about what she is trying to achieve – ideally a feature of work with any client group.

There are various key relationships, development stages, and life transitions which can be usefully explored when considering life story work up to the age of around 21. Following is a list of potentially important areas to reflect upon with clients:

- Has the client been able to maintain good relationships with his parents?
- Has there been abuse or neglect?
- What role did the client take up in the family (submissive or dominant)?
- Has the person been able to maintain positive relationships with siblings?

- What is the culture of the family; is there dysfunction in the lives of parents and siblings?
- What was the experience of primary and senior school, and relationships with fellow pupils?
- Was the client bullied or did he bully?
- What was the client's relationship like with teachers and authority?
- Were there discipline problems?
- Did the client under-achieve, relative to his social circumstances?
- How is distress managed (flight/freeze/fight – passivity/aggression/assertiveness)?
- How does the client meet needs for power, status, safety?
- What needs and desires are particularly important to the client?
- Are there issues with drugs, alcohol, mental health, suicide and self-harm, general criminality, gambling, debt, risk-taking, or general sexual addiction and compulsivity related to impulse control?
- Has the person been able to obtain social capital: education; occupation; constructive family and social relationships? (The presence or absence of social capital can provide information about resilience; ability to take on board new information; problem solving; prioritizing; objectivity; deferring gratification; empathizing with others; management of relationships. These are all core skills related to the ability to control deviant impulses and to protect children from such impulses.)

Other pertinent later life story areas which may be fruitful to explore include:

- Sexual orientation
- Any formative early sexual experiences (abusive or otherwise)
- Early fantasies that have endured in any way
- At the time of burgeoning sexual awareness and adolescence, how did the person relate to the opposite sex (prospective girl/boyfriends), and how did he view himself as a sexual being?
- Number of casual sexual encounters
- Number of adult relationships, and length of relationships
- Any signs of sexual deviancy or preoccupation: inappropriate internet use; sado-masochistic tendencies; partner swapping or group sex
- Any pattern of how the client functions in relationships
- Convictions, allegations of domestic abuse, police call-outs, medical records
- Beliefs about the role of men, women, children, and parenting
- How important is the role of being a parent to the person's self-concept, and to fulfilling the client's own needs and desires?
- Has the person had any relationships which seem constructive?
- Has the person been able to flee abusive relationships?
- Has the person ever been able to live on their own?
- What are the dynamics of the current relationship?

- Is there any dependency or intimidation in the current relationship?
- Who calls the shots and holds the power in significant relationships in terms of age; physical size; intelligence; education; occupation; finance; physical attractiveness; verbal persuasion?

The above list of potential areas to explore is not exhaustive, and should not be worked through as a tick list, eschewing the client-centred aspect of counselling. Some of these areas may be relevant to one client and not to another. Over the subsequent chapters, many of these topics and themes will be evident in the case studies presented, albeit configured differently with different clients.

Attachment and trauma issues

There is an extensive and significant body of evidence linking past deficits to future problems. Poor attachment between parents, significant others, and children has a significant impact on future functioning (Ainsworth et al., 1978; Crittenden and Landini, 2011). With regard to how deficits in upbringing can inform sexual offending, the theoretical risk framework of sexual risk (Beech and Ward, 2004) cites developmental attachment theory as relevant to sexual abuse. Building on the general attachment, child-developmental work of Bowlby (1969), Marshall (1989) found that family backgrounds of sexual offenders are typified by neglect, violence, disruption, and erratic or rejecting parenting. Smallbone and Dadds (1998) similarly found that poor attachment to parent figures, particularly mothers, was predictive of general anti-social behaviour and sexual offending. Moreover, there is a wealth of research and clinical data on how deficits and trauma in childhood heighten the likelihood of sexual crime (Bentovim et al., 2009). In the light of all the research data indicating how a person's past is linked to adult functioning, exploration of a client's childhood can be an important part of providing counselling to a person with sexual offending problems.

Ward and Keenan (1999) suggest that individuals brought up in dysfunctional circumstances (i.e. where there have been poor attachments and trauma) and perhaps a family or relationship network in which sexual abuse is tolerated or encouraged, can develop faulty 'implicit theories' or 'schema' about the world, relationships, and sex. This can produce distorted thinking, which can be activated at times of high emotional or sexual arousal. For instance, typical distorted thoughts that I have observed over the years of working with individuals who have exhibited sexually abusive behaviour, are variations of the following:

- S/he was leading me on.
- They're all up for it.
- S/he's a prick tease.
- S/he came on to me.
- S/he wasn't a virgin.
- I wasn't getting sex from my wife.

- I'm only attracted to youngsters.
- A wife shouldn't deny her husband sex.
- S/he may as well learn from someone s/he knows.
- The way she was dressed, she was asking for it.
- She was a right bitch, always making trouble.
- She's/they're out to get me.
- They need to know who's boss.
- I don't like the adult world, I get on better with children than adults.
- You can keep the real world; I'm a big kid really; I've never grown up.
- It just happened.
- I was drunk/stoned.
- I can't remember anything.
- It was a one-off.
- Things just got on top of me.
- S/he was enjoying it.
- S/he didn't resist.
- They're not so innocent.
- We have a special relationship.
- It's legal in some cultures.

These examples of distorted thinking are not exhaustive, but provide a flavour of the way individuals can talk about their sexual offending. A note of caution should be sounded here: therapists working with these clients will have to decide if such or similar statements are indicative of a genuine, deep-lying, world view or whether the individual is merely trying to rationalize after the event in order to avoid shame, social censure, and the legal consequences of offending. Moreover, it is important to not conclude that a client has a distorted world view from a one-off remark or isolated phrase. An entrenched way of thinking is usually indicated by repeated statements, supported by a pattern of anti-social events across an extended period of time.

Case study: Thomas

When Thomas was approximately 11 years old, he started to be bullied at school, with students saying that he was fat and a bit weird. He used to hate going to school and would dread breaks, when he would either be all alone in the school yard, or be picked on by the other kids. On Sundays, he would feel sick at the thought of the next day and would cause arguments and rows in the family, because he was feeling so bad. His parents would get very angry and scream and shout at him, and would sometimes hit him. The girls in Thomas's class began to change. Some of them started to get a lot bigger, wearing bras and make-up. As time went on, a few of them began going out with older boys, and one or two of the good-looking boys in his class started going out with girls. He secretly liked Susan, although she and the other girls called him 'fatso,' never using his first name like they did with the other boys. Whilst masturbating, Thomas used to think of pop stars and some of the girls at school, including Susan. The boys at school all used to talk about touching and feeling girls and Thomas would feel sick that none of this was happening to him. At home, things went from bad to worse. Thomas eventually stopped going to school altogether, and social services became involved. His mother used to cry about the situation, and his father would shout at him all the time. The only person who was nice to him was his little sister, Chloe. Chloe was like a smaller version of all the girls at school. She even looked a bit like Susan. Chloe would often jump up on Thomas, and sometimes kiss him on the cheek. Thomas would also play fight with her on the floor. Thomas used to enjoy the touch of his little sister's smooth skin, and the way she smelt. Sometimes his penis began to go hard when he was playing with her. Thomas loved his sister, but used to get angry with her for being spoilt, as he saw it. His parents would always buy her things, and speak nicely to her.

One evening, Thomas had his money stopped and was told to stay in his room because, during a row, he had smashed an ornament he had bought for his parents as a Christmas present. Upstairs in his room, he heard his parents and his sister and brother all laughing and joking together, downstairs. Thomas was filled with such rage that he felt he could kill them all. Half an hour later, at 8pm, his sister was sent to bed as it was her bedtime. Thomas had recently been thinking of Chloe when he was masturbating, but had pushed these thoughts to the back of his mind because he thought that this was bad. However, now he didn't care, and began to think about how it would be to feel Chloe's private parts. He even began to think of how it might feel to have Chloe touch his penis, or for him to put his penis inside Chloe's vagina, or even Chloe's mouth. One of the boys at school said that he had done this to Susan, although Thomas was not sure whether or not to believe him. Thomas tossed the thought of touching his sister to and fro in his mind, until he decided to do it. He kidded himself that if he touched his sister when she was sleeping, nobody would know about it. He also kidded himself that touching his sister down below wouldn't do any harm, and that he would only do it this once, to see what it felt like. After all, he told himself, why should everybody else have all the fun? Why should he miss out? Thomas went into his sister's bedroom and began touching Chloe's private parts. Chloe woke up, but didn't say anything. Thomas kidded himself that Chloe didn't mind what was happening because she kept quiet, not saying anything. For the next few days, he was frightened that Chloe might say something and began being especially nice to her. On the day that he abused Chloe a second time, his brother Jonathan came home with a cup he had won playing football and was going out to the cinema with his new girl-friend. Since he last abused Chloe, Thomas had continued to play fight with her and encourage her to jump on his lap. Even though his sister was only seven years old, Thomas kidded himself that Chloe could not have minded being touched sexually, because she still wanted to play with him. Thomas took advantage of playing with Chloe to rub himself against her and to touch her in private places, when he played with her. One night, when Chloe was sleeping, Thomas went into her room, laid on top of her, and tried to put his penis in her vagina. Chloe woke up and screamed and Thomas's mother rushed into the room to see what was happening. Soon afterwards, Thomas was taken into care.

Predisposing factors to Thomas's offending

The circumstances of Thomas's young life can be seen to have predisposed him to develop a view that the world is hostile. Often such a perspective derives from poor attachments with parent figures, when early normative negative experiences (e.g. hunger, cold) and anxiety-provoking excursions into the world (e.g. bumping into objects when crawling) are not soothed by consistent attuned parenting. Thus, the child internalizes a sense of the world as a hostile place and grows up to be traumatically hyper-vigilant, overreacting to relatively low levels of physical and psychological threat. When early negative experiences are particularly extreme (i.e. severe neglect and abuse) the view of life as essentially hostile usually becomes firmly embedded. Such experiences can adversely impact on brain development and the neuro-chemical processes which regulate mood states (Creeden, 2004).

We do not know if Thomas suffered such early poor attachment experiences, but the parenting he receives as an older child certainly seems insensitive and not attuned to his developmental needs. He has low self-esteem, is overweight, in his brother's shadow, bullied and isolated at school, and unhappy at home. At a formative time of increasing sexual curiosity, when hormones are starting to rage, he is rejected and humiliated by the peer-age girls and one in particular, Susan, to whom he is appropriately attracted.

Thomas's masturbating over pop stars and girls at school is normative, and does not suggest a paedophilic orientation, as such. Deviant sexual arousal begins when he starts to think of his sister whilst masturbating. Even though Chloe is only 7 years old and pre-pubescent when he sexually abuses her, his sexual arousal pattern is probably short of paedophilic. What seems to be happening is that Thomas is using his sister as a substitute for the girls he really wants but cannot have, in particular Susan, who although still legally a child, would be post-pubescent, having developed secondary sexual characteristics such as curves and breasts.

This is an important distinction for counsellors to consider. Is the abuser attracted to the childlikeness of the child, or is the abuser using the child as a substitute for a peer-age adolescent or adult partner, and superimposing fantasies on the child's body? With regard to Thomas and individuals similar to him, what can start off as opportunistic sexual experimentation with a young child, in the absence of being able to have sexual contact with a peer, can turn into a stable paedophilic arousal template. The abuser starts to fantasize about the previous abuse of the child and gravitates to other children, not developing the interpersonal capacity to have sexual relationships with peers as he grows into full adulthood.

Thomas may be in danger of developing a view of children as sexual by abusing his sister on more than one occasion, and entertaining the notion that sex with children causes no harm, kidding himself that Chloe will not suffer as a result of his actions. Grievance can also be seen in his thinking and distorted self-talk: 'Why should everybody else have all the fun? Why should I miss out?'

The motivation for sexual offending is often complex and multi-factorial. For instance, Thomas has ambivalent feelings about his sister. She is one of 'them', one of his family whom he resents, but he clearly also has brotherly affection for Chloe as she seems to be the only person who is nice to him. The much needed comfort he experiences as she innocently makes physical contact with him through play is a further trigger for abuse.

Many young males would be in a similar position to Thomas – having problems at school and not being popular with girls – but would not sexually abuse a sister or anyone else. The reason that Thomas ended up perpetrating abuse is due to a random and highly unfortunate collection of predisposing factors, coalescing at a particular time.

Thomas comes for counselling

Thomas comes for counselling at the age of 26. He says he has not reoffended since being put into care, after sexually abusing his sister.

He says that they tried to give him therapy in care but he would never talk about his abuse of his sister, Chloe. However, he is now racked with guilt about what he did, and thinks he may be able to talk about it for the first time. Chloe and his family say they forgive him, but he's not sure if he believes them. He works with computers and lives on his own. He has one or two male workmates, with whom he sometimes goes out and gets drunk. He is in regular contact with his family but has a strained relationship with them. He says he masturbates between one and three times a day, and spends at least two hours after work looking at internet porn. The images are legal but he is worried because he is increasingly looking at more violent sexual images. He is also worried because a colleague at work has just gone to jail for looking at abusive images of teenage girls. He says he wants a girlfriend but feels that he needs to lose at least six stone in weight, due to his overeating.

Therapeutic work with Thomas

At the start of counselling, the client usually informs the counsellor of his sexual offending behaviour, alleged behaviour or fears about committing a sexual offence. Often, these are minimized accounts, which lack coherent detail. Consequently, these matters need to be explored in greater depth, further on in the therapeutic process.

After the broad content of counselling had been agreed upon (see Chapter 3), the counsellor informed Thomas that many people he works with like to tell him their life story first, so he can get an idea of what led up to their offending. This allows the counsellor, and the client, to put the offending into context. The counsellor explained to Thomas that other clients like to discuss their sexual offending in detail first, as they have been dreading doing this very thing and want to get it over with. Thomas decided he wanted to start by talking about his life story.

The counsellor started this process by asking about the first memory Thomas could recall. Even if this memory seems relatively inconsequential, it orients the client to the past.

Thomas:	I don't know really. It must be me riding a three-wheeler bike around and around in the kitchen, and my brother pushing me off it, and my parents being too busy to notice.
Counsellor:	From the way you are describing it, it sounds like an unpleasant memory.
Thomas:	It used to happen all the time. They were always taken up with their business or having friends around for dinner parties or something.

Counsellor:	How did you cope with that as a child?
Thomas:	I just got on with it. I used to go off on my own and steal cake and biscuits.
Counsellor:	I know it's a long time ago, but how do you remembering feeling, being on your own and stealing the cake and biscuits?
Thomas:	I can't remember, but I've always been a loner – I like my own company.
Counsellor:	Tell me what you like about it.
Thomas:	Nobody can bother you, can they?
Counsellor:	And the stealing of the cake and biscuits?
Thomas:	I just like food – always been a greedy sod.
Counsellor:	Were there times when you chose not to steal food?
Thomas:	When I wasn't hungry, and when my parents had been nice to me – it wasn't that often. Maybe that's unfair. It could have been worse. My mother and my father never battered me or anything. It was just that they were always all for my brother, and later for my sister, Chloe.

In the extract, after the counsellor had acknowledged Thomas's subjective experience of a difficult childhood, he used various strengths-focused questions and techniques: a coping question, showing respectful curiosity about the rewards of stealing cake and biscuits, and a question inquiring how Thomas had managed not to give in to the temptation to steal. As well as establishing a strengths-focused dialogue, the counsellor attempted to encourage Thomas to look at his problematic past in fresh ways. The purpose was to begin a process by which Thomas could develop self-compassion with regard to the, albeit dysfunctional, coping mechanism he used as a child (the stealing of comfort food, isolating himself). The counsellor also wanted to convey the message that he was not going to jump on previous negative behaviour in a judgemental way (offering a different model to Thomas's parents) but wanted to respectfully explore with Thomas the possible meanings of such behaviour.

The counsellor proceeded to attempt a strengths-focused sculpt of Thomas's family situation. This can be done using various forms of representative kit: stones, objects, drawings, or paintings to represent the family system. The counsellor used chairs with Thomas to symbolically represent his family of origin: Thomas, his brother, his sister, and their two parents. The counsellor asked Thomas to tell him where to place the chairs in relation to each other, with the configuration chosen providing insight into the family dynamics, as Thomas viewed them.

Thomas placed the chairs symbolically occupied by his brother and sister next to the parental chairs. He placed his own chair further away. Once Thomas was happy with the shape of the chairs, the counsellor asked another series of strengths-focused questions:

- Can you re-arrange the chairs as you would have ideally wanted them to be?
- What would your relationship be like with each member of the family, if it could have been just as you wanted it to be?

- What would your parents' relationships have been like?
- What sort of things would you have been doing with each member of the family?
- What sort of things would you have been doing as a family together?

In response to the questions, Thomas described an ideal family in which his parents worked fewer hours and had more time for the children, particularly for him, and more time for themselves. He said there would have been far less stress in the household, and everybody would have had a lot more time together, rather than his parents being so driven and competitive. He described more relaxed holidays than the activity-driven skiing and sailing holidays enjoyed by his brother, but not by him. Rather, he talked of holiday activities which involved the family playing cards and board games, and lying around on the beach together, joshing about. He spoke of being appreciated by his parents as much as they appreciated his siblings.

This exercise can bring up powerful emotions for a client, as it cuts through intellectualizing, getting to the nub of what a client feels he missed out on. Usually what comes up is fundamental material: security, validation, stimulation, happiness, and boundaries. Often there will be a link between the very nurturing experiences denied and triggers for sexual offending.

With regard to Thomas, having worked with this therapeutic sculpt, he was able to identify the following risk triggers:

- Feeling left out
- Being rejected, especially sexually rejected
- Feeling an entitlement to sexual touching, being deprived of this and rejected
- Feeling a sense of grievance
- Emerging feelings of anger and shame
- Being alone with a vulnerable child
- Kidding himself the sexual touching wouldn't do any harm
- Kidding himself that his sister did not mind the abuse

The sense of stigma about committing a sexual offence had prevented Thomas from talking about the details of his offending to anybody, previously. It was important, therefore, for the counsellor to conduct some therapeutic work on Thomas's own victim issues, and to help him to gain some insight into his offending (Chapter 9 deals with victim issues specifically). This would allow Thomas to develop self-compassion, providing him with sufficient ego strength to comprehensively address his offending issues for the first time. The family sculpt was part of this process.

Thomas was able to begin to appreciate what he had been denied as a child and how he had suffered significant emotional deprivation through his parents' insensitive treatment of him. In addition, he was able to make links between what he predominantly valued at this current time in his life – feeling safe, wanted, and affirmed – with the nurturing he lacked as a child.

Thomas's years in care as a teenager denied him usual developmental opportunities to socialize. Residential homes for adolescents who abuse are frequently risk averse, fearing that a young person may sexually offend in the community, on the institution's watch. Hence, young people in this situation are often provided with few opportunities outside of the institutional home setting to learn social and relationship skills, because of fears they will offend if allowed to be with other young people. Hence, the counsellor and Thomas discussed and role-played social and courtship skills and brainstormed ways in which Thomas could search for opportunities to find a fulfilling relationship with a peer sexual partner. They explored the issues of eating, masturbating, and using the internet as a way of regulating negative emotional states. They also addressed managing sexual fantasy (these themes are looked at in greater detail in subsequent chapters).

As the counselling developed, they addressed the details of Thomas's offending: how he groomed his sister through physical play, used the opportunity of being alone with her to commit the offences, and employed cognitive distortions to justify abusing her. The counsellor explained to Thomas the distorted thinking commonly used by individuals to delude themselves that it is OK to have sex with children. This psycho-educational intervention was aimed at raising Thomas's ability to self-monitor when he might be entertaining such perspectives (Chapter 7 explores such offence-focused interventions in greater depth). The counsellor explored with Thomas how he could manage risky thoughts, triggers, and situations, should they occur in the future. Thomas was still in contact with his family. By the end of counselling, he was able to write letters of apology to family members, including Chloe, taking full responsibility for his offending. These letters were not sent as it was considered that this would bring up too much pain for the family.

N.B. The impact on the victims of receiving such a letter should always be carefully considered, as any contact coming from a person who abused them could be re-traumatizing. Usually, the therapeutic benefit is in the individual who has offended simply writing the letter of apology, and there is no need for such letters to be sent. The use of these letters is explored in more depth in Chapter 9.

Conclusion

Thomas suffered various dysfunctional childhood experiences, explored through life story work. This enabled him to make sense of his past and to become more aware of how consequential distorted thinking and dysfunctional ways of coping became triggers for sexual offending. Through the therapeutic relationship, Thomas was able to develop sufficient ego strength to overcome his internal shame and to address his offending issues. Developing self-compassion was key. An important part of the counselling was working with Thomas on his self-esteem and social skills. This would hopefully enable him to meet his needs and desires in pro-social ways, including eventually having a mutually satisfying relationship with an adult peer partner. These changes in identity and lifestyle would act as protective factors against further offending.

References

Ainsworth, M.D., Blehar, M., Waters, E. and Wall, S. (1978) *Patterns of attachment: A psychological study of the strange situation.* Hillsdale, NJ: Lawrence Erlbaum Associates.

Baim, C. and Guthrie, L. (2014) *Changing offending behaviour: A handbook of practical exercises and photocopiable resources for promoting positive change.* London: Jessica Kingsley Publishers.

Beech, A.R. and Ward, T. (2004) 'The integration of etiology and risk in sexual offenders: A theoretical framework', *Journal of Aggression and Violent Behaviour,* 10 (1), pp. 31–63.

Bentovim, A., Cox, A., Bingley Miller, L. and Pizzey, S. (2009) *Safeguarding children living with trauma and family violence: Evidence-based assessment, analysis and planning interventions.* London: Jessica Kingsley Publishers.

Bowlby, J. (1969) *Attachment and loss. Vol. 1: Attachment.* New York: Basic Books.

Creeden, K. (2004) 'The neurodevelopmental impact of early trauma and insecure attachment: Re-thinking our understanding and treatment of sexual behavior problems', *Sexual Addiction and Compulsivity,* 11 (4): pp. 223–247.

Crittenden, P.M. and Landini, A. (2011) *Assessing adult attachment: A dynamic maturational approach to discourse analysis.* New York: Norton.

Edwards, D. (2014) *Art therapy,* 2nd edition. London: Sage.

Jennings, S. (1992) *Dramatherapy with families, groups and individuals: Waiting in the wings.* London and Philadelphia: Jessica Kingsley Publishers.

Marshall, W.L. (1989) 'Intimacy, loneliness and sexual offenders', *Behaviour Research and Therapy,* 27 (5): pp. 491–503.

Smallbone, S.W. and Dadds, M.R. (1998) 'Childhood attachment and adult attachment in incarcerated adult male sex offenders', *Journal of Interpersonal Violence,* 13 (5): pp. 555–573.

Ward, T. and Keenan, T. (1999) 'Child molesters' implicit theories', *Journal of Interpersonal Violence,* 14 (8): pp. 821–838.

Chapter 5

Life story themes
Developing profiles

Introduction

This chapter will continue to explore life story themes, focusing particularly on power and relationships. Three profiles of individuals who sexually offend will be presented, to develop further understanding of the different motivations underpinning sexual abuse. The case study, 'Jay', features an adolescent offender who comes to counselling in his 20s. Unlike Thomas, in Chapter 4, he is globally anti-social, identifying with teenage, criminal gang culture. As with Thomas, the case study illustrates a particular developmental pathway, leading to an adult man posing a sexual risk.

Power in relationships

Attitudes to sex and relationships are key areas of exploration in life story work with individuals at risk of sexual offending. Hanson and Bussiere (1998) found that attachment problems, particularly with mothers, were consistent with difficulties in forming stable adult relationships, and also with sexual offending. In addition, poor attachments can lead to a lack of empathy, and a tendency to sexually objectify others (Marshall et al., 1993).

It is not uncommon for males who sexually assault and rape women to have missed out on experiences of healthy maternal nurturing. When they then find themselves in relationships and encounters with women, past maternal deficits can distort their perception, making them acutely sensitive and destructively reactive to being denied respect, affirmation, or sexual gratification. Unconscious rage can then be triggered, resulting in rape: the drive to humiliate in order to compensate for a felt lack of power (Brownmiller, 1975; Prentky and Knight, 1991). If, during childhood, a boy has been denied appropriate boundaries and models of men respecting women, a core belief of male entitlement can develop, often an underlying factor in the rape and sexual assault of women.

Same-sex rape attacks do occur (Scarce, 1997), and are under-reported, but the majority of rape is perpetrated by men on women and children (King et al., 2000). Perpetrators of rape or sexual assault are more likely than perpetrators of other violent offences to be known to their victims (Pinor and Meier, 1999). When rape or stranger sexual assault does occur, as in the Jay case study featured in this chapter, many offenders have records of general criminality and anti-social behaviour (Scott et al., 2006).

Notions of power have been heavily emphasized in the feminist perspective on sex offending. The various feminist positions are nuanced. However, from a radical feminist viewpoint, psychological causal theories of sexual crime have been criticized (Herman and Hirschman, 1977). Rather than viewing sexual abuse as a problem of pathology, feminist commentators such as MacLeod and Saraga (1988) argue that sexual offending should be seen as a problem of patriarchy. Hence, there should be a focus on challenging notions of male entitlement: men feeling they have a right to sexual gratification from and power and control over women and children. Calder (1999) comments on how the feminist perspective has made a valuable contribution to the treatment of males who sexually offend, particularly within prison and probation service treatment programmes, where chauvinistic and sexist attitudes are routinely challenged.

Three useful profiles

In my clinical experience with this client group, I have found it useful to explore three characteristic profiles of males who sexually offend. I term these 'The Inoffensive Offender', 'The Patriarch', and 'Jack the Lad'. Each will be introduced in turn, with the subsequent case study (Jay) illustrating themes pertinent to The Patriarch and elements of Jack the Lad.

Ultimately, individuals who sexually offend cannot be put into neat boxes. But characteristic profiles that are easy to remember can help the therapist gain insight into the various motives behind sexual offending, the sorts of relationship offenders can make with victims, and different grooming patterns involved in an offence. Moreover, beliefs, attitudes, and behaviour of persons who have committed sexual crime can be seen not so much as constituting a fixed state, but as occupying shifting points on a continuum.

The Inoffensive Offender

- Emotional congruence with children
- Emotional loneliness
- Problems with forming adult relationships
- Anxious personality type
- Views the world as a scary place, so seeks solace in the world of children

This type of individual is not inoffensive in fact, as he can commit serious sexual crimes, but he can appear that way to others. The Inoffensive Offender tends to view and experience the world of adults and adult relationships as hostile and threatening, so he seeks sanctuary and solace in the world of children. Children tend to be less judgemental and are easier to impress. An unfortunate cycle can develop in which a person can avoid contact and intimacy with adults. Consequently, he does not gain the social skills and usual experiences of the adult world that can facilitate the forming of relationships, particularly intimate relationships, with people his own age. Of course, many individuals who are prone to anxiety and seek escape from the pressures of the adult world may share the characteristics of this profile, without committing sexual offences.

A particular issue with this sort of offender is that professionals, including counsellors, as well as family members with a responsibility for protecting children, can be lulled into a false sense of security by the individual's compliant and inoffensive presentation. Often the offender is not merely being manipulative – putting on a harmless front – although this can be the case. Many of these individuals are genuinely vulnerable and needy, and, as explained later, can suffer significant social rejection. This can result in some of those close to them, including counsellors, wanting to act as rescuers, resulting in a minimized perception of risk.

The Patriarch

- Enjoys power and control
- Intimidates people
- Has problems controlling anger
- Believes that he is entitled to put his needs and desires before those of others

The Patriarch can be seen as the polar opposite of the Inoffensive Offender. An Inoffensive Offender generally wants to ignore the power dynamics between himself and a victim, viewing himself as a child or a child victim as an adult. The Patriarch tends to want to emphasize the power difference (within his own mind, if not publicly), gaining gratification from being 'top dog'. Many similarities can be seen with men who are domestic abusers.

The Patriarch often displays overt signs of egotistical entitlement. Both the Inoffensive Offender and the Patriarch Offender can perceive the world as essentially hostile, but in different ways, largely conforming to the flight/freeze or alternatively the fight reaction when faced with threat. The Inoffensive Offender experiences the world as dangerous, uses avoidance as a coping mechanism, and is often too anxious to act assertively and take up appropriate power. The Patriarch also experiences the world as hostile but, conversely, takes up inappropriate power, subjugating others and taking what he wants, as a reaction to perceived threat or limitation.

The challenge people face when living, or working, with this latter sort of individual, is coping with intimidation: the temptation is to walk on eggshells around them, to avoid conflict. If a counsellor experiences such feelings, then this probably provides a clue to what it is like for a child or partner living with such a man.

Jack the Lad

- Behaves generally irresponsibly
- Behaves in anti-social ways
- Poor emotional management
- Indulges in pleasure without thinking too much of the consequences

This individual can come across as the last sort of person you think would sexually abuse children, presenting, for want of a better term, as a 'normal bloke'. He is more likely to offend against teenagers than to be attracted to pre-pubescent children, but is liable to take pleasure where he can get it, without much thought for the consequences or the impact on others. There is often an emotional immaturity, or even a narcissistic element, to his character. Signs of lack of emotional regulation might include being in debt, substance misuse problems, criminality, or a chaotic employment record. This type of offender may be married and/or have had numerous adult sexual partners. He can be successful with women although often ends up with a younger partner he can more easily impress.

In my doctoral research (Smith, 2009), offenders who more closely fitted The Patriarch and Jack the Lad profiles said they felt relatively safe in prison and in the community, although they had committed some of the most serious sexual crimes. One was a double rapist; another had committed serious sexual offences against underage boys. However, neither conformed to the stereotype of a sex offender, as one of them illustrated.

> *In my flat, where I live, if you were a vulnerable old man, with horn-rimmed glasses and looked the part – the stereotype – then you could have problems, but I haven't met any problems.*
>
> (Offender 10)

Many of the other offenders in the study looked as if they would indeed have trouble defending themselves, conforming to the Inoffensive Offender profile which reflects more closely the cliché of the inadequate individual 'in a dirty raincoat'. These more vulnerable offenders had, by and large, committed less serious sexual crimes than the 'hard man', 'blokey' guys. It would seem that conforming to the public image of a sex offender, regardless of the seriousness of the sexual crime, compounds the difficulty of social integration. A probation officer in the study critically reflected to this effect.

> *I think it was something about his whole demeanour that I didn't like. . . . But there was something I couldn't put my finger on about him, you know the guy I mentioned before, with two rape convictions, I would certainly go out and have a drink with him. I wouldn't go out with the other guy.*
>
> (Probation Officer 10)

Case study: Jay

Jay has always lived in a caring family; he was the only boy and had five older sisters. As a boy, his parents had big plans for him as they believed that men should be head of the family and home. But Jay found school difficult. He was slow to pick up reading and writing, and did not shine academically. Because of this, he would fool around and, at senior school, he was often given detention. The most important person in Jay's family was his uncle, his father's older brother, who owned two businesses. He was a very successful man. Jay's father, however, worked as a taxi driver, and used to drink too much. At one time, when Jay was about 14 years old, he left the family to live with another woman for six months, but then came back home when Jay's behaviour at school deteriorated. Around this time, Jay started getting into fights. In one fight in particular, he lost control, needing to be dragged off the boy in question.

Jay began to be friendly with a group of boys who used to get in trouble with the police. Like the others, he began smoking and drinking. One of his sisters told their mother and father about this, but Jay denied it and his sister was told off by her parents for lying. Various girls in the school used to like Jay, thinking he was good looking. He went out with a few of them and tried to have sex with them. When one refused he moved on to the next girl. He also knew many girls around the same age as himself, who were daughters of his parents' friends. Some of these girls used to like Jay as well but he was never really interested in them, as he knew they were 'nice girls' who would only want to talk and kiss.

When Jay was still only 14 years old, he passed a young girl in the street and grabbed her breast. A month later, he did the same thing to another girl. All his friends would talk about having sex with girls, and one or two girls who hung around the group used to have sex with more than one boy on the same night. This never happened to him, only to the hardest boys, the leaders of the gang. Jay had been really excited when he grabbed the girls' breasts, although he was also frightened that he would get into trouble. When nothing happened, he was relieved that he had got away with it. He told his friends about it when they got drunk together one night, laughing with them about the shock on the girls' faces. A few weeks later, Jay was walking in the street and saw an older girl he thought was a prostitute. He asked her for sex, but she laughed at him. He followed the girl into the park. He was a strong boy for his age and dragged the girl into some bushes and tried to rape her, hitting her across the face to keep her quiet. The girl managed to get away and screamed for help. That day, Jay was arrested by the police and was put into a special residential unit. He was really upset and frightened to find himself away from his family, who have stuck by him, despite being really shocked by his offending.

Predisposing factors to Jay's offending

In the case of Jay, we see a very different offending trajectory than that of Thomas in Chapter 4. Unlike Thomas, Jay was doted on from an early age. His early attachments with parents seemed to be good. However, he had been socialized into believing he is more important than his sisters, and inculcated with a sense of entitlement that he will get what he wants.

The expectation that he will be 'top dog', as it were, was frustrated by his learning difficulties at school and the sense of shame he feels in not living up to his family's high expectations of him. Hence, he gravitated to an anti-social, non-academic peer group, where what he had going for him (physical strength, good looks, and popularity with girls) was valued and respected. When his father left home, Jay started getting into fights, using physical violence as a release for the hurt and anger he was unable to articulate in other ways.

His sense of superiority to females was consolidated when his parents refused to believe his sister's account of his anti-social behaviour. He was not interested in relationships with girls in his family's social network, whom he could not use for his sexual gratification. His tendency towards sexual objectification of women, along with his sense of entitlement, likely informed his choice to grab a girl's breast in the street. As with his anti-social behaviour at school, he got away with this and so repeated the assault.

Jay's inflated expectations were frustrated somewhat by the tougher boys in his gang who, by virtue of their leadership roles, had more sex with girls than he was having. In an effort to impress them and elevate his status in the gang, Jay boasted of his sexual assaults on the two girls. Within the cultural norms of the group, such behaviour was legitimized, consolidating Jay's distorted thinking about sex, power, and females.

If it is not curtailed, sexual offending often becomes more extreme, and this was the case with Jay. The attempted rape of the older girl is the result of anti-social schemas which have developed over time. These distal risk factors coalesced with acute risk factors: Jay's expectations for sex being denied and the humiliation he felt when the older girl laughed at him. There were many elements predisposing Jay to The Patriarch and the Jack the Lad offender profiles.

At the age of 25 Jay comes for therapy. He has not reoffended since coming out of the Young Offenders Unit when he was 17. Since then he has settled down back into the family home, and is working for his uncle. He entered an arranged marriage when he was 20, and now has a 2-month-old daughter and a 4-year-old son. He has been arrested for talking to two 14-year-old girls in a sexual way in internet chat rooms, and trying to meet up with one of them. The police have found nothing on his computer apart from legal pornography. His young wife (22) seems very submissive. She believes he will be no risk to his children, and believes the 14-year-old girls tried to seduce her husband. However, social services are worried about Jay's long-term risk to his daughter when she becomes a teenager, the submissive nature of his wife, and the fact that police were called out to a domestic abuse incident at the family home, after a neighbour had reported screaming and shouting. When the police arrived, they noticed swelling around his wife's eyes, but she said that she had walked into a door.

Therapeutic work with Jay

Jay appeared highly defensive when he entered the counselling room. The counsellor asked him how his journey had been and Jay's body language and tone of voice communicated, in no uncertain terms, that he did not want to be in the same room as the counsellor.

Counsellor:	Jay, why have you come here today?
Jay:	No choice, have I? They told me to come.
Counsellor:	But you could have stayed in bed, said you were ill, said 'sod it'.
Jay:	(staring sullenly)
Counsellor:	Tell me, why did you come?
Jay:	If I didn't, social services wouldn't let me see my kids, would they?
Counsellor:	Jay, I can tell from your attitude that this is the last place you want to be today, so it's clear to me that you're prepared to make a big effort for your family.
Jay:	(softening). It's the only thing that matters to me. I just want to get back home to them.
Counsellor:	Tell me honestly, Jay, what's the worst thing about coming here today?
Jay:	They've all got me down as a paedo, haven't they? They want me to say that I fancy kids, and that I'm going to have sex with my own daughter. They're sick, sick, man!

Often, when mandated clients (or others who feel they have been pressurized into undertaking therapy), come to see a counsellor, they feel anxious and resentful, displaying differing levels of resistance and hostility. Such clients frequently come out with unreasonable statements: attempting to shift blame and evade responsibility, showing little appreciation of the perspectives of others, particularly social services or anybody else preventing them having contact with their children or loved ones.

Jay protested to the counsellor about being labelled a paedophile, a 'paedo'. On one level this is understandable. Who would want this label? However, he had committed three very serious sexual crimes as an adolescent, two of which were against teenage children. More recently he was arrested for talking to two 14-year-old girls over the internet and asking to meet up with one of them. He showed no sign of acknowledging any of this to the counsellor and no objective awareness that, given this history, professionals were inevitably going to view him as a sexual risk to children, including his own child. The apparent submissiveness of his younger wife and indications of domestic abuse compounded concerns for child protection professionals and for the counsellor also.

In the light of such responsibility shifting, the counsellor felt the pull to express disapproval. The counsellor self-observed the temptation to play to the disapproving public gallery in his mind's eye. Yet he knew that it is not the business of a counsellor to indulge in this sort of judgementalism. To do so, even at a subtle level through tone of voice, facial expression and body language – which the client will sense – is likely to lead to more defensive blame shifting by the client, compromising the therapeutic process, and doing little to protect victims.

The counsellor believed that with Jay there was little chance of breaking down his denial and minimization of his past offending. He had never talked in detail about his previous sexual crimes. He was continuing to shift responsibility for talking to the teenage girls on the internet by saying that they had pursued him, and that he was 'stupid' enough to agree to meet up with the 14-year-old girl in question.

The word 'stupid' is often a face-saving term used by individuals to describe all sorts of criminal activity, implying a momentary lack of judgement or an aberration from otherwise pro-social character and behaviour. Challenging such minimization of criminal intent (or in the context of sexual abuse, premeditated grooming behaviour) head on, had rarely been successful, in the counsellor's experience.

Most individuals the counsellor had worked with, especially young men with fragile egos, want to save face. Keeping face also seems to be a cultural norm of Jay's background, with the maintenance of honour and respect a very strong value, especially amongst males. The counsellor did not consider that Jay, just like most of the clients he worked with who have committed sexual offences, was in denial in a classical Freudian sense (i.e. that his offending was so shameful that he had disassociated from it and could not bring it to conscious awareness). The counsellor was fairly certain that Jay, like the majority of clients, was aware of what he had done and might or might not have private feelings of regret and remorse which he could not express whilst refusing to talk about his sexual offending in any detail.

In order for any meaningful rehabilitative counselling to be completed with Jay, it was necessary to find a way of addressing underlying issues, whilst keeping his ego intact. Unlike with Thomas in Chapter 4, Jay was not at a motivational stage to discuss his offending at any depth. Hence, the counsellor worked with 'what is', reassuring Jay that he would not be asking him to talk about his offending, but would provide him with information about how and why sexual offending occurs, the impact on victims, and how he can avoid placing himself at risk of being accused of sexual crimes in the future. In addition, they agreed to explore the differences between respectful and abusive relationships, including the impact of domestic violence on partners and children, and to undertake cognitive-behavioural anger management work. The psycho-educational interventions would include providing Jay with fictional case studies to explore and raise awareness of relevant issues. Following is a flavour of the sort of psycho-educative work the counsellor conducted.

At a stage where the counsellor considered he had established a good therapeutic relationship with Jay, and having gained Jay's agreement to conduct psycho-educational work, the counsellor asked Jay if they could look at the following case study together. Jay agreed.

Mel was brought up with her mother, father, and her brother, Matthew. Her mother used to drink a lot and spend many days in bed sleeping off a hangover from the night before, although her mother was never cruel to her. Her father was always at work, and she spent a lot of time with Matthew, who was three years older than her. Often she and Matthew had to fend for themselves and cook their own meals, when their mother was going through a bad time. Mel was bright and would often tease Matthew about being a bit slow, although he was popular because he was good looking and was also good at rugby. They used to be close when they were younger and sometimes cuddled up together upstairs, when their father was working shifts and the loud music from downstairs meant that their mother was getting drunk. When Mel was around 12, her brother changed. He started missing school and hanging around with the rough boys. One afternoon, when her mother was sleeping in the bedroom, he suddenly began putting his hands down Mel's top. After that he would regularly touch her up, rubbing himself against her and making her have oral sex. She told her mother, who didn't believe her and said if she carried on saying things like that, the authorities would come and take her and Matthew into care, as she had been taken into care as a child. This shocked Mel, as she did not know that her mother had ever been in care. Mel was angry with her mother but, at the same time, felt sorry for her, seeing her sobbing. A bit later, Matthew slapped her across the face, saying that their mother had told him to leave her alone. After this, her brother bothered her less, apart from a few occasions when he came home drunk or on drugs. When Mel had sex education lessons in school, she thought it was a joke because of what had happened to her, and when her friends started talking excitedly about snogging boys, she thought to herself, *if only they knew what I have done.* Maybe Matthew was right when he called her 'a little slut'. Mel began to lose interest in school work, and started hanging around the girls who bunked off school, who smoked and drank alcohol. She felt better around these girls. Mel used to get more attention from boys, with some of them saying she was really fit. She found home depressing, and the only time she felt good about herself was when she was getting drunk and dressing up to go into town, and later to pubs and clubs. She could then forget everything, especially when she got chatted up by a good-looking boy with a car who would compliment her, and make her feel good about herself. She started to sleep with boy after boy when she was drunk, thinking they would stick around. They never did. She would feel used the next morning and promised herself she wouldn't let it happen again. By the time the next weekend came around, she would get drunk again, thinking that if she could only get a boyfriend to love her, life wouldn't seem that bad.

The counsellor explored with Jay the traumatic effects that sexual abuse had on Mel, propelling her into a lifestyle of sexual risk taking. Jay was able to understand that, as a result of the sexual abuse by her brother, Mel dropped out of school and began to misuse substances, to blank out traumatic memories. The counsellor also discussed with Jay how Mel's low self-esteem, and her experiences of sexual objectification, had led her into having sex with men as a substitute for being valued and affirmed for herself. Jay acknowledged that if he had seen Mel in a pub or club, he would have seen her as a sexual object and available, not relating to her as a human being. He would have likely exploited her vulnerability.

The counsellor asked Jay to draw a square on a piece of paper, listing ways in which some men may view young females such as Mel. Jay wrote the following:

- Up for it
- Showing too much flesh

- Slag
- Bit of alright
- Naughty

The counsellor then asked him to draw a circle, listing the characteristics of the person behind the sexual object. Jay came up with the following:

- Somebody's daughter
- Schoolgirl
- Needing protection
- Badly treated in the past
- Parents might have had high hopes for her
- A person just like me
- Having insecurities
- Somebody's future mother
- Having a family who might love her and care about her
- Somebody easily hurt
- Person with potential
- Person with talents and skills

The purpose of this exercise was to help Jay to de-objectify females. Sometimes when I work with clients I suggest that they imagine people they are having inappropriate sexual fantasies about living their everyday lives – waking up with a cold, celebrating a birthday, attending the funeral of a loved one – working out with the client any image that will assist in breaking the sexually objectifying spell.

To continue this theme of sexual exploitation, and in the light of Jay's offences, the counsellor asked if he could think about different types of rape. Jay could only think of stranger rape. The counsellor informed him that rape could also occur within a relationship or marriage, or could take the form of date rape. The counsellor discussed how rape and sexual assault could occur in war zones, gang culture, and occasionally in prisons, including male rape: rape in general often being as much about humiliating the victim, revenge or exercising power, as it is about sex. Jay did not verbally respond to this information, but looked thoughtful and seemed emotionally uncomfortable. The counsellor considered that Jay was probably seeing how he had sexually behaved in the past towards females in a new and negative light. It can sometimes occur in sessions that clients have a sudden cognitive shift in thinking, or leap in consciousness, whereby previous behaviour is conceived in a more mature way.

The counsellor considered that it would be constructive to work with Jay in a preventative way, given his history. He asked if it was OK if they discussed date-rape situations involving underage girls, and whether he could handle this. He added that this might help him avoid situations in the future where allegations may be made against him. Jay sheepishly agreed.

The counsellor asked him to think of the signs that a girl could be under the age of consent (16 in real life, 18 in the virtual world of the internet). The counsellor informed Jay that the age of consent for any sexual activity on the internet, such as sending sexually explicit texts or images, or communicating with a young person in order to meet up with them for sex, is 18. Jay came up with the following signs that a girl could be under the age of consent:

- Got to get home early
- Young looking
- Sounding childish (in real life and on the internet)
- Not fully physically developed
- Not talking about work
- Talking about school
- Talking about teenage activities
- Not being able to drive

The counsellor inquired what questions a person could ask to check somebody's age. Jay suggested:

- What jobs have you had?
- Getting her to talk about work
- When did you leave school?

The counsellor prompted Jay to think about the signs that men may misread, thinking that a woman may want sexual intercourse when she does not. Jay came up with the following:

- Flirting
- Giving you eye contact
- Giggling
- Dancing up close in a sexual way
- Being confident about kissing and sexual touching
- Making sexual noises of enjoyment

The counsellor further inquired what would be the early signs that a woman did not want to have contact with a man who started chatting her up in a bar, or who was driving her home, or who had come in for coffee. The counsellor and Jay discussed the following:

- Turning away
- Looking away
- Refusing a drink
- Not wanting to dance
- No eye contact

- Walking away
- Cutting off conversation
- Becoming fidgety
- Becoming quiet

The counsellor then asked what would be the signs that a woman wanted to stop sexual contact short of intercourse or any other further sexual activity. The counsellor and Jay discussed the following:

- Saying 'no'
- Pushing you away
- Saying 'enough, enough'
- Crying
- Getting angry
- Breaking off contact

Finally, the counsellor requested that Jay think about the signs that a woman did not want to have sex, if she was in a relationship and living with a man. Jay and the counsellor came up with the following:

- Being tired
- Having a headache
- Emotionally out of sorts
- Not aroused, not interested in sex at that time
- Falling asleep

The counsellor asked Jay how a person might kid himself that it was OK to force sex in any of the situations listed so far. They arrived at the following:

- Thinking 'no' really means 'yes'
- If she didn't want it, why is she doing all this (flirting etc.)?
- She let me spend all that money on her
- She sleeps around. Why does she not want to sleep with me?
- She wants it (sex) as much as me

These examples are obviously not exhaustive, and the responses will differ from client to client. When conducting this sort of psycho-educational work, I wait first for the client to come up with examples. However, I am not averse to then suggesting other examples a client may have not thought of, all of which can lead to an awareness-raising interchange with the client.

One note of caution for counsellors to consider when working with a client who may be abusive to a partner: consider if such work might threaten the client's ego to the extent that he may react by venting anger on his partner when he gets home, feeling the gratifying rush of compensatory power. Some practitioners and agencies will not work with clients when there are domestic abuse issues, unless the partners are separated. I find this position inflexible. In some cases of high risk this policy may constitute best practice. However, in many cases, partners will not leave one another, and the risk is not sufficient for the authorities to force a separation. To do nothing may be to miss an opportunity to increase safety for the partner, children, and the general public. Some good practice points should be considered with a supervisor, or other professionals, before embarking on the sort of work the counsellor carried out with Jay earlier:

- How likely is it that the client might act out negative feelings experienced in counselling towards those he lives with (or with the counsellor)?
- Is there any way that that this can be monitored, possibly through liaison with other professionals?
- Are there constraining factors that would probably prevent the client acting out any feeling of humiliation and anger towards others?
- What has been the level of violence and abuse in the past?
- Is the therapeutic relationship sufficiently positive to minimize negative feelings as the result of challenging work?
- Is the counsellor capable of discussing challenging issues in a strengths-focused way to minimize the client's sense of incompetence and to maximize competency?
- It may not be safe for a female counsellor to conduct this sort of work with a male who has sexually offended and shown anger against females, especially if the counselling is taking place in a relatively isolated venue. The same sort of health and safety risk assessment should be considered, however, regardless of whether the counsellor or client is male or female.

As noted in Chapter 2, counsellors should be vigilant about any risk with regard to being similar to the victims the client has offended against, in terms of age or appearance, for example. The female probation officer quoted here talked about feeling wary of this client group.

> *Yes, yeah, and it can be quite uncomfortable to think that when somebody may be viewing you in a sexual element, and I suppose that is uncomfortable, if you think anybody is, that you're not particularly keen on.*
> (Probation Officer 3)

Stanley and Goddard (2002) found that threats and intimidation can adversely affect the ability of workers to make accurate assessments and provide effective interventions. Most sexual offences are perpetrated by males on females (Grubin, 1998). Therefore it is logical that female therapists, in the round, may feel more at risk than male therapists. Erooga (1994: 211) suggests that female workers 'may feel covertly victimized during the process of working with offenders', and may also feel 'a generalized anger with men' for their abuse of power, which can be manifested in the dynamics of the working relationship. Whilst counsellors should not put themselves at risk, a therapist who is able to work constructively with such dynamics of transference and projection, in concert with an able supervisor, can offer the client a transformative therapeutic experience.

Many female probation officers, for instance, carry out sexual offence-focused work with male offenders, although they usually operate in a communal work setting, with panic alarms in the interviewing room. A prime component of such input can be the male experiencing a positive therapeutic relationship with a female, with the offender benefitting from the experience of having a relationship with a woman without perceiving her in terms of chauvinistic stereotypes: the 'angel' (mother or wife) or the 'whore' (sexual object). This would mean the counsellor modelling firm boundaries and assertiveness, appropriate use of humour, relating through her humanity as well as her professional role, gaining the client's respect if possible, and feeding back, from a female perspective, in a non-moralizing and judgemental way, how it feels to be objectified and disempowered.

Conclusion

If Jay is contrasted with Thomas in Chapter 4, a very different etiology of offending emerges. There was no obvious mistreatment or history of attachment problems, apart from parental over-indulgence and the parents failing to teach Jay respect for females. He had bullied others rather than being himself a victim of bullying. Unlike Thomas, he was popular with girls and did not suffer from a deficit of social skills with regard to making relationships with them, although clients like Jay may have problems in developing intimacy within relationships. There were no obvious indications that Jay was attracted to children below the age of puberty. However, he posed a sexual risk to young teenage girls and a risk of physical violence to his wife, and potentially to others by whom he might feel humiliated. Unlike Thomas, he was not at a motivational stage to talk about his previous offending in detail. The focus in counselling with Jay was not so much on attending to past attachment or trauma issues, but on lowering his risk through strengths-focused psycho-educational and cognitive-behavioural input, challenging male entitlement, and his related sexual objectification of females.

References

Brownmiller, S. (1975) *Against our will*. New York: Simon and Schuster.

Calder, M. (1999) *Assessing risk in adult males who sexually abuse children*. Dorset: Russell House.

Erooga, M. (1994) 'Where the professional meets the personal', in T. Morrison, M. Erooga and R.C. Beckett (eds.) *Sexual offending against children: Assessment and treatment of male abusers*. London: Routledge, pp. 203–220.

Grubin, D. (1998) *Sex offending against children: Understanding the risk*, Police Research Series, Paper 9. London: Home Office, Policing and Reducing Crime Unit. Available from: http://fairplayforchildren.org/pdf/1291334387.pdf [22 August 2016].

Hanson, R.K. and Bussière, M.T. (1998) 'Predicting relapse: A meta-analysis of sexual offender recidivism studies', *Journal of Consulting and Clinical Psychology*, 66 (2): pp. 348–362.

Herman, J.L. and Hirschman, L. (1977) 'Father-daughter incest', *Signs: Journal of Women in Culture and Society*, 2 (4): pp. 735–756.

King, M.B., Coxell, A. and Mezey, G.C. (2000) 'The prevalence and characteristics of male sexual assault', in G.C. Mezey and M.B. King (eds.) *Male victims of sexual assault*, 2nd edition. Oxford: Oxford University Press, pp. 1–16.

MacLeod, M. and Saraga, E. (1988) 'Challenging the orthodoxy: Towards a feminist theory and practice', *Feminist Review*, 28 (1): pp. 16–55.

Marshall, W.L., Hudson, S.M. and Hodkinson, S. (1993) 'The importance of attachment bonds in the development of juvenile sex offending', in H.E. Barbaree, W.L. Marshall and S.M. Hudson (eds.) *The juvenile sex offender*. New York: Guilford Press, pp. 164–181.

Pinor, N.W. and Meier, R.F. (1999) 'Gender differences in rape reporting', *Sex Roles: A Journal of Research*, 40 (11): pp. 979–990.

Prentky, R.A. and Knight, R.A. (1991) 'Identifying critical dimensions for discriminating among rapists', *Journal of Consulting Clinical Psychology*, 59 (5): pp. 643–661.

Scarce, M. (1997) *Male on male rape: The hidden toll of stigma and shame*. Cambridge, MA: Perseus Books.

Scott, D., Lambie, I., Henwood, D. and Lamb, R. (2006) 'Profiling stranger rapists: Linking offence behaviour to previous criminal histories using a regression model', *Journal of Sexual Aggression*, 12 (3): pp. 265–275.

Smith, A. (2009) *Sex offenders and the probation officers who supervise them: How relevant are strengths-based approaches?* Doctoral thesis for Cardiff University School of Social Sciences. Available from: http://orca.cf.ac.uk/55909/ [31 May 2017].

Stanley, J. and Goddard, C. (2002) *In the firing line: Violence and power in child protection work*. Chichester: Wiley-Blackwell.

Chapter 6

Life story themes

Counselling victims of abuse who have gone on to sexually offend

Introduction

This chapter will begin with some brief comments about issues related to the widespread notion that an individual is more likely to sexually offend if he has been a victim of sexual abuse. The links, such as they are, between suffering abuse and becoming an offender will then be discussed in greater depth. The remainder of the chapter is devoted to exploring the fictional case study of 'Martin,' a young man with borderline intellectual disabilities. The client has been in institutional care since committing a sexual offence when he was 14 years old. He has now been sent to counselling, following his disclosure that he was sexually abused as a child by a ring of four men, led by his now-deceased father.

Pertinent victim issues

Many people who have been sexually abused do not go on to sexually offend against others. A meta-analysis found that out of 1,717 offenders, around 28.2% reported a history of childhood sexual abuse (Hanson and Slater, 1988). This leaves just over 70% of the sample who had not themselves been sexually abused. Bentovim et al. (2009) make the point that if an individual is a victim of sexual abuse, it is aggravating features such as ongoing neglect, violence, and absence of compensatory nurturing which often tip the balance with regard to victims going on to sexually harm others.

Many victims of sexual crime take exception to being defined by their abuse, rejecting the notion that they are 'survivors' or even 'thrivers', therapeutic terms often used by practitioners (Dolan, 1998: 1–11). They argue that the belief that if a person has suffered sexual abuse he will likely sexually offend is both erroneous and constitutes repeat victimization in terms of being labelled. Moreover, some individuals who sexually offend report no victim or traumatic experiences in their backgrounds:

> I've had a brilliant upbringing. . . . I wasn't abused. I was loved. I was looked after.

> (Offender 5)

One of the main tenets of the strengths-focused approach is to work in concert with the client's motivation. In my experience, clients are more willing to talk about their offending issues once they have had their own concerns acknowledged and addressed, the experience of being sexually abused being one such possible concern.

> So if you're working with somebody on a one-to-one . . . and say if he really isn't going to move on this objective, let's look at something else until he is ready to talk about the other one.

(Probation Officer 3)

This sort of client-centred approach was clearly valued by a respondent who had sexually offended.

> She's done them [interventions] at the right time. She had to go at my pace; . . . it's taking it stage by stage. It's no good coming in here talking about the ex-wife [whom he had mistreated], because I was not interested you know. . . . So that wouldn't have worked.

(Offender 4)

Links between being a victim and a perpetrator of sexual abuse

Despite the caveats, trauma of all kinds, including sexual abuse (as discussed in Chapter 4) can adversely impact on pro-social functioning, even negatively impacting on neurodevelopment (Creeden, 2004). Jesperson et al. (2009) found in a meta-analysis that those who offended sexually against children were three times more likely than general offenders to have been sexually abused. There are various reasons for this.

Sexual abuse can alter a victim's arousal template, causing sexual fantasies about the abuse and leading to sexual offending (Bramblett and Darling, 1997; Hudson Allez, 2014). Victims can both hate the abuse but, at the same time, enjoy aspects of it. This process has been termed 'opponent process theory' (Solomon, 1980), whereby unpleasant effects of sexual abuse are replaced by pleasant effects. This phenomenon can lead to self-disgust, confirming destructive notions that may have been put into the victim's mind through grooming by the offender:

- There must be something bad about me.
- I must have been giving out signals, inviting the abuse.
- It couldn't be that bad, if I enjoyed bits of it.

The process by no means occurs with all victims and, in my experience, the majority of victims hate the abuse and experience no pleasure from it. However, it is important for the counsellor to be open to the possibility that a victim may have enjoyed aspects of the abuse and to convey to the client that, if so, this can be heard non-judgementally.

'Repetition compulsion 'and 'destiny neurosis' are Freudian terms describing how clients can be compelled to revisit sites of past trauma, including sexual abuse (Freud, 2010, first published 1920). In this way, individuals seek to control or understand sites of historical distress through familiarization (Fenichel, 1946), as a sort of unconscious, self-help aversion therapy. This process can be seen to offer an explanation as to why internet offenders who have themselves suffered abuse insist that they searched for images of children being sexually abused out of curiosity rather than a quest for sexual satisfaction, although such clients may also be minimizing their sexual interest in children. Moreover, with regard to sexual abuse, familiarization can then turn into pleasure (e.g. a person being made to perform oral sex developing a particular sexual inclination for this).

In a patriarchal and a capitalist society which values strength and success, the position of the male victim does not sit comfortably. Hence, male victims of sexual abuse can compensate for this 'one-down position' by seeking the 'top dog position', abusing and disempowering others, having learnt the painful lesson that this is a way of getting what you want in life (Woods, 2003).

In families where sexual abuse has occurred over a protracted period, or where intergenerational abuse is part of the culture, sexual boundary breaching or offending can become normalized. It is only when the victim (or the adolescent offender) leaves the home environment and has corrective experiences in a wider world that he comes to view sexual abuse from a normative perspective (i.e. that it is morally wrong and harmful).

Victims of sexual abuse can be prevented from disclosing for a host of reasons. The following list is not exhaustive:

- The victim wanting the abuse to stop, but not wanting the offender (if a loved one) to go to prison
- The shame of exposure, felt by family and/or victim
- Ties of family loyalty preventing the victim disclosing
- Pressure from family members (overt or subtle) to keep the abuse secret
- The victim having been groomed into feeling sorry and responsible for the offender
- Not wanting child protection professionals involved
- The victim fearing s/he won't be believed
- Fear concerning the exposure and distress of the legal process
- Fear of the abuser, sometimes because actual threats have been made
- Fear of being scapegoated and rejected by the family, and blamed for causing shame to the family and the possible break-up of the family, if the offender will have to be removed or children taken into care

Victims are also prevented from recognizing and integrating abusive experiences because of trauma ties and identification with the abuser (Fonagy, 2006). For some victims who have been abused in childhood the pain of acknowledging that a parent (whom the victim has relied upon and still might rely upon) is a perpetrator, is too great. Putting up with continued abuse, or idealizing one's childhood or the abusing parent is less threatening to the damaged ego. Where a parental abuser is strong and dominating, the victim may have been groomed to still rely upon the perpetrator (psychologically or practically) into adulthood. Where the parental abuser is weak and vulnerable, the victim may have protective feelings, especially if the offender has aged and become helpless. Victims can become locked into the familial system, caring for the family member who perpetrated the abuse and those who allowed it to happen. The shame, fear of the abuse ever coming to light, and often the sheer dysfunction of some abusive families can cut them off from the wider community, creating a situation where victims and perpetrators become locked in a domestic world where secrecy is the unspoken rule. Victims can come to believe at a pre-verbal, instinctive, unconscious level, that they are primarily valued for their body. Through abusive sex the victim becomes commoditized and dehumanized: a sexual object to be used and discarded. If the abuse has involved oral, vaginal, or anal penetration, the boundaries of personhood have been significantly invaded. Finkelhor and Browne (1985) proposed a traumagenic model of sexual abuse, which crystallizes many of these themes.

As well as leading to avoidance of sex, sexual victimization can also lead to participation in risk-taking environments and behaviours, where victims can use drugs, alcohol, and promiscuous sex to escape and manage post-traumatic symptoms. Such risk-taking behaviour and concomitant deficits in emotional regulation, can not only lead to increased risk of repeat victimization, but also to higher risk of becoming a perpetrator through involvement with anti-social groups which hold values permissive of sexual abuse.

Case study: Martin

Martin (32) has borderline intellectual disabilities and is living in supported accommodation. He has spent his entire adult life in care institutions, under the Mental Health Act, since he was taken away from his farming family at the age of 14, after being accused of sexually abusing Lizzie, a 7-year-old girl. Lizzie alleged that he had given her a lift on a tractor and suggested that they went into a barn to look at some nesting birds. In the barn, he had tried to kiss her and put his hand into her knickers, but had run off when she started screaming. There have been reports of him masturbating in public.

In the various institutions in which he has lived, some female staff members said they felt uncomfortable as he would stare at their breasts. He told one female staff member that he thought about her all the time, and imagined having sex with her. A number of female fellow residents in institutions over the years have said that he has rubbed up against them and, at other times, made inappropriate sexual remarks. Five years previously, a female resident had accused him of attempting to rape her, with staff noticing beforehand that they had begun what seemed to be a jokey, flirtatious relationship. No further action was taken as there was no evidence of an attack, and the female resident had made similar allegations about other patients.

Currently, Martin is living in a flat of his own, within a supported housing complex. He is not allowed to go out alone into the community, and is always accompanied by a support worker. Support workers report that he sometimes stares at children when they are out with him. Martin has received psychological input from various psychiatrists in the past, and he continues to be assessed as high risk. For a number of years, he has insisted that he is no risk to children and wants to be allowed to go out into the community, and eventually to work on his mother's smallholding, which she struggles to run on her own. His mother still regularly visits him. Martin recently told his support worker that, for the last few months, he has been having dreams of being taken to a room somewhere as a young child – he thinks when he was around 13 years old – and being sexually abused by his father (now deceased) and three other men. He thinks that this happened but he had blanked it out. He remembers the men drinking, and being made to give the men oral sex. His mother says that she knows nothing about such abuse, but that her late husband did have an alcohol problem and was violent towards her. They separated soon after Martin was taken into care. Some mental health staff members involved with Martin believe that he is being manipulative, claiming that he is a victim so that there will be sympathy for his pleas to be allowed more freedom in the community. Other staff members believe that he is not sophisticated enough to attempt this. A counsellor from outside the mental health system has been employed to explore with Martin possible victim issues, and how these might impact on risk management.

Predisposing factors to Martin's offending

Given Martin's borderline intellectual disabilities, and the fact that he had spent his entire adult life in institutional care, the counsellor had arranged for one of Martin's support workers to bring him to the first session. Martin seemed friendly and outgoing. An intellectual disability was apparent, with Martin seeming younger than his age, although it did not seem pronounced. Martin was not particularly nervous, so once initial introductions were completed, the counsellor asked Martin if it was alright to continue without the support worker. Martin agreed.

Counsellor: So tell me, Martin, why are you seeing me today?

Martin: I've asked for more help. I've been remembering things that happened to me, and I want a more independent life.

Counsellor: What would life be like if you had a more independent life?

Martin listed various ways in which he wanted more independence, including being allowed to go into town on his own, move back to help his mother on the farm, and to have a girlfriend. The counsellor asked Martin if he could say what the first step would be in trying to achieve these goals.

Martin: Talk about issues.

Counsellor: Could you say what issues?

Martin: I need to prove myself, don't I, that I'm not going to mess around with kids and do to them what my father and his mates did to me, and what I did to Lizzie (the neighbour's little girl sexually abused by Martin in the barn).

Counsellor: Tell me Martin, where would you place yourself on a scale of nought to 10, with nought meaning no risk of abusing children and 10 meaning high risk?

Martin: Nought, no chance.

The counsellor then asked Martin where he would place himself at the time when he had offended against Lizzie. Martin placed himself at 10. The counsellor considered that the two extremes (nought and then ten) were probably due to Martin's concrete thinking style, a result of his intellectual disability. Rather than overtly challenging the reality of these two extreme risk measures, the counsellor remarked that this seemed to be a huge change, and asked Martin how he had managed it. He provided the following reasons:

- I was only young back then.
- I know right from wrong now.
- I don't want to be locked up for the rest of my life.
- I wouldn't want anybody to go through what I've gone through.

The counsellor asked Martin if he was referring to himself being sexually abused in this last statement. Martin went quiet and looked down.

Martin: This is what I've come here for as well, to talk about that.

The counsellor, being experienced in working with abuse, knew that each victim's experience is different, and many victims can go on to lead happy, constructive lives. Nevertheless, the following factors are usually aggravating features, often leading to higher levels of trauma and acting out by harming self or others:

- If the abuse was prolonged
- If the victim was very frightened by the abuse
- If the victim feels unprotected from further abuse, and lives in a state of fear
- If the abuse was carried out by a trusted family member the victim relied upon for security (e.g. a parent figure)
- If the abuse was particularly invasive (i.e. oral sex, intercourse)
- If the victim was not believed by family members, and blamed for causing trouble
- If the victim was made to feel responsible for the abuse
- If the victim was particularly vulnerable, with existing emotional and welfare problems

The counsellor did not want to just focus on victim issues and never get around to dealing with Martin's offending. She already sensed that she was starting to feel protective towards Martin, with fantasies emerging of rescuing him from a repressive residential regime. However, the counsellor had sufficient self-awareness to acknowledge that she had her own issues with mental health services. For a while she had worked in the system, and she had felt undervalued by it and blocked in her career. It had been the consultant psychiatrists' opinions which held sway, not hers, despite most of them having received little psychotherapy training. It was important that she (the counsellor) did not allow her own sense of grievance to contaminate the therapeutic relationship, over-identifying with Martin as a victim of the system, aligning herself with Martin against the mental health establishment.

Whilst bearing these issues in mind and making a mental note to take them to supervision, the counsellor knew that Martin had focused on his offending with various psychiatrists and had not, to date, addressed being a victim of sexual abuse. This definitely seemed to be the place to start, if Martin was willing. The counsellor wanted to give Martin ample opportunity to discuss any possible traumatic reactions to abuse whilst not insisting (no matter how subtly) that there must inevitably be traumatic symptomology to discuss. The following strengths-focused questions can help a counsellor with regard to achieving a balance:

- From what you're saying, I feel there could be more to this. Am I on the right track?
- Would it help to talk about this?
- If you talk about this today, what support is around for you when you leave here?

- How can you be supported when you go home?
- Would you like to say more about what happened?
- Do you want me to ask you more about that?
- What would help you to talk about this?
- Would you see this behaviour as abuse?
- Would it be helpful to agree a word or a signal for when you want to stop talking or want me to stop asking questions?
- What were the immediate challenges for you after the abuse stopped?
- What was the worst thing you had to cope with when you were abused?
- What were the long-term challenges for you after the abuse had stopped?
- What were the qualities in you that made you survive the abuse?
- What were the qualities in you that made you move on and prosper?
- Is this helping, or do we need to do something else or talk about it in a different way?

There are various reasons for facilitating a client who has also sexually abused to talk about his experiences as a victim. These reasons are mainly connected to the client developing ways of living a better-quality life, where needs and desires are met constructively rather than unconstructively, thereby decreasing the risk of further sexual offending. Therapeutic/rehabilitative gains can include the following:

- For the client to cathartically discharge emotions about the abuse, which may have been seeping out destructively in other parts of life
- To allow the client to make meaning of the abuse and to construct a helpful account of what occurred
- To help the client put the abuse into a life-affirming perspective and challenge cognitive distortions that the abuse was their fault in some way and that there is something essential about their person that is indelibly soiled
- To help the client dispel any notions that sexual abuse is normative and not harmful
- To help the client manage destructive thoughts, emotions and behaviour, causing harm to self and others
- To help the client have empathy and compassion for the victim part of themselves, so that they can develop empathy and compassion for other victims, including those they have personally victimized.

Counsellor: Can you say, Martin, if you are ready to tell me what happened when you were abused?

Martin: (nods his head, implying yes).

Counsellor: Martin, if you want to stop talking about what happened at any time, or you want to take a break, or if you find any question I ask you too difficult, just say so and we can have a rest. Some people find it easier to agree a sign, like raising a hand if they want a break.

Martin:	I can stick my thumb up.
Counsellor:	Yup, nice one, that's fine. From time to time, I will check in with you to see if what we are talking about is helpful, and whether you want to do more of it, or try something different.

When talking with a client about memories of abuse, especially if it is the first time the client has addressed the issue, it is important for the counsellor to create the conditions in which the client feels in control of the pace of disclosure or trajectory of the exploration and feels that he can stop at any time. All abuse, including sexual abuse, involves a misuse of power and control. Revisiting the abuse in a therapeutic setting should, ideally, be a corrective experience, in which the client feels in control, experiencing renewed agency.

Fortunately, most counsellors are well-practised at talking to clients about victim issues, whilst being more unfamiliar with offending issues (the subject of Chapter 7), so most therapists will have their own tried and tested ways of discussing sexual abuse with clients. Presented in this book are some ideas, taken from structured ways of working with offenders (with victim issues) within the criminal justice system, but given a strengths-focused slant. These ideas are not offered as alternatives to the therapist's own ways of working, but as possible additions.

Counsellor:	Martin, I understand that you have indicated that some pretty serious things happened to you of a sexual nature. What bits of it have been the most challenging for you?

The counsellor chose the word 'challenge' to suggest that whatever has happened can be overcome or coped with, inviting the client to believe in a transformational narrative of possibility and competence – a strengths-focused approach also used by the following probation officer in her work with this client group.

> *So breaking it down and to recognize the pain, and also to recognize how strong he is to have come through that and still actually be alive, because many people wouldn't.*

(Probation Officer 3)

Martin:	Well I'm not sure if it (the abuse) happened, or how much of it happened.
Counsellor:	Can you say what you can remember happening?
Martin:	I remember walking with my father, I was holding his hand. I hate the fucking fog. I've always hated the fog. Then I remember my father and two men drinking. There was music on, ZZ TOP. My father and his mates used to be into motorbikes. Then, it's a bit embarrassing to say . . .
Counsellor:	That's fine; just say as much as is comfortable.

Martin:	My dad made me suck his dick, and the dicks of the other two. I remember they held me down, and Dad saying 'Be careful, we don't want to leave any bruises.'
Counsellor:	How many times did it happen?
Martin:	I don't know.
Counsellor:	Did it happen once or more than once?
Martin:	More than once. I remember my dad used to take me to the barn, when my mother visited Gran at the weekend to do her shopping. Once, a woman was there, and she made me watch while they did it [have sex] with her. But then it stopped when I did what I did to Lizzie in the barn.
Counsellor:	Can you say how old you were, Martin, when the abuse occurred?
Martin:	I think it was when I was 13, because my dad bought me a mini motorbike for my 14th birthday, saying it was because I had been a good boy, and not said anything about what was happening to me. After the sessions, my dad and his mates would take me to town to McDonald's, telling me it was only a bit of fun, and Dad said if I said anything to Mum, he'd kill me.
Counsellor:	Was anything else said to you?
Martin:	He would always say that my time would soon come with the 'local sluts'. He always used to use words like that. I can't remember anything else.

Martin did not seem unduly upset by the disclosure. The counsellor found herself questioning whether or not the disclosures were true, feeling guilty about this as she knew victims of sexual abuse are often not believed. The counsellor compassionately acknowledged her thoughts and feelings, knowing that there is a connection between the therapist being present and compassionate to her/himself, and facilitating this in clients.

Martin's apparent lack of emotional affect may have been related to his intellectual disability, or that simply sufficient time had passed to heal the emotional impact of the abuse. Natural healing processes occur in the lives of people all the time – although, as noted earlier, in some cases victims of trauma, including child victims, are irretrievably damaged. Clients' emotional responses to both suffering and committing abuse have often been dulled by the frequent telling of the tale to different professionals, although this was not the case with Martin. Moreover, Jones (2004), studying child victims' experiences of severe trauma in wartime Bosnia, found that many children who had suffered or witnessed horrendous events showed remarkable resilience. The children who were allowed to 'distance' themselves from the suffering, rather than talking about it to counsellors, seemed to find a measure of healing through natural processes.

However, in my experience, many victims of sexual abuse have been significantly distressed by their experiences and value the opportunity to explore them within a safe therapeutic environment, defrosting the frozen trauma through the warmth of the therapeutic relationship. Often the therapeutic response needed is for the therapist to act as compassionate witness, encouraging the client to be present to whatever thoughts and feelings the client's defences are allowing to emerge, before the process moves on to developing coping strategies.

With regard to Martin, the counselling proceeded as follows.

Counsellor: Martin, you say you are not sure if the abuse happened. How have you coped with that and with only having certain memories of it?

Here, the counsellor used the strengths-focused language of resilience, choosing the verb 'coping'.

Martin: Just get on with it, like.
Counsellor: Just getting on with it; that sounds like quite an achievement. What do you do when you just get on with it?

One of the tenets of the strengths-focused approach is careful attention to language used by the client. We see this here, with the counsellor adopting Martin's language – 'just get on with it.' A further strengths-focused principle is employed in which the client is asked to describe a generalization in concrete terms.

Martin: I just say to myself it wasn't my fault; it was them who were in the wrong for doing it.
Counsellor: Yes, it's really good that you can place the responsibility where it belongs. But can you say a bit more about why it was so wrong?
Martin: People shouldn't do that to kids, should they? It's filthy.

The counsellor was encouraged that Martin was not displaying any distorted thinking about the abuse. He knew it was wrong, and he was not responsible for it. But the counsellor considered that, if possible, it would have a rehabilitative effect if Martin could name his own feelings about being a victim. This could then lead to him engaging with the consequences of the abuse he was subsequently responsible for, hence developing increased victim empathy, the theme of Chapter 9. One note of caution here, however, is that some clients with certain forms of intellectual disability have limited capacity for empathy with others. In such cases, the harmful consequences of abusive actions on the client's own life can be used as extrinsic motivational material. The effectiveness of a probation officer adopting such a pragmatic approach is commented here:

> *'Well, it's up to you [the probation officer said]. I'm here to help you, but it's up to you as a person. If you want to move [on], that's fine. If you don't want to move on, you spend a lot longer in prison.' And that's what made me think about my past.*
>
> (Offender 3)

With regard to Martin, the therapeutic process continued as follows.

Counselling: Martin, if I could explain an exercise I would like to do with you, and then you can say if you would be OK with doing it. Imagine that a younger, immature Martin is sitting in a chair over there. What would he say about the feelings and thoughts he has had about the abuse?

After a period of the counsellor encouraging reflection by using open questions, prompts, empathic statements, and summaries, Martin came up with the following:

- Angry that if the abuse didn't happen, he [Martin] might not have abused and ruined his life
- Angry that his father had died without saying he was sorry, but feeling sad his father had died
- Angry about his father beating his mother
- A bit angry with his mother for not noticing anything
- Frightened after each time he was abused, in case it happened again
- Feeling dirty
- Worried that he would abuse other people and turn out like his father
- Ashamed of himself that he has turned out to be like his father.

The counsellor then explored with Martin at length, always searching for practical detail, what Martin would say to his immature self:

- It wasn't your fault.
- You're a good person.
- You're sorry for abusing the little girl in the barn.
- You want to live a good life and be kind to people.
- There's hope for the future.

The counsellor used different forms of Socratic questioning to facilitate Martin to come up with those statements, although art and experiential therapies might prove more effective with some clients than the talking method, especially those with intellectual disabilities.

The counsellor asked Martin to complete a list of the usual negative thoughts he had about the abuse, and any related negative behaviours. The counsellor then prompted Martin to think about exceptions to the problem: positive thoughts, behaviours, and circumstances which help him deal with negative mood states and cognitions. These were then put into an evolving New Life Safety Plan, as discussed in Chapter 3. At the beginning of each session, this New Life Safety Plan was briefly checked with Martin, to review progress over the previous week, and amended following latest developments. The style of the interaction with Martin was straightforward and concrete, to take into account his intellectual disability.

With clients who are more intellectually and conceptually developed, the style would be more sophisticated. However, similar principles would apply.

Conclusion

The majority of victims of sexual abuse do not go on to sexually offend. The lazy belief that they do constitutes discrimination and repeat victimization. Many, although not all, individuals who commit sexual crime have suffered from trauma and attachment problems. Victims of sexual abuse are more likely to go on to sexually offend if their abuse is accompanied by other forms of neglect and mistreatment, particularly violence. Hence, it is a combination of factors which causes people to commit sexual offences, including sexual abuse being eroticized or normalized, and victims becoming abusers in an effort to compensate for lost power. As discussed in Chapter 1, to provide therapy to clients who have sexually abused is to work with shame, and the same is true of working with victims of sexual abuse who have gone on to offend. Sexual offending is often kept secret in family and community networks, because of stigma and the serious consequences of exposure. Counsellors who work on victim issues should seek to empower the client, offering a corrective therapeutic experience to the disempowerment of abuse. If a client can learn to tolerate and cope with traumatic symptomology, developing self-compassion, this can lead to greater capacity to reflect on offending risk triggers and the client developing greater compassion for his victims and others, acting as protective factors against further offending.

References

Bentovim, A., Cox, A., Bingley Miller, L. and Pizzey, S. (2009) *Safeguarding children living with trauma and family violence: Evidence-based assessment, analysis and planning interventions*. London: Jessica Kingsley Publishers.

Bramblett, J.R. Jr and Darling, C.A. (1997) 'Sexual contacts: Experiences, thoughts and fantasies of adult male survivors of child sexual abuse', *Journal of Sex and Marital Therapy*, 23 (4): pp. 305–316.

Creeden, K. (2004) 'The neurodevelopmental impact of early trauma and insecure attachment: Re-thinking our understanding and treatment of sexual behavior problems', *Sexual Addiction and Compulsivity*, 11 (4): pp. 223–247.

Dolan, Y. (1998) *One small step: Moving beyond trauma and therapy to a life of joy*. Watsonville, CA: Papier-Mache Press.

Fenichel, O. (1946) *The psychoanalytic theory of neurosis*. New York: Norton.

Finkelhor, D. and Browne, A. (1985) 'The traumatic impact of child sexual abuse: A conceptualization', *American Journal of Orthopsychiatry*, 55 (4): pp. 530–541.

Fonagy, P. (2006) 'The mentalization-focused approach to social development', in. J.G. Allen and P. Fonagy (eds.) *Handbook of mentalization-based treatment*. Chichester: Wiley-Blackwell, pp. 53–100.

Freud, S. (2010) *Beyond the pleasure principle*, trans. James Strachey. Seattle, WA: Pacific Publishing Studio. First published 1920.

Hanson, R.K. and Slater, S (1988) 'Sexual victimization in the history of sexual abusers: A review', *Annals of Sex Research*, 1: pp. 485–499.

Hudson Allez, G. (2014) *Sexual diversity and sexual offending: Research, assessment and clinical treatment in psychosexual therapy*. London: Karnac Books.

Jesperson, A.F., Lalumiere, M.L. and Seto, M.C. (2009) 'Sexual abuse history amongst adult sex offenders and non-sex offenders: A meta-analysis', *Child Abuse and Neglect*, 33: pp. 179–192.

Jones, L. (2004) *Then they started shooting: Growing up in wartime Bosnia*. Cambridge, MA and London: Harvard University Press.

Solomon, R. (1980) 'The opponent process of acquired emotion', *American Psychologist*, 35 (8): pp. 691–712.

Woods, J. (2003) *Boys who have abused: Psychoanalytical psychotherapy with victims/ perpetrators of sexual abuse*. London: Jessica Kingsley Publishers.

Chapter 7

Offence-focused interventions

Introduction

Apart from the particular feelings and charged ethics pertaining to such an emotive subject as sexual crime, much of the content of the previous chapters – contracting, negotiating goals, life story work, and victim issues – will be familiar territory to most practising counsellors and therapists. What is probably less familiar is talking to clients about their sex offending. This chapter will concentrate on discussing the challenges of talking about sexual abuse in detail with perpetrators and the therapeutic/rehabilitative need for such an intervention. The Martin case study, presented in Chapter 6, will again be utilized. Whereas the last chapter focused on Martin's own victim issues, this chapter will concentrate on his offending.

Some issues around offence-focused work

Previous chapters in this book have illustrated the importance of addressing matters such as attachment and trauma issues, and the psychodynamics of the client's history, including victimology. Most counsellors and therapists are familiar with this territory. How clients construct and manage the reality of their lives is the meat and drink of most counsellors' practice. Those who have not worked within the criminal justice system are far less familiar with talking in detail about sexual offending.

In the past, there has been criticism of one-to-one case work with offenders, including individuals who have sexually offended. The main criticism has been directed at one-to-one case work based on psychodynamic and non-directive Rogerian therapy, where therapeutic gains are generally conceived in terms of the practitioner offering interpretations and supportively facilitating the offender to reflect and discharge emotion (Burnett, 2004). Various research studies emerged (Losel, 1995; McGuire and Priestley, 1985; Lipton et al., 2002), which recommended that more directive cognitive-behavioural therapy was the most effective way to reduce the risk of reoffending, including sexual reoffending (Chapman and Hough, 1998). A key component was facilitating individuals to understand their feelings, thoughts, and circumstances prior, during and after the sexual offence, using various cyclic models of sexual offending (Finkelhor, 1984; Wolf, 1984). Through this process the individual would be better able to identify and manage relevant risk triggers, and gain a deeper appreciation of the consequences of his sexual crimes on victims and others, which would likely act as a deterrent to reoffending.

In their time, the Finkelhor and Wolf models, and indeed the Eldridge cyclic models (1998) provided seminal insight into how, rather than merely why, individuals committed sexual offences, breaking sexual offending down into cyclic patterns with discrete stages. For instance, the Finkelhor model breaks offending down into four steps:

1   Motivation
2   Overcoming internal inhibitors
3   Overcoming external inhibitors
4   Overcoming victim resistance

If using this model, I prefer to use everyday language that clients can more easily relate to:

1   Wanting to do it
2   Kidding yourself it's OK
3   Clearing the coast
4   Making the victim give in and not tell

However, these models can be over-deterministic and mechanistic with inexperienced practitioners or those ideologically committed to cycles, sometimes trying to shoe-horn offenders into them, rather than working with each person and his unique set of experiences, holistically. I have worked with many offenders where these models have been used in sex offender group work treatment programmes they have attended. Whilst offenders retain some important information about their offending, they often fail to remember the theoretical terms, or get confused by the order of the cycle they have been taught. I prefer to use a generic cognitive-behavioural model, with everyday language that can be applied to all aspects of life, not just sexual offending, avoiding the risk of adding to the client's sense of stigma through the use of forensic terms. Table 7.1 presents an example model, used to illustrate typical sexual offending phenomena.

Before describing how the model shown in Table 7.1 can be applied, using the Martin case study, it might prove helpful to discuss the resistance some counsellors feel to working in an overtly offence-focused way. As part of training days I conduct with counsellors and therapists, I sometimes set up role-play exercises, so participants can practise talking to clients about the details of the sexual offence. Often when I set up this exercise, I sense resistance. It can be more difficult to re-gather the group after a coffee break. There can be some nervous hilarity. Trainees

Circumstances	Feelings	Thoughts	Behaviour (grooming)
In circumstances where anything goes/ loose sexual boundaries	Feeling angry	S/he's leading me on	Gaining carer's trust to gain access to child
	Feeling resentful		
	Feeling aggrieved	Children can enjoy sex with adults	
	Feeling lonely		Making the carer dependent, fearful, or responsible
Unsatisfactory relationship, life circumstances or event	Feeling depressed	Kids are up for it these days	
	Feeling nothing		
	Feeling everything is futile	It won't do any harm	Make sure that the sex is good with partner, so she'll never suspect
Access to victim (including via the internet)	Feeling humiliation	Only this once	
		We have a special relationship nobody else understands	
	Feeling more comfortable with children		Talk about how disgusting sex offenders are
In a position of power over victim			
	Feeling sexual desire	It happened to me at this age, and it didn't cause me any harm	Choose victim in most need of attention or less likely to tell
Victim is vulnerable	Feeling, or wanting to feel, emotionally close to victim		
Victim is unlikely to tell		I won't get caught	Make victim feel special
	Feeling the child victim is a peer	Nobody will believe her/him if they tell	
Drinking and drugs masking conscience			Make jokes and talk about sex to children
	Feeling the excitement of the forbidden	Everyone will believe me	
On own with victim			Use cuddling and play fighting to touch the child sexually
	Feeling in control	I'm too clever, I'll never get caught	
	Feeling powerful		
	Feeling sadistic pleasure in causing pain	My life is horrible, why should I care?	Give the child cigarettes, alcohol, or drugs; show pornography
		You only live once	Commit the act or acts of sexual abuse
			Use guilt or fear to keep victim quiet

can also procrastinate by focusing on the need to establish a trusting therapeutic relationship before talking about the offence, even though I have been at pains to explain that this should be assumed, with the theoretical client having come prepared to discuss his previous offending. Such resistance in the training room is not apparent when role-playing other therapeutic issues, such as contracting with a client, or goal-setting. In one particular session, a participant was honest enough to say that he felt a bit 'tawdry', having to trawl over the details of the sexual offence in question.

One explanation for the uncomfortable feelings around talking about sexual abuse, particularly when perpetrated on children, has been provided by Douglas (2002). She notes how certain topics such as sex, and particularly sexual deviance, are associated with pollution or contagion beliefs: *if I get too close, maybe the stigma will rub off.*

Erotic transference and related issues

Some counsellors are anxious that a client might become aroused by the subject matter, or aroused by the counsellor. This rarely happens, in my personal experience. Sexual arousal is very contextual and most of the clients I work with are in crisis, distressed, or deeply ashamed. Sexual pleasure is the last thing on their mind in the session. However, it is important not to be complacent, and when I worked as a volunteer counsellor on a telephone helpline, I did have some calls from a small minority of clients who seemed as if they were gaining some sexual gratification from the call, with sounds of heavy breathing and shuffling in the background, indicative of masturbation. I have also been told many anecdotes, by female telephone counsellors in particular, involving this sort of behaviour.

When I conducted my research with probation officers, a number of female officers spoke about being viewed sexually by male clients with whom they worked. The following is an example.

> *Obviously, depending on the offence, but certain offences, I'm very conscious at times that I'm young, female, fairly slim, so I have to be careful that I'm not being groomed. . . . Some of it is gut feeling, not tangible, but there might be the odd comment; 'oh you look very nice today,' not even that obvious. You have to just be careful about what their offence is; what their victim spec is.*
>
> (Probation Officer 3)

Sexual attraction, or erotic transference between counsellors and clients, generally, is a well-documented issue (Birchard, 2015: 51–52); counsellors have a professional responsibility to maintain boundaries and to take any sexual transference and counter-transference issues to supervision. However, attraction between clients and therapists in the general run of things is different from the specific issue of an offender getting aroused by talking about his sexual crimes. If a counsellor senses this is happening, then it is again best to take this matter to supervision. If it feels safe enough, then the counsellor can share her/his observation with the client and this can lead to reflection, behaviour modification, and constructive change. In extreme cases, where the client continues to become aroused, consideration can be given to changing the therapeutic tack or stopping the counselling altogether, if it seems to be proving counterproductive.

As noted elsewhere, practitioners should be especially vigilant if clients have committed sexual offences against victims the same gender and age as the counsellor. Sensible precautions should be taken, such as not seeing such clients in isolated therapy rooms and ensuring that the counsellor does not inadvertently provide details about where she lives. It would be my view that therapists of both sexes should dress in a modest fashion, not wearing clothes that emphasize the individual's sexuality and are inappropriate for the occasion. These basic boundaries are applicable to all client groups, not just individuals with sexual offending problems.

Language

Sometimes a counsellor's resistance to talking about sexual offending in detail can be related to simple uncertainty about which words to use. When I first ever talked to a person about the details of the sexual offending he had committed, I recall feeling uncertain and uncomfortable about what language to use, how explicit to be. It seemed a bit like trying to disarm an unexploded bomb. What if I say the wrong thing and it goes off, or causes a delayed explosion after the counselling has ended, resulting in a sexual offence occurring?

With regard to talking about sex, Birchard (2015: 44) offers some useful guidance for working with clients with sexual addictions, which can be applied to sex offenders, positing that it is best to avoid euphemisms, technical language, and crude terms which may arouse. When talking about sexual abuse, it is also important not to collude with a client that sex with a child is legitimate. For instance, if an adult man refers to 'the sexual relationship with X' when talking about a 14-year-old girl, in reply I would rephrase this as 'when you had sex with X', as this emphasizes that the adult is responsible for sexual conduct, not the child. The term 'relationship' implies mutuality and consent when a child is not legally able to give such consent and would not be sufficiently psychologically mature to do so. If the client continued to linguistically construct abuse as legitimate sex, I would at some point say that I was uncomfortable using this language, explain why, and attempt to negotiate a form of words with which we were both comfortable. Such a conversation can prove constructive, as it can increase the client's awareness of how and why he is attempting, either consciously or subconsciously, to construct socially unacceptable behaviour in acceptable terms. The pros and cons of the client continuing on this course can then be discussed.

Case study: Martin

The Martin case study presented in Chapter 6 is again illustrated here to re-familiarize the reader with the history.

Martin (32) has borderline intellectual disabilities and is living in supported accommodation. He has spent his entire adult life in care institutions, under the mental health act, since he was taken away from his farming family at the age of 14, after being accused of sexually abusing, Lizzie, a 7-year-old girl. Lizzie alleged that he had given her a lift on a tractor and suggested that they went into a barn to look at some nesting birds. In the barn, he had tried to kiss her and put his hand into her knickers, but had run off when she started screaming. There have been reports of him masturbating in public.

In the various institutions in which he has lived, some female staff members said they felt uncomfortable as he would stare at their breasts. He told one female staff member that he thought about her all the time, and imagined having sex with her. A number of female fellow residents in institutions over the years have said that he has rubbed up against them and, at other times, made inappropriate sexual remarks. Five years previously, a female resident had accused him of attempting to rape her, with staff noticing beforehand that they had begun what seemed to be a jokey, flirtatious relationship. No further action was taken as there was no evidence of an attack, and the female resident had made similar allegations about other patients.

Currently, Martin is living in a flat of his own, within a supported housing complex. He is not allowed to go out alone into the community, and is always accompanied by a support worker. Support workers report that he sometimes stares at children when they are out with him. Martin has received psychological input from various psychiatrists in the past, and he continues to be assessed as high risk. For a number of years, he has insisted that he is no risk to children and wants to be allowed to go out into the community, and eventually to work on his mother's smallholding, which she struggles to run on her own. His mother still regularly visits him. Martin recently told his support worker that, for the last few months, he has been having dreams of being taken to a room somewhere as a young child – he thinks when he was around 13 years old – and being sexually abused by his father (now deceased) and three other men. He thinks that this happened but he had blanked it out. He remembers the men drinking, and being made to give the men oral sex. His mother says that she knows nothing about such abuse, but that her late husband did have an alcohol problem and was violent towards her. They separated soon after Martin was taken into care. Some mental health staff members involved with Martin believe that he is being manipulative, claiming that he is a victim so that there will be sympathy for his pleas to be allowed more freedom in the community. Other staff members believe that he is not

> sophisticated enough to attempt this. A counsellor from outside the
> mental health system has been employed to explore with Martin pos-
> sible victim issues, and how these might impact on risk management.

Therapeutic work with Martin

Prior to the offence-focused work, the counsellor had undertaken victim work
with Martin as outlined in Chapter 6. The counsellor had also undertaken some
preparatory motivational work with Martin: asking strengths-focused questions to
identify what he wanted to gain out of counselling and his wishes, generally, with
regard to the position he found himself in. The stage of counselling had now been
reached where a significant degree of rapport and trust was established and Martin
had agreed to specifically address his offending issues.

First, the counsellor provided Martin with an explanation and outline of the
model shown in Table 7.1, and summarized here:

1   Circumstances
2   Feelings
3   Thoughts
4   Behaviour

Generally, when working with this basic cognitive-behaviour model, it works best,
in my experience, if the counsellor asks the client to apply it to a recent event.
With some clients I have already laid the foundations for this sort of offence-
focused analysis by using this model to explore significant life events, how the
client managed these, and how the client could have responded differently. Often,
repeated feelings, thoughts, and behaviour patterns will emerge. The strengths
of these patterns can be highlighted, with the client also learning to apply more
constructive and satisfying ways of responding to life.

In terms of offence-focused work, I explain to the client that the model can be
applied to any behaviour that causes problems (e.g. eating or drinking too much,
smoking or driving too fast). The counsellor can then apply the model to a relatively unthreatening unwanted behaviour – smoking, for instance. In the exchange
that follows, the counsellor begins the offence-focused intervention in a very non-
threatening way, using the example of herself drinking too much red wine. If
using this technique, the counsellor should not choose something that is seriously
problematic, as this would constitute inappropriate disclosure and might embar-
rass the client. The tenor should be relatively light-hearted, without trivializing.

Counsellor: Martin, the four stages can be applied to me drinking too much
red wine. OK; what are the *circumstances* when I drink too much?

Well, it's usually after a hard day's work and at the weekend, or when I want to celebrate. What would be my *feelings* in these situations? Usually, I'm either feeling tired or upset, and want to escape from these feelings or console myself. I can also be feeling happy or excited and I use alcohol to maintain or increase these feelings. I also like the taste. As for my *thoughts*, well a sort of civil war goes on inside me. Part of me thinks, 'I want to be healthy and slim,' 'I don't want to be reliant on alcohol,' and 'I don't want to say something I might regret, and feel bad about later.' However, I also kid myself that it's OK to drink too much by thinking: 'I know loads of people who drink more than me,' 'I deserve it because I've had a bad day,' 'I'll reward myself because I've done well,' and 'You've only got one life.' With regard to my *behaviour*, I might change my route home to pass the garage to buy a bottle and drink some of it on my own after my partner has gone to bed (i.e. clearing the coast, because I don't want to feel bad or be challenged about my behaviour). I then drink the rest of the bottle. Martin, have you known someone with a bad habit they wanted to give up? Perhaps they've given it up for a while, but then gone back to it.

Martin: My mother; she was always trying to give up smoking.

Applying the model in this way, especially with the counsellor telling a story of indulging in problematic behaviour against herself, as it were, can begin to desensitize the client to the shame of having committed a sexual offence, so that he is more able to talk about his offending and make sense of his behaviour. One of the positive aspects of the model is that it de-stigmatizes sexual abuse to some extent, positing that similar psychological, behavioural, and environmental processes are involved in a whole range of unwanted behaviour, not just sex offending. This is not to suggest that there is a moral equivalence between smoking or drinking too much and committing a sexual offence. Beginning with a fairly innocuous example of another person trying to give up smoking is, however, a non-threatening way into the conversation.

Counsellor: Why do you think your mother smoked, or people smoke in general?

Martin: I don't know, because they like it. I think kids used to smoke in school to look cool.

Counsellor: I think that might be the case. Anything else?

Martin: My mum used to say she had to have a fag when she was stressed.

Counsellor: Yes, stress is another reason. OK: we have liking it, looking cool, and a way of coping with stress. So if smoking does all these good things, why give it up?

Martin: It's bad for people, causes cancer doesn't it?

Counsellor: Anything else?

Martin: Money?
Counsellor: Health reasons, money, and many people don't think smoking is
               cool these days and might disapprove, maybe. OK: you've got all
               these good reasons for giving up, so how do people kid themselves
               it's OK to do it, to smoke I mean?
Martin: I dunno.

Given Martin's intellectual limitations, he may have found it difficult to put himself in the mind of another person, although he may just not be used to thinking in the way the counsellor was asking him to think. In my experience, most
clients will be able to come up with how people square it with themselves to do
something that a different part of them does not want to do. Such ambivalence is
universally human. What can often be of additional help is for the counsellor to
come up with suggestions if the client is stuck, as long as this is not done in an
overly didactic fashion. It is good practice to be client-centred, usually counterproductive to give advice, and research has shown that clients are more likely to
change when they speak out the reasons for change themselves rather than being
told them by the therapist (Miller and Rollnick, 1991). However, it can also be
awareness-raising for clients to be invited to entertain ideas and concepts they
have not yet considered.

Counsellor: Well, these are some of the ways smokers have told me that they
               kid themselves it's OK to go back to smoking:
               'My granny lived until she was 90, and she smoked all her life.'
               'Cancer will never happen to me.'
               'You've got to die of something.'
               'What's the point in life if you can't enjoy yourself?'
               'I've been good all week; I deserve a reward.'
               'I'll only smoke this one.'
               'I've smoked one pack, so I may as well carry on.'
               'I'll give up once I'm not under so much stress.'
               'I've had such a bad time, I deserve a treat.'
               'Sod it! I'm going to do what I want to do.'

The ways in which people commonly justify going back to smoking can obviously be applied to other unwanted behaviours, including the sort of cognitive
distortions that facilitate sex offending. Exploring how unwanted or anti-social
behaviour occurs in this way can help clients to make links with their own criminal actions, whether they verbalize these links or only consider them in the privacy of their own minds.

Counsellor: Right, Martin, we looked at the circumstances, feelings, thoughts,
               and behaviour; why people want to do stuff they shouldn't do, and
               how they kid themselves it's OK to do it. Now let's look at how

people behave to 'clear the coast' in order to do things they know that others might disapprove of or they themselves are afraid of. In the case of driving too fast, people tend to do this when there are no speed cameras nearby, or late at night when nobody is around. Often alcoholics will drink in secret. How do you think smokers cover their tracks?

Martin: My mum used to suck mints, because my father didn't like her smoking, and she would do it when there was nobody around. I could always tell, though, because her clothes used to smell.

Counsellor: So the main thing, then, is doing it when nobody is around, when the coast is clear.

Once the client is familiar with the model, it can then be applied to a fictional case study involving sexual abuse, such as the one which follows. Good-practice guidance on using case studies in therapy, generally, can be found in Chapter 8.

David was taken into a children's home when he was 14 because his parents were drug addicts and they couldn't look after him. After a few months, he was placed in a foster family. The foster parents were both teachers and had a son, George (aged 8), and a daughter, Harriet (aged 13). David didn't feel at home in what he considered to be such a posh house, and would often stay in his bedroom. His foster parents were kind but they were very strict, unlike his own parents, who would let him get away with anything. Although he would often go hungry at home because there was never any food in the house, he really missed his parents. He was never hungry at his foster parents', but they made him eat around the table with the rest of the family. Harriet was a bit stuck-up, but was one of the prettiest girls he had seen, and she was nice to him. Each night he used to masturbate about having sex with her, like he used to see his parents and their friends doing when they were stoned at parties in his house. He knew Harriet would never allow him to do anything to her, but this didn't stop him planning how to get her alone. She was really good at school work and he knew that she liked to help other people, being a right goody two-shoes. He decided that he would ask for help with his homework, when there was nobody else in the house. He didn't think she would put up much of a fight if he tried it on with her, and might be too scared to tell her parents. He might even get her to feel sorry for him. Anyway if he was caught, sod it! All that would happen is that he would just be taken back into care. He had nothing to lose. When the opportunity came, he was in two minds. Harriet had been nice to him. He didn't want to hurt her. But then perhaps she wanted it to happen. The way she smiled at him sometimes made him think she might fancy him. He had had a shit life so far, not like these snobs with their nice life. No, he decided to go for it. When the time came, he lay on his bed and called Harriet in, asking her to help him. She joined him on the bed and said 'let's have a look,' starting to read the assignment. It was then that he forced himself on her.

The counsellor asked Martin if he would prefer to read the above case study himself, or for her to read it out and then Martin could follow it on the page. Martin said he wanted to do it himself. Once he had read it, the counsellor read sections out again (in order to consolidate understanding), and asked Martin to comment.

Counsellor: 'David was taken into a children's home when he was 14 because his parents were drug addicts and they couldn't look after him. After a few months he was placed in a foster family.' OK, Martin, how do you think it was at home for David?

Martin: Pretty rotten.

Counsellor: Anything else?

Martin: Well, if his parents were taking drugs all the time, they would have been out of it. He would have felt all on his own, perhaps.

Counsellor: I wonder what that would have been like on a day-to-day basis, getting up in the morning, coming home from school, in bed at night listening to his parents and friends downstairs, being in the home when there was no school.

Martin: He would probably have to look after himself. It says, doesn't it, that he wasn't fed. He might have been afraid in bed at night, listening to his parents getting high. He might have been afraid that one of his parents might take an overdose. One of the kids who was in care with me – his mother did that.

The counsellor was impressed with how well Martin could put himself in David's shoes and was pleased that she could genuinely compliment Martin on this. This paying of genuine compliments, where possible, is a feature of the strengths-focused approach. Martin clearly had the ability to empathize with another person's experience, despite his intellectual disability. If Martin could empathize with David, he had the potential to empathize with the harm caused to his victim, Lizzie, whom he had sexually abused in the barn. Asking clients to analyze fictional case studies, when they are not experiencing the anxiety of having to talk about their own offences, can provide such valuable information.

Counsellor: Martin, I'm impressed with your ability to put yourself in David's shoes. You're good at this stuff. Tell me, if life was so bad at home for David, why do you think he had mixed feelings about going into foster care? After all, at least he got fed well in foster care.

Martin: Well I know what it's like to go into care, taken away from my family. I fucking hated it.

The counsellor considered that it was worthwhile exploring Martin's feelings about going into care, as this had not yet come up. This was tangential to the offence-focused nature of the session but the counsellor considered that it was important to go with what seemed to have therapeutic 'juice', rather than be hamstrung by an inflexible agenda. Exploring, expressing, and honouring Martin's feelings about this unhappy and frightening time in his life took up the remainder of the session. At the end, the counsellor agreed with Martin to resume the case study work in the next session. When they next met, Martin read the case study out again, to refresh his memory.

Counsellor: Martin, last week we talked about how difficult it was for David at home, but that he had mixed feelings about going into foster care. Can you say more about this?

Martin: I think he feels out of place. They are a bit snobby, aren't they, and he probably feels embarrassed about sitting around the table to eat with the family. We never did this at home. And they are strict, too, which he wouldn't have liked.

Counsellor: Like last week, Martin, I'm really impressed by your understanding of this.

When giving compliments and affirming clients, it is important to know how to pitch it, in order not to sound phoney or patronizing. If the counsellor had been working with a more mature or sophisticated client, he may have communicated affirmation by a simple nod and a facial expression.

Counsellor: OK. Why do you think that David wanted to do it – sexually abuse Harriet?

Martin: He fancies her, doesn't he? It says something about her being the prettiest girl he had ever seen.

Counsellor: I think that's right. Anything else?

Martin: Don't think so.

Counsellor: Apart from fancying her, can you say anything else about how he feels about Harriet? Does he like her or not?

Martin: I think he does like her. But he also thinks she's a snob, and a goody two-shoes.

Counsellor: OK. He's tossing the thought around in his mind about whether to abuse her, isn't he, playing around with the idea?

Martin: He's in two minds.

Counsellor: Yes, I think so. But why is he in two minds, if he fancies her?

Martin: Well, he knows that he'll get into trouble doesn't he, if he forces himself on her, like?

Counsellor: That seems to be part of it. Anything else?

Martin: He knows it's wrong, probably.

Counsellor: And why is it wrong?

Martin: She's only a young kid, and she doesn't want it. Forcing people is not right.

The analysis of the case study was again revealing very useful information. Clearly Martin understood that forcing somebody into sex, especially a young child, is morally wrong. Another client may have only focused on the pragmatic consequences of getting caught.

Counsellor: If he knows that it's wrong, and he shouldn't do it, how does he kid himself that it's OK to do it, to sexually abuse Harriet? Take a bit of time to read through the case study again.

Martin: He thought she wouldn't put up a fight. She was a bit spoilt. He said basically, fuck it, I've had shit in my life, so why shouldn't other people? Anyway, he didn't mind going back into care, because he didn't like it much with the foster parents anyway.

Counsellor: Anything else? Have a look at the sentence beginning 'but then perhaps. . . .'

Martin: Oh, he thought that she fancied him and wanted it to happen, because she was smiling at him.

Counsellor: Any truth in that, do you think?

Martin: Nah, she's only a kid, isn't she? She's just trying to be nice.

Another client with genuine distorted thinking about children and sex could have said something like, 'Well, maybe she was being flirty.' This was not the case with Martin.

Counsellor: I think you got them all, Martin – the ways David gets over his conscience by thinking, by kidding himself it would be OK to abuse Harriet. The 'fuck it' bit, 'I've had a hard time of it' train of thought, it's a bit like when someone kids themselves they should go back to smoking, isn't it, or drinking or eating too much, or driving too fast, like we talked about before?

Martin: Yeah.

What the counsellor is trying to do here is to encourage the client to make internal links between the examples of unwanted behaviour discussed previously, the offending in the case study, and the client's own offending.

Counsellor: OK. How does David behave to clear the coast, get the victim alone with him?

Martin: He gets her to help him with his homework, when everybody else is out. And he's lying on the bed.

Counsellor: That's basically it. How does he behave to make Harriet give in?

Martin: He's bigger and stronger than her. And by lying on the bed, it'll be easier to get on top of her, and make her give in.

Counsellor How do you think the victim is feeling?

Martin: Terrified, probably. She probably doesn't know what's happening to her.

At a later stage in the counselling with Martin, when victim empathy and the impact of sexual abuse on victims was being tackled, the counsellor came back to this case study, and explored with Martin the possible consequences of the sexual abuse on Harriet and her family, in much more detail. This sort of awareness-raising work is discussed in the following chapter.

The next stage of offence-focused work with Martin was to discuss with him possible escape routes David could have taken. When conducting this sort of work, the counsellor can explain that the pathway towards a sexual offence is often made up of seemingly small, unimportant decisions. At each point of decision making, there will also be an escape route that, if taken, can avoid or reduce the risk of a sexual offence occurring. The counsellor asked Martin if he could identify escape routes David could have taken. With some prompting, Martin came up with the following:

- Talked to somebody about missing home
- Told his social worker how he felt about being with his foster family
- Not masturbated about somebody he was living with, but masturbated about someone older that he wasn't in such close contact with
- Reminded himself that Harriet is only a child
- Reminded himself that Harriet is a nice person
- Reminded himself that sexually abusing Harriet might devastate Harriet and the family
- Not asked Harriet to go into his room when nobody was in the house
- If he was tempted, to go out of the house when he was alone with Harriet
- Stopped, when Harriet told him to

Directly addressing offending behaviour

So far, all the offence-focused work with Martin has been based on hypothetical and fictional examples. Having gradually desensitized Martin to talking about the taboo topic of sexual offending, and having raised his awareness of how such offending occurs, it was now time to talk to him about the offending he himself had committed against Lizzie. The counsellor employed the externalizing technique of referring to 'Immature Martin' and 'Mature Martin', as this provides the therapeutic space for Martin to maintain a sense of having an essentially 'good self', whilst talking about having committed such shameful behaviour.

Counsellor: Martin, we agreed last week that we would discuss Lizzie this week, yeah?

Martin: (He nods sheepishly.)

Counsellor: OK. What would you say now, at your age, to 'Immature Martin', who abused Lizzie in the barn?

Martin: Don't do it. It'll ruin your life.

Counsellor: Tell me how you were feeling about yourself, back then, when you knew Lizzie, but hadn't abused her yet.

Martin: I don't know really. She used to come with her father, and used to hang around me.

Counsellor: How well did you know her?

Martin: Not well.

Counsellor: How would you describe your relationship with her?

Martin: Didn't have much to do with her really.

Counsellor: Tell me about the first time that you were alone with her.

Martin: Can't remember being alone with her.

Counsellor: Tell me what thoughts and feelings you had about her.

Martin: I didn't have any thoughts and feelings about her. The time in the barn was the first time we were alone together, I think. I can't remember much about what happened.

Counsellor: No thoughts or feelings about her at all?

Martin: No.

Counsellor: How old were you, Martin, when the abuse of Lizzie took place?

Martin: 14, I think.

Counsellor: Most boys fancy people – girls at school, friends, or pop stars and celebrities off the TV. Was this happening for you?

Martin: No, not really.

Counsellor: OK, so you say that you had no thoughts and feelings about Lizzie, and you didn't fancy other people either, so how do you think it came about that you touched Lizzie sexually in the barn?

Martin: I don't know.

Counsellor: I know this may be a tough question, Martin, but can you say what you actually did to her?

Martin: (Looking down at his shoes.) I can't remember.

Counsellor: Is it OK if I tell you what I've been told happened?

Martin: (Nods, yes.)

Counsellor:	Well, I read that you asked her if she wanted a lift on the tractor and suggested that the two of you went into the barn. Then you tried to kiss her and put your hands down her knickers. She screamed and ran off. Have I got these details right?
Martin:	(Nods, yes.)

Martin does not deny the abuse but, despite the counsellor's best efforts and pre-paratory work beforehand, Martin is not at a motivational stage to want to dis-cuss his offending in any meaningful detail, probably feeling too embarrassed and ashamed to do so, and not having the capacity to overcome these feelings. The counsellor, therefore, 'rolls with the resistance' and tries a strengths-focused tack, offering Martin the opportunity to demonstrate awareness of the mistakes he made, and how he could behave differently in the future.

Counsellor:	Tell me what 'Mature Martin' would say to 'Immature Martin' about what he should and shouldn't have done. Let's take it from the top. What was the first thing 'Immature Martin' should have done?
Martin:	Not offered to take Lizzie for a ride on the tractor.
Counsellor:	The second thing?
Martin:	Not taken her into the barn.
Counsellor:	And once in the barn?
Martin:	Not tried to touch her.
Counsellor:	Why should 'Immature Martin' have avoided this?
Martin:	Because it would mean a whole world of trouble.
Counsellor:	What, trouble for Martin?
Martin:	Yep.
Counsellor:	Any other reason?
Martin:	Because it was wrong.
Counsellor:	Can you say why it was wrong?
Martin:	Because she was only a child, wasn't she?
Counsellor:	And why should children not be touched sexually?
Martin:	I dunno, maybe because they are too young to know what's going on, and don't have feelings like that.

In future sessions the counsellor would work with Martin on a psycho-educational basis, providing him with basic information about the following:

- Age of consent issues
- Why sexual abuse is wrong
- The impact of sexual abuse
- How to form relationships with girls his own age
- How to know when it is OK to touch and not OK to touch
- How to behave respectfully in relationships and courtship situations

However, in this session the counsellor explored with Martin how to avoid risky situations in the future.

Counsellor: OK, Martin, what would be the golden rules 'Mature Martin' would put in place, to make sure that he is never in a situation where he could be accused of sexual offending or where sexual abuse could take place?

Martin: I would never do it again.

Counsellor: OK, I'll take you at your word, but tell me about the golden rules you could put in place to make sure nothing else happens like that in the future.

Martin: Never talk to a young child when I'm on my own with them – not even be on my own with them.

Counsellor: Anything else?

Martin: Never touch anybody who doesn't want to be touched.

Counsellor: These seem good rules, Martin. In the next few sessions we can talk more about making relationships, and the difference between respectful, safe relationships and disrespectful relationships. You've really done well in this session.

Much of the work with Martin described in this chapter involved structured exercises, initiated by the counsellor. This may be a foreign way of working to some counsellors and therapists, and the more traditional talking method, based on following what the client brings to the session, may be more appropriate with some clients. However, if a counsellor is familiar with and has internalized the generic cognitive-behavioural model, this can then inform the asking of useful offence-focused questions.

From a strengths-focused perspective, the cognitive-behavioural model can be criticized as being problem based, encouraging the client to explore sites of failure. A cynic could also say that the model teaches individuals how to sexually offend, although it can be argued that the means by which individuals go after what they want, described by the model, are pretty universal and hard wired into the psyche. The therapeutic and rehabilitative task, therefore, is to bring the, often subconscious, processes – especially during the time when a client is emotionally and sexually aroused and at immediate risk of committing a sexual offence – into conscious, self-reflective awareness.

Another criticism of the model is that getting the client to unpack his offending in such detail can trigger shame, and even traumatize the client. Avoidance of this is in large part down to the therapist's clinical ability to identify when he is not respecting the client's defences, and forcing the client to look at behaviour that he is unmotivated, or does not have sufficient ego strength as yet, to look at.

The questions suggested in the list that follows avoid most of the criticisms raised so far. They are organized around basic cognitive-behavioural principles, but given a strengths-focused slant. However, counsellors should feel free to depart from this structure and to use the questions in any way that seems useful. To reiterate, as with all strengths-focused questions and interventions, the counsellor should avoid confronting denial and cognitive distortions head-on, should 'roll with the resistance', utilizing the language of the client where appropriate, show plenty of empathy, and keep on asking clarifying questions (i.e. *tell me more; what would that look like in real life?; can you say anything else?; if that was happening, how would you be feeling, thinking, acting?*) These questions can be tweaked for use with clients of differing intellectual capacities and levels of sophistication:

- You must have been around children and young people many times, when no abuse has taken place. What has been different about those times?
- What helps to take your mind off sex? Are there any thoughts, places, people, photographs, smells, memories, and activities which make you think of something else?
- Tell me about the times when you have no interest in sex. What are you feeling, thinking, or doing?
- What would have been safe, OK sexual fantasies for you?
- I have some suggestions about how to avoid situations in which you may be tempted to offend, or may be at risk of further allegations being made against you. Can I share them with you, and you can give me your reaction?
- Many people feel sexually attracted to some people, but they know it would be wrong to have sex with them, for example, a friend's partner. Have you had to resist such temptation in the past? How have you done this? What have you told yourself?
- What do you tell yourself, when you think that having sex with children is wrong?
- How could you reassure professionals that you are making efforts to avoid risky thoughts?
- What circumstances would help to keep you and others safe?
- Which people would need to be around to ensure that children are safe?
- What would need to be in place so that others would think that children are safe with you?
- I have some suggestions. Can you tell me if you think they would be useful, the pros and cons of using these ways?

Conclusion

Many therapeutic skills of counsellors and standard ways of working with general clients can also be used with individuals at risk of sexual offending. However, being offence-focused, in addition to standard therapeutic interventions, is an important part of the work with most clients with sexual offending issues, in my view. Ideally, counsellors should become comfortable in working in this offence-focused way. The ideal is for the client to admit to the abuse committed and to be willing and able to understand the emotions, thoughts, behaviour, and circumstances prior to, during and after the offending, and to empathically engage with the harm caused to the victim and others. In reality, many clients will be too defended and ashamed to go to these dark places, or will be too fearful of the consequences of admitting to their offending, making such in-depth offence-focused work unfeasible. It is still possible, nevertheless, to conduct significant constructive work with such clients, using strengths-focused interventions and questions, working hypothetically and with fictional case studies.

References

Birchard, T. (2015) *CBT for compulsive sexual behaviour: A guide for professionals*. London and New York: Routledge.

Burnett, R. (2004) 'One-to-one ways of promoting desistance: In search of an evidence base', in R. Burnett and C. Roberts (eds.) *What works in probation and youth justice: Developing evidence-based practice*. Devon and Portland, OR: Willan, pp. 180–197.

Chapman, T. and Hough, M. (1998) *Evidence based practice: A guide to effective practice*. London: Home Office Publication Unit.

Douglas, M. (2002) *Purity and danger*. London: Routledge. First published in 1966, by Routledge and Kegan Paul.

Eldridge, H.E. (1998) *Therapist guide for maintaining change: Relapse prevention for adult male perpetrators of child sexual abuse*. Thousand Oaks, CA: Sage.

Finkelhor, D. (1984) *Child sexual abuse: New theory and research*. New York: The Free Press.

Lipton, D., Pearson, F.S., Cleland, C.M. and Yee, D. (2002) 'The effectiveness of cognitive-behavioural treatment methods on offender recidivism', in J. McGuire (ed.) *Offender rehabilitation and treatment: Effective programmes and policies to reduce re-offending*. Chichester: Wiley-Blackwell, pp. 79–112.

Losel, F. (1995) 'The efficacy of correctional treatment: A review and synthesis of meta-evaluations', in J. McGuire (ed.) *What works: Reducing reoffending*. Chichester: Wiley-Blackwell, pp. 79–112.

McGuire, J. and Priestley, P. (1985) *Offending behaviour: Skills and stratagems for going straight*. London: Batsford.

Miller, W.R. and Rollnick, S. (1991) *Motivational interviewing: Helping people change*. New York: Guilford Press.

Wolf, S. (1984) 'A multifactor model of deviant sexuality', Paper presented at 3rd International Conference on Victimology, Lisbon, Portugal, November 1984.

Chapter 8

Psycho-educational interventions

Introduction

Psycho-educational initiatives are commonly used with individuals who have committed sexual offending, often as part of a rehabilitative programme within the criminal justice system. Marshall et al. (2011: 50) comment that such psycho-educational interventions are usually delivered in manual form, remarking critically that this can constitute a reduced form of psychotherapy, a concern probably echoed by many counsellors. Working in a pedagogical way might seem alien to psychodynamic, existential, transpersonal, and humanistic therapists who may view therapy more as a client-centred process, responding to whatever the client brings to the session. Even some strengths-based therapists may have reservations about teaching, given that many strengths-based approaches privilege answers coming from clients themselves. Nevertheless, in my experience, certain psycho-educational exercises seem to work well with some individuals, especially those who are younger, have borderline intellectual disabilities, or are mandated clients. Psycho-educational interventions can be particularly effective with those who have been sent to counselling to specifically raise their awareness of risk management issues and the impact of sexual offending on victims. This chapter will illustrate how to collaboratively impart information related to human functioning generally and sexual abuse specifically. The chapter will also consider good practice, with regard to using case studies in rehabilitative ways.

General points

As with all interventions, the counsellor needs to make a clinical appraisal of whether the material would be too threatening and upsetting for the client to consider. Moreover, the structure that follows is intended to provide readers with an idea of how psycho-educational work can be conducted. The exercises which follow are not meant to be used as part of a rigid formula. Different aspects of what is presented can be used at different times with different clients, depending on the clinical judgement of the practitioner and the client's motivational flow in the here-and-now.

A number of information sheets are presented in this chapter, which can be given to clients. A folder can be provided, in which the information sheets can be kept, if the counsellor judges that the client would not find this infantilizing. At strategic points in the therapeutic process, the information can be referred to, if this seems apposite and helpful. The information on these sheets covers some basic points. The data are not meant to be exhaustive, but to generally raise awareness of risk issues and stimulate productive conversations between counsellor and client.

Chimp brain/human brain

I borrow the terms *Human Brain* to refer to the rational part of the brain (the prefrontal cortex) and *Chimp Brain* for the part of the brain producing primitive emotional reactions (Peters, 2012). Often clients relate well to the terms Human Brain and Chimp Brain, the descriptions tending to make intuitive sense to them. I find that, generally, clients take these concepts on board and internalize them, referring to them periodically throughout the sessions when discussing their choices and behaviour. When working with individuals who have sexually offended, they will say 'My Chimp Brain was in charge when I was doing that.' This explanation can act as an externalizing device, allowing clients to talk more freely about sexual behaviour and thoughts which they and society consider shameful.

Fight/flight/freeze

I also use a very simplified version of the neuro-scientific explanation of how the fight/flight/freeze response can be 'emotionally hijacked' by the limbic system of the brain (Goleman, 1996), especially for people who have been exposed to stress, danger, or trauma (Briere and Scott, 2006). How our primitive ancestors operated the fight/flight/freeze responses to threats to life in order to survive (i.e. being chased by animals) can be discussed. The conversation can then move on to how we humans still use the fight/flight/freeze responses when we feel threatened in social situations and relationships, leading to behaviour which can harm ourselves and others. The counsellor can expand the discussion, explaining how people who have been traumatized by danger, violence, or abuse can become hyper-vigilant about threat. They can develop PTSD (post-traumatic stress disorder), being flooded by chemicals such as adrenalin and cortisol which evolved to stimulate quick reactions, but which limit consequential thinking (Panksepp, 2005). Often clients are able to relate these conditions to themselves or individuals they have known, providing insight into behaviour.

I point out that we can all react by going into fight, flight, or freeze, but some of us are more prone to one response than another. This explanation can provide insight into how we habitually behave in personal relationships and social situations. Those clients more prone to the flight or freeze response, and who tend to be more avoidant, can come to see how they may have felt fearful and disempowered in relationships and social settings. This can lead to understanding how they may have compensated by seeking safety, power, and agency through escaping the adult world into relationships with children or criminal online sexual activity. Those prone to the fight response can come to understand how they might have used disproportionate degrees of personal power and aggression in order to ward off threat and to meet needs and desires and, in doing so, have abused others.

Cognitive-behavioural model

As explained in the last chapter, in order to help clients create objective distance from and a richer sense of their history and behaviour, I present a simple cognitive-behavioural model of human functioning (Beck, 1976). I endeavour to negotiate the terms of the model so that the language makes sense to the client, reverberating with actual experience. As explained in Chapter 7 and shown in Table 7.1, typical wording would be:

1   Circumstances
2   Feelings
3   Thoughts
4   Behaviour

The model is then discussed, with the aid of a flip chart or through free-flowing conversation, and related to how the client has met challenges:

- In the family of origin;
- At school;
- In work, with peers; and
- In relationship with partners, children, and significant others.

More often than not distinct patterns emerge, which can provide clues to the origin of sexually harmful behaviour, and ways of reducing and managing such behaviour.

Mindfulness

I explain to the client that we can manage destructive urges and behaviour in two main ways. The first is distracting oneself from unpleasant or problematic feelings by replacing negative thoughts and behaviour with positive thoughts and behaviour, as with the cognitive-behavioural model presented. The other way is to learn to be present to unpleasant or problematic experiences, when we are being flooded with fear, anger, or lust, as our Chimp Brain takes charge. If we can practise observing feelings and thoughts in a compassionate, non-judgemental manner, applying a detached curiosity to whatever is happening in the here-and-now, this can create time and space for our Human Brain to take charge again, so we can make better decisions.

If it seems appropriate, I introduce a Mindfulness meditation exercise which can help to control the Chimp Brain. The client can be requested to relax and breathe deeply, given the option of closing his eyes. He is then asked to imagine thoughts and feelings as twigs floating down a stream and to observe these thoughts and feelings (the twigs) pass on in the current, until they go out of view and are replaced with other thoughts and feelings which will, in turn, also pass out of view. I explain that it is important to develop compassion and kindness for oneself and for whatever negative or shameful feelings and thoughts are experienced. This will calm the Chimp Brain and lead to more kindness and compassion towards others (Gilbert, 2009; Neff, 2011). If clients take to Mindfulness meditation, there are many helpful books on the subject, such as that of Dunkley and Stanton (2013).

What is sexual abuse?

In addition to the models described earlier, which can provide individuals with increased insight into how they function in order to gain more control of their functioning, clients can be provided with basic information about sexual abuse. This input can be introduced by suggesting that it is useful for people to have a sound understanding of what sexual abuse actually is. Although this can seem obvious, the ensuing discussion can open up fruitful areas of therapy. The counsellor can brainstorm feelings and thoughts that the term 'abuse' evokes. This can lead to reflection on anything from a client's own victim experiences through to suffering caused from the stigma of being labelled a sex offender. The conversation can develop through a mutual exploration of the following different forms of abuse:

- Emotional neglect
- Physical neglect
- Emotional abuse
- Physical abuse
- Sexual abuse
- Sexual exploitation

This discussion can provide the client with the stimulus and permission to reflect on his own experiences of these different forms of mistreatment, both from the perspective of victim and perpetrator. The counsellor then explores with the client what defines behaviour that is abusive. The following information sheet, covering these matters, can be given to the client to stimulate further discussion. A full-size copy of the information sheet can also be found in Appendix 11.

What is sexual abuse?

- Sexual contact between an adult and a child under the age of 16 (18 via the internet)
- Unwanted sexual contact between one adult and another
- Unwanted sexual contact between an older or more powerful person and another
- Sexual abuse can take the form of: general touching in a sexual way, touching sexual parts, oral sex, vaginal sex, anal sex, talking in a sexual way, using sexual innuendo, exposing oneself, performing sexual acts in front of others, viewing sexual material in front of others, and viewing indecent images of children

Who commits sexual abuse and where does it typically occur?

Providing information to clients about where sexual abuse typically occurs can, again, stimulate links with previous behaviour. The client may never talk about these links, continuing to deny sexual offending because of shame and fear of the consequences of admitting to the crime. Nevertheless, the information provided might enable the client, in the privacy of his own thoughts, to identify and manage signs of risk, helping to prevent situations occurring in which a sexual offence is more likely to be committed.

A brainstorming exercise can be conducted, asking the client to think of places and situations in the family home and the community where sexual abuse is more likely to occur, and exploring how these risky situations can be avoided. A discussion can then take place about who commits sexual abuse, emphasizing that most abuse takes place in family and friendship groups and is committed by ordinary men known to the family and children.

Below is an information sheet regarding these topics, that can be given to clients. A full-size information sheet appears in Appendix 12.

Who commits sexual abuse and where does it typically occur?

- Most sexual abuse is committed by men, often fathers, stepfathers, or men who are known to the children.
- Adolescents also commit high levels of sexual abuse.
- Teenage girls, under the age of 16, are the most common victims of sexual abuse, although boys and girls suffer much sexual abuse that is never reported.

- Contrary to popular fear, it is relatively rare for children to be abused by people in the street whom they don't know.
- Most sexual abuse occurs in the home. Sexual abuse commonly occurs around the following activities:

  Bath time
  Bedtime
  Baby-sitting
  Applying medicinal creams
  Physical play with children
  Adults being drunk and/or on drugs
  Lack of sexual boundaries in the home

Why does so much sexual abuse go unreported?

The client can additionally be asked to reflect on why many people prefer to think that sexual abuse is usually committed by strangers and monsters, and not by ordinary individuals (the majority being men) in family situations and friendship groups. The client can be asked to reflect on why it is so difficult for family members to report abuse, and why many victims are not believed. Such conversations can provide the counsellor with valuable insight into whether the client has distorted thinking about sexual issues, as explained in Chapter 4. This can then provide the basis for targeted therapeutic work directed at anti-social or offence-permissive beliefs, attitudes, and behaviour. The discussion can also bring to the surface feelings of shame, not only about abuse committed, but about the stigma and impact of sexual offending on the lives of the loved ones of victims, such as parents, siblings, and other family members.

Below is an information sheet that can be given to clients about these issues. A full-size information sheet appears in Appendix 13.

Why does so much sexual abuse go unreported?

- Victim was groomed to think abuse was not serious or wrong
- Didn't want parents to find out
- Didn't want friends to find out
- Didn't want authorities to find out
- Was frightened
- Didn't think s/he would be believed
- Had been threatened by the abuser
- Often there is no physical evidence

- Child and traumatized witnesses unreliable
- Details of historical abuse difficult to remember
- Adversarial system is good at undermining victims
- Victims can love their abusers (not just trauma ties), but hate the abuse

---

Why people deny abuse and the reasons for admitting to it

The topic of why so much abuse goes unreported can lead to an exploration of how victims of sexual abuse can be doubly victimized when their disclosures are not believed, and how the suffering of victims can be lessened if the person who has abused admits to the offence committed. This can lead into a conversation about denial.

Providing clients with information about denial can create an objective space in which the individual can view the reasons for and against maintaining the position of denial. It can be interesting to observe the client's body language, facial expression, and tone of voice when engaged in this sort of psycho-educational work, such observations providing indications of the following:

- If the client is likely disassociated from his offending
- If it is likely that the client has been desensitized by the sheer number of times he has resisted efforts by the police and other professionals to get him to admit to the abuse perpetrated
- If the client is likely to be emotionally in touch with the harm caused by the offending but is frightened of expressing this because to so do would be to admit to the crime and face the consequences of admission
- If the client is on the verge of breaking out of denial and admitting to offending

As already noted, psycho-educational consciousness-raising work can encourage clients to make links between previous and current attitudes and behaviour. This can motivate the client to make more informed, less damaging, and kinder choices about future conduct, independent of whether or not the client may publicly admit to having sexually offended. The following is an information sheet concerning denial, which can be given to clients to facilitate discussion and reflection. A full-size copy can be found in Appendix 14.

Reasons why people deny sexual abuse

The person is deeply ashamed and embarrassed about the offence.
He has too much to lose by publicly admitting guilt (e.g. job, money, status, family, friends, the opportunity to continue offending).

There may be great pressure from the family to conceal the offending for fear of the effect on them.

He may not trust the professionals with whom he is engaged, with regard to these offences.

Reasons to admit to sexual abuse

To prevent the victim suffering further through doubt being thrown on the validity of the abuse.

Admitting the abuse and apologizing can help the healing process for the victim and the family.

To enable professionals to help you understand and manage the thoughts and feelings which triggered the abuse, making it less likely that further abuse will occur.

To enable empathy with the victim's suffering. Getting in touch with the suffering caused and consequences for others of abusive actions can act as a deterrent to future abuse. If an individual is prepared to go through the pain of fully recognizing the suffering he has caused this can result in genuine remorse, and an increased determination not to cause such suffering again.

Using case studies

Case studies have been used throughout this book to help ground theory with practice, and the same principle can be used with clients. Readers are free to use any of the case studies presented in this book in their own therapeutic practice. Frequently, clients who find difficulty in relating to and internalizing theoretical concepts can grasp narratives and stories. Case studies work particularly well with adolescent clients, and clients with borderline intellectual disabilities. Case studies also work well with clients who are in denial. Whereas it is impossible to discuss with such clients their own offending, because they insist it did not happen, many are more than happy and able to usefully reflect on relevant offending issues hypothetically, by analyzing fictional accounts of abuse.

When using a case study it is important to be sensitive, in order to not alienate the client. Below are some good practice recommendations.

• Use a case study which includes pertinent themes to the client's offending, but is not obviously the same as the abuse in question.

• Do not use a case study that includes far more serious sexual offending than the client has been convicted or accused of, as this is likely to be experienced as stigmatizing, provoking resistance.

• Use case studies at the appropriate level of sophistication for the client.

- Explain to the client there might be material in the case study that he might find upsetting.
- Ask the client's permission to use a case study, explaining that it is a way of helping to understand how sex offending happens and can be avoided.
- The therapist should always use clinical judgement as to whether or not the client is sufficiently emotionally robust to engage with the material in any case study.

Once agreement to use a case study has been negotiated, the client can be provided with a copy, with the practitioner retaining a copy for him- or herself. Following is an example of a typical case study that can be used with clients. This scenario is revisited in Chapter 9, which deals with victim empathy, with the protagonist, Michael, seeking counselling later in his life to address what has happened.

Case study: Michael

Michael (40) met Janet on an internet dating site. He seemed a bit shy but very nice, and gentler than her previous partner, who had been intimidating and emotionally abusive to her. After they had been seeing each other for three weeks, he moved in with her and her three children: two boys (8 and 10) and a girl (6). Janet thought he was great with the children. He would often take them to the park and play football with the two boys, and he always brought sweets home for them on the day he received his benefits. Janet worked part time and it was nice having someone to care for the children after school. It was also useful, when she was exhausted after work, that Michael offered to help with the children's homework and bath times. Sometimes Janet would ask Michael to babysit if she was going out and he would offer to take Suzie, her daughter, swimming while she took the boys to football practice. When he got a job, he would bring presents for the children on payday and seemed to spoil Suzie, buying her more things than the boys. When Janet spoke to him about this, he just said it was because she was the only girl; the boys had each other. Janet thought no more about it. She did sometimes wonder what they got up to as they seemed to spend so much time together, but Janet put it down to the fact that little girls need a father figure and Suzie did not see her dad anymore.

It wasn't until Suzie mentioned to Janet that she had touched Michael's 'willy' that Janet realized that Michael had been abusing Suzie.

Janet talked to Suzie some more to try to find out exactly what had been happening and then immediately contacted the police and social services. Michael was arrested and held in custody. Suzie had to be interviewed by specialist social workers and then examined by a doctor to see if there was any physical evidence of abuse. It took a lot of persuading, but eventually Suzie told her mum and the social workers that Michael had started off playing 'tickling' games that she did not mind at first. But then he started putting his hand under her clothes to tickle her. She said she told him she didn't like it and he stopped for a while. Sometimes when he was putting her to bed he would watch her while she went to the loo and got undressed and then would start trying to tickle her under the bedclothes. She woke up one night and he was lying in bed beside her and he was touching her vagina. He told her not to tell anyone or she would be in big trouble and he would have to go away. The next day he took her out to McDonald's and treated her to her favourite meal. Suzie also explained that Michael often came into the bathroom when she was in the bath and would help her to wash and dry herself. On the basis of Suzie's evidence, Michael was charged with several counts of indecent assault. When the charges were put to him, he denied that he had done anything wrong. He said that he had never touched Suzie, but that she often came into the bathroom when he was in there and liked to watch him having a wee. He also said that Suzie would get into bed with him and tickle him. He told police that ever since he moved into the home, Suzie had 'fancied' him and followed him around.

Therapeutic work with the Michael case study

The client is asked whether he would like to read the case study himself, or whether he would like the counsellor to read it out loud, with the client following the text on the page. Some clients with reading difficulties, who choose to read the case study themselves, nevertheless read aloud, never having mastered the skill of silent reading. The counsellor can then reread aloud relevant segments of the narrative, asking the following sort of questions at the end of each segment:

*   What do you think is happening at this point?
*   What do you think are the feelings, thoughts, and motivations of the characters at different points in the narrative?
*   What were the main triggers to the offending?

- How did the person gain the parent's trust to be alone with the child?
- How did he kid himself that it was OK to offend?
- How did the person groom the victim?
- How did the person make the victim give in to the abuse?
- What could the person have done differently to avoid offending?
- What were the main points of decision?
- At these points what other decision could have been made, to avoid offending?
- In the future, what would be the danger points and risk triggers for this person?
- What could the person do to avoid the danger points and manage the risk triggers?
- What could the person do if he noticed that the risk triggers were emerging in his life?
- What would be the challenges the person would have to overcome to manage the risk triggers safely?

Conclusion

The use of psycho-educational interventions may be foreign to many counsellors and therapists and the sort of reflection, insight, and consciousness raising which they are designed to encourage may well be achieved through the free-flowing talking method, or experiential exercises. However, they offer another set of tools for the therapeutic tool box. The learning that can occur from this sort of structured work (particularly that related to victims and families) can prepare and inform clients to take part in one of the most difficult aspects of therapy for people who have sexually offended – victim empathy work – the subject of the next chapter.

References

Beck, A.T. (1976) *Cognitive therapy and the emotional disorders*. New York: Guilford Press.

Briere, J.N. and Scott, C. (2006) *Principles of trauma therapy: A guide to symptoms, evaluation and treatment*. London, Thousand Oaks, CA and New Delhi: Sage.

Dunkley, C. and Stanton, M. (2013) *Teaching clients to use mindfulness skills: A practical guide*. London and New York: Routledge.

Gilbert, P. (2009) *The compassionate mind*. London: Constable.

Goleman, D. (1996) *Emotional intelligence: Why it can matter more than IQ*. London: Bloomsbury.

Marshall, W.L., Marshall, L.E., Serran, G.A., and O'Brien, M.D. (2011) *Rehabilitating sex offenders: A strength-based approach*. Washington, DC: APA Books.

Neff, K. (2011) *Self-compassion: Stop beating yourself up and leave insecurity behind*. New York: Harper Collins.

Panksepp, J. (2005) *Affective neuroscience: The foundations of human and animal emotions*, Series in Affective Science. Oxford: Oxford University Press.

Peters, S. (2012) *The chimp paradox: The mind management programme for confidence, success and happiness*. London: Vermillion.

Chapter 9

Facilitating victim empathy

Introduction

The therapeutic process is different for each client. An opportunity can advantageously arise at any time to facilitate the development of greater concern for the well-being of others, including the people a client may have mistreated sexually or harmed in other ways. In addition, the psycho-educational awareness raising work described in Chapter 8, addressing the client's own victim issues (Chapter 6) and the offence-focused interventions illustrated in Chapter 7, can all lay the foundations for specific victim empathy work, as can the whole reflective experience of counselling. This chapter will discuss the interrelatedness of client denial and failure to show empathy for victims, and how this can challenge the counsellor's capacity to communicate positive regard. The rehabilitative gains of victim empathy are demonstrated, and various ways of facilitating empathy are discussed. The case study, Michael, which was introduced in Chapter 8, is revisited in order to illustrate relevant points.

Denial and victim empathy

The issues of denial and lack of victim empathy are intertwined. As is hopefully self-evident to readers of this book, it is possible to provide constructive counselling to individuals in denial or those who minimize their offending. Denial might take the classic Freudian form, where a person disassociates from reality because it is simply too distressing to bear. More frequently in the case of individuals who have committed sexual offending, denial is absence of public admission of sexual crime because of shame or fear of the consequences, whilst the person remains well aware of the sexual abuse perpetrated. In both instances, it is highly problematic for the client to display victim empathy because there is no recognition (at least publicly) that he has sexually victimized another.

Denial and minimization of sexual offending are no longer viewed as straightforward risk factors, with regard to reoffending (Hanson and Bussiere, 1998; Hanson and Morton-Bourgon, 2004). However, Hanson revisited his research with

Nunes et al. in 2007 and found that incest offenders (men who offended against victims related to themselves, often regarded as 'low risk') who denied their crimes, were at increased risk of sexually reoffending. Having said this, denial as a risk factor still does not appear in risk-assessment tools.

Despite this ambiguous research evidence, admitting to having done something wrong, appreciating the harm caused to others, and being genuinely remorseful is, arguably, a common value shared by most human beings. Intuitively, a person who acknowledges his guilt and wrongdoing in relation to harming a child sexually would seem more likely to wish to avoid being a perpetrator again. A person who can empathize with the suffering caused to the victim is more likely to have undergone moral development, not wanting to cause further victims to suffer, as is apparent in the statements from sex offenders which appear further on. It can be argued that encouraging the client to develop such increased interpersonal perspective taking is to encourage an important personal resource and life skill, and is therefore consistent with a strengths-focused approach.

An absence of such remorse, especially when a child has been sexually abused, attracts fairly universal opprobrium, including amongst professionals working with this offending client group, as is obvious from the statements of probation officers in Chapter 1, when referring to denial and minimization. I will remind the reader of one such response.

I just thought he was an absolute disgrace because of how he minimized things.

(Probation Officer 12)

Counsellors, like probation officers, may have to overcome a negative response to a client in denial or one who minimizes harm and who does not show empathy for vulnerable victims.

Denial and lack of victim empathy are now generally viewed, in most cases, as being caused by shame and fear of the consequences of admitting to sexual crime (Ward et al., 1998; Bumby, 2000). As stated at the beginning of the book, counsellors working with people who have sexually offended will soon realize that much of the work involves helping clients to overcome shame which usually presents, in part, as denial, minimization, and lack of victim empathy.

As discussed in Chapter 1, many of the men I interviewed about their rehabilitation reported that talking about the details of their offending and the harm caused to victims was the most difficult aspect of treatment. Again, I will repeat one statement to emphasize the point.

You sit back and think 'Phew!' All of the sudden you go from just being well, ah well, get over it, to being . . . saying to yourself, 'you horrible, evil, vindictive bastard!'

(Offender 9)

However, many offenders said that this most difficult aspect of treatment (engaging with the details of their sexual offending and the harm caused to victims) was also the most valuable:

> *I was put into a situation on the programme; what it must have been like being in her [the rape victim's] shoes, and that brought home how much I destroyed somebody's life and family, and also my family and friends as well. I feel that was the biggest step I made. The biggest thing as well to go through; it was enormous and I feel that that helped me so much.*
>
> (Offender 3)

Raising the client's awareness of the impact of sexual abuse, generally

Many clients will not be at a motivational stage to publicly admit to sexual offending. In such cases, one of the key messages of this book is the importance of the counsellor working with, not against, the motivation of the client. If a client will not go to this darkest place, as it were, then there are many constructive ways of working with denial and minimization from a strengths-focused perspective, which are illustrated throughout the text.

Despite making the most of and working with whatever motivations a client brings into the therapy room, the rehabilitative ideal, in my view, is for the client to admit to the sexual abuse perpetrated, and fully internalize the harm caused to the victim/s. Unless the client is seriously callous, narcissistic, or psychotic – which few clients are – fully engaging with the impact and consequences of sexual abuse for victims and related others should act as a further deterrent to reoffending, as the statements of the research respondents, earlier and in Chapter 1, suggest.

This process can begin by facilitating the client to get in touch with her/his own victim experiences, as explained in Chapter 6. Even if the client has not suffered sexual abuse, most people have suffered disempowerment of some kind, whether it has taken the form of emotional or physical mistreatment or neglect. If a client engages with his own victim experience, this can be starting point for engaging with the victim experiences of others.

The client can be asked to reflect on different forms of abuse. This conversation tends to restrict engagement to an intellectual level, but this is fine as a start. Engaging the client at a theoretical and cognitive level about harm caused to others is designed to sensitively soften defences, with the aim of encouraging the client to eventually relate at an emotional level with harm caused to a specific individual.

A further step in this gradual exposure process is to ask the client to consider the impact of sexual abuse on victims generally. Psycho-educational work, similar to that described in the last chapter, can be utilized to this end. For example, the following information sheet can help to facilitate reflection. A full-size copy appears in Appendix 15.

Impact of sexual abuse

Each individual's experience of sexual abuse is different. However, the following factors tend to be aggravating features.

The more frightened the victim was by the abuse

If the victim felt/feels unprotected from further abuse, and is living in a state of fear

If the abuse was carried out by a trusted family member the victim relied upon for security (e.g. a parent figure)

If the abuse was particularly invasive (e.g. oral sex, intercourse)

If the victim was not believed by family members, and blamed for causing trouble

If the victim was made to feel responsible for the abuse

If the victim was particularly vulnerable, with existing emotional and welfare problems

The next information sheet describes the possible longer-term consequences of sexual abuse for the victim. Again, a full-size information sheet appears in Appendix 16.

Longer-term possible consequences of sexual abuse

Not being believed and being labelled as a troublemaker

Rejected, scapegoated by family because of reporting abuse

Guilt because of reporting abuse

Falsely believing there must be something wrong with them for attracting the abuse

Low self-esteem

Trust issues

Feeling different from others

Mental health/psychological problems

Drug/alcohol problems

Low educational and occupational achievement

Relationship problems

Promiscuity

Difficulty in forming sexual relationships

Caught in cycle of abusive relationships

Social isolation

Problems with authority figures

These lists are not exhaustive, but can stimulate further discussion and raising of consciousness.

Using case studies to increase victim empathy

The use of case studies was discussed in Chapter 8, including good-practice considerations. Case studies such as the following can be used for specific victim empathy work.

Case study: Mark

Jude was brought up with her mother, Sharon. Her mother was never cruel to her, but she suffered from depression. When Jude was around 12, Sharon met a man, Mark (35), who moved in and became a stepfather figure to Jude. Initially, Jude thought that Mark was a good laugh and she liked it that her mother was happier since being with him, and seemed to drink less. She would sometimes get irritated with Mark when he used to play the joker too much, hanging around when her friends were there, offering them all fags and telling stupid jokes. Jude also became increasingly uncomfortable about Mark. He used to stand close behind her when she was washing up and, on a couple of occasions, he had barged into the bathroom when she was having a shower. Jude did not say anything to her mother, because she didn't want her mother to become unhappy again. However, one day when he had been particularly touchy-feely, she told her mother that she and her friends were getting fed up with Mark hanging around them. Her mother got angry, calling her friends troublemakers, and banned them from coming to the house.

After this Mark changed, getting into more arguments with Sharon after they had been drinking. One night, after her mother had gone to bed, Mark asked Jude if she had ever had a boyfriend, and did she want to look at a film about 'how it's done'? Jude told him he was disgusting and that she would tell her mother. Mark laughed at her, saying that her mother couldn't get enough of him, and she would do anything to keep him. He said he bet that Jude would follow her mother, once she 'got a taste for it'. Jude put a brave face on it, telling him to 'fuck off' and went up to bed, shaking with fear. She remembered the times she had overheard her mother having sex with Mark, and felt very lonely and a bit jealous. She began to worry that maybe Mark was right; maybe she and her mother were no good. Almost asleep, she heard the door open and Mark enter her bedroom. Jude couldn't breathe, smelling the alcohol and tobacco on Mark's breath. As he got into bed and began to touch her and call her horrible names, she turned away and then froze, trying to blank everything out. She felt some wet on the back of her legs, and then he left the room.

The next morning, she was afraid to get out of bed, in case she saw Mark. He came in and she caught her breath, thinking the same thing would happen again. He had a mug of tea in his hand, which he handed over to her, saying he was sorry about last night, but he was drunk and it wouldn't happen again. He said it would be a shame to upset her mother over such a silly incident. Jude was confused. Was it just a silly incident? For the next few weeks Mark kept his distance, but Jude couldn't get what had happened out of her mind, and got scared every time her mother and Mark began drinking.

Around two months later, Mark visited her in bed again and the same thing happened. This time the incident wasn't mentioned. Sharon and Mark announced that they were getting married and it was at this point that Jude told her mother what Mark had done to her. Sharon slapped her across the face, saying she was jealous, had never liked Mark, and wanted to ruin her happiness. When Mark found out, he denied everything and, on one occasion when he was alone with Jude, he caught her around the throat and said if she ever told anybody else or the police, he would kill her for making her mother so unhappy. It was at this point that Jude ran away from home to live with her aunt. It was agreed that Jude could live at her aunt's, as long as she stopped making wicked allegations. Jude agreed.

Empathy work with case studies

When exploring a case study such as this one with a client (see Chapter 8 for tips on how to do this), the counsellor can concentrate on five distinct elements:

- The victim's experience of the grooming stage leading up to the abuse
- The victim's experience of the actual abuse
- The victim's experience shortly after or in between abuse episodes
- The victim's longer-term experience after the abuse
- The experiences of the loved ones of the victim

Following are questions which can be asked, related to each of the above stages. These questions should not be asked one after another; only a few of them might be applicable to any given client, and the list is primarily meant to provide a general flavour. The material is apt to invoke shame and self-disgust in clients who have abused in a similar way to Mark, so the counsellor must use clinical sensitivity in order not to cause the client too much distress, whilst not protecting him from the emotional impact of engaging with the pain caused to others. To go to this dark place, the client must have trust that the counsellor is not going to be judgemental and is fundamentally committed to his overall welfare. Using a fictional case study can allow the client to engage with the harm caused by sexual abuse and to make internal links with his own offending, whilst not requiring the client to accept the label of a sex offender and related consequences of admitting to the crime.

The victim's experience of the grooming stage leading up to the abuse

- Can you tell me how Jude might have felt about Mark coming into the house?
- Can you think of any key points when Mark crossed the line into inappropriate behaviour?
- How do you think Jude experienced this behaviour?
- Did Jude give off any signals that she was uncomfortable with aspects of her relationship with Mark before physical abuse started ?
- How do you think she felt when Mark ignored these signals?
- Why do you think that Jude didn't tell her mother when she first started to feel uncomfortable around Mark?
- Can you think of any ways in which Mark subtly suggested that Jude was leading him on?
- How do you think it would have felt to Jude if she began to believe that she was responsible for an inappropriate relationship developing?
- Does what you learnt from the counselling so far give you any insight into how this stage of the abuse might have been for Jude?

The victim's experience of the actual abuse

- How do you think it was for Jude the first time the abuse occurred?
- What sorts of thoughts and feelings might she have been experiencing during the abuse?
- When the abuse occurred on subsequent occasions, how do you think it might have been for Jude?
- What do you think it felt like for Jude to keep the abuse secret?
- What do you think stopped her from telling?
- How did Mark, subtly and not so subtly, dissuade Jude from disclosing the abuse?
- Does what you have learnt from the counselling so far give you any insight into how it might have been for Jude during the actual times of abuse?

The victim's experience shortly after or in between abuse episodes

- Can you think of all the thoughts and feelings which Jude might have been experiencing in between the incidents of abuse?
- How do you think it was for her, facing people, between the incidents of the abuse?
- How do you think it was for her being with Mark between the incidents of abuse?
- What do you think she feared happening if she told about the abuse?
- When do you think she was most worried about the abuse happening again?
- Does what you have learnt from the counselling so far give you any insight into how this stage of the abuse might have been for Jude?

The victim's ongoing long-term experience after the abuse

- What do you think that the long-term consequences might be for Jude after the abuse?
- How do you think it might have affected her relationship with others: her mother; authority figures; friends; romantic and sexual relationships?
- How do you think the abuse might have impacted on her self-esteem?
- How do you think the abuse might have impacted on her view of the world?
- How might she blame herself for the abuse?
- Does what you have learnt from the counselling so far give you any insight into how being sexually abused might have impacted on Jude?

The experiences of others connected to the victim

- Tell me how do you think it was for Sharon, looking back at what had happened to her daughter?
- How do you think Sharon felt about introducing Mark into Jude's life?
- How do you think Sharon coped with not having done anything, when Jude initially said she felt uncomfortable about her relationship with Mark?
- How do you think the abuse impacted on the relationship between Sharon and her daughter?
- How do you think what happened has impacted on Sharon's view of herself as a mother and person?
- How do you think the abuse might have impacted on how Sharon views relationships with men and the world in general?
- Does what you have learnt from counselling so far give you any insight into how being sexually abused might have impacted on Jude's mother?

Raising the awareness of clients about suffering caused to their victims

After exploring the harm caused to victims of sexual abuse on an intellectual level through information giving and discussion, and then on a hypothetical level through exploration of a fictional case study, the final stage of victim empathy work is to facilitate the client to engage with the likely harm caused to his victim or victims. As already stated, if the client is prepared to do this, all well and good. If not, this should not rule out conducting the victim empathy work described above. The following case study, introduced in Chapter 8, provides the background of a client, Michael, who seeks counselling years after his offending, in order to talk about his crime.

Case study: Michael

Janet (35) met Michael (40) on an internet dating site. He seemed a bit shy but very nice, and gentler than her previous partner, who had been intimidating and emotionally abusive to her. After they had been seeing each other for three weeks, he moved in with her and her three children: two boys aged 9 and 11 and a girl aged 7. Janet thought he was great with the children. He would often take them to the park and play football with the boys, and he always brought sweets home for them on the day he received his benefit. Janet worked full time and it was nice having someone to care for the children after school. It was also useful, when she was exhausted after work, that Michael offered to help with the children's homework and bath times. Sometimes Janet would ask Michael to babysit if she was going out and he would offer to take Suzie, her daughter, swimming while she took the boys to football practice. When he got a job, he would bring presents for the children on payday and seemed to spoil Suzie, buying her more things than the boys. When Janet spoke to him about this, he just said it was because she was the only girl, the boys had each other. Janet thought no more about it. She did sometimes wonder what they got up to as they seemed to spend so much time together, but Janet put it down to the fact that little girls need a father figure and Suzie did not see her dad any more.

It wasn't until Suzie mentioned that she had touched Michael's 'willy' that Janet realized that Michael had been abusing Suzie. Janet talked to Suzie some more to try to find out exactly what had been happening and then immediately contacted the police and social services. Michael was arrested and held in custody. Suzie had to be interviewed by specialist social workers and then examined by a doctor to see if there was any physical evidence of abuse. It took a lot of persuading, but eventually Suzie told her mum and the social workers that Michael had started off playing 'tickling' games that she did not mind at first. But then he started putting his hand under her clothes to tickle her. She said she told him she didn't like it and he stopped for a while. Sometimes when he was putting her to bed, he would watch her while she went to the loo and got undressed and then would start trying to tickle her under the bedclothes. She woke up one night and he was lying in bed beside her and he was touching her vagina. He told her not to tell anyone or she would be in big trouble and he would have to go away. The next day he took her out to McDonald's and treated her to her favourite meal. Suzie also explained that Michael often came into the bathroom when she was in the bath and would help her to wash and dry herself. On the basis of Suzie's evidence, Michael was charged with several counts of indecent assault. When the charges were put to him he denied that he had done anything wrong. He said that he had never touched Suzie, but that she often came into the bathroom when he was in there and liked to watch him having a wee. He also said that Suzie would get into bed with him and tickle him. He told police that ever since he moved into the home, Suzie had 'fancied' him and followed him around.

Michael was sent to prison for 10 years, serving five years in custody and five years on licence in the community. He is on the Sex Offender Register for life. Whilst in prison he went onto a sex offender group work programme. He is now 57 and has not offended since being released from prison 10 years ago. He lives on his own, works as a security guard, and plays in a pub darts team. At times he feels suicidal after he's been drinking, when he thinks of what he did to Suzie. He's become friendly with Donna (50), the barmaid at his local pub, and had consensual, mutually enjoyable sex with her when they were both drunk. She wants a relationship and he is keen. Michael has been seeing a counsellor for a number of weeks, and a good therapeutic bond has been built up. He says that he wants to talk about what happened with Suzie. He always avoided doing this on the group work programme in prison, but wants to face it now, before committing himself to Donna. He and the counsellor have agreed to talk about what happened with Suzie in the session described here.

Therapeutic work with Michael

Counsellor: So Michael, do you still want to talk about what happened with Suzie?

Michael: I had second thoughts about it coming here today, but I want to face it now. I never really did on the programme in prison.

Counsellor: So why now?

Michael: Well, I know if the relationship is to go anywhere with Donna, I'll need to tell her about my past. And being as I'm on the Register (Sex Offender Register) I'll have to inform the police if we move in together. I want to be able to tell Donna that I've talked about what happened to a counsellor.

Counsellor: OK, can you tell me about your relationship with Suzie, before the abuse happened?

Michael: I liked her, not in that way. She was a bit spoilt . . . (silence).

Counsellor: Tell me what you think were the good things about the relationship with Suzie.

Michael: I used to give her attention. Her father didn't want to know. It also helped her mother that I used to lend a hand with the kids.

Counsellor: What do you think were the not so good things?

Michael: Well, the way things turned out. What I did to her.

Counsellor: Am I right, Michael, that you are talking about sexually abusing Suzie – are you OK with using that term?

Michael: I don't like it, but that's what happened.

Counsellor: Michael, when do you think you first crossed the boundary to behaving inappropriately with Suzie?

Michael: (Silence.)

Counsellor: When can you remember first becoming sexually aroused, with regard to Suzie?

Michael: I remember when she was sitting on my lap once, and I had an erection.

Counsellor: I respect your honesty in admitting that. What happened when you had the erection?

Michael: I can't remember.

Counsellor: Michael, clearly you stayed in the house after that and the relationship became sexually abusive. How did you kid yourself that it was OK to remain in the house, and continue to have contact with Suzie?

Michael: I suppose I told myself, after the first time Suzie was on my lap and I had the erection, like, that it was just one of those things. It wouldn't lead to anything and I was doing a good job, helping out with the kids.

Counsellor: What would you say to that Immature Michael back then; what should he have done? [The counsellor and Michael had previously agreed to use the terms 'Immature Michael' and 'Mature Michael' to refer to his previous and present self.]

Michael: Leave the house immediately, make some excuse, and get out of there.

Counsellor: Why do you think Immature Michael didn't do that?

Michael: He was lonely. He liked the attention he was getting from the kids, and having a family to be part of.

Counsellor: How come, Michael, that you got to be alone with Suzie, to abuse her?

Michael: I used to do homework with her in her bedroom, and tuck her up into bed, and do things she liked, such as swimming.

Counsellor: How many times in all did you abuse Suzie?

Michael: I dunno. About half a dozen I suppose.

Counsellor: Over what sort of period?

Michael: Three weeks maybe.

Counsellor: I know this is difficult, but what did the abuse consist of?

Michael: What do you mean?

Counsellor: What did you actually do to Suzie?

Michael: Touching.

Counsellor: Can you say where you touched her on the body? Was it outside clothes, inside clothes?

Michael: Both. Mostly her bum and vaginal area.

Counsellor: Did you insert any part of your hand into her vagina?

Michael: I may have inserted my finger once or twice.

Counsellor: OK Michael; you're doing very well. I just need to ask you, was there any oral sex involved, or did you penetrate her with your penis?

Michael (Looking down) No.

When talking to clients about the abuse they have committed (also see Chapter 7), it is possible to get too hung up on the physical details of the abuse to no therapeutic or rehabilitative value. However, in order to facilitate a client to engage with the harm caused, it is necessary to encourage them to reflect on how the victim would have experienced the type of physical abuse enacted upon the body. To achieve this, some details usually need to be established.

Counsellor: Michael, can you tell me about when you first sexually abused Suzie?

Michael: She climbed on my lap another time. I think I had another erection, and I moved her around on my lap to stimulate me.

Counsellor: How do you think Suzie experienced that at the time?

Michael: She was probably too young to notice anything.

Counsellor: OK, she was young. She may have noticed something or she may not have noticed anything. Say she did notice something. How do you think she would have experienced what was happening to her?

Michael:	She would have probably been confused – frightened, maybe.
Counsellor:	How do you think she would feel later on, if memories of that time on your lap came back to her?
Michael:	Dirty, maybe?
Counsellor:	Michael, you are doing very well. I know this is not easy. You say that you abused Suzie on about half a dozen occasions. How do you think she might have felt between the instances of abuse?
Michael:	I can't say. I really don't know.
Counsellor:	Can I repeat some of the things that victims say when they talk about abuse of this sort. Are you up to hearing this?
Michael:	Carry on.
Counsellor:	OK, well the first thing to say is that victims have different reactions to being abused. But many talk about how the fear between episodes of abuse – waiting for it to happen again, as it were, can be as bad as the abuse itself. Maybe Suzie was too young to have these thoughts. But many victims blame themselves for not reporting the abuse earlier, and are doubly victimized because they think that the abuse is somehow their own fault and, as you say, they can feel dirty.

The counsellor leaves a period of silence for Michael to internalize this information, and then uses what is called 'assumptive questioning', basing a question on knowledge about how sexual abuse and grooming usually happens.

Counsellor:	Michael, how did you manage to keep Suzie from talking about what was happening, during the period you were abusing her?
Michael:	I guess I would keep being nice to her, and treat her special like, hoping she wouldn't say anything.
Counsellor:	How do you think, in hindsight, Suzie may look upon you treating her special?
Michael:	It probably sickens her.
Counsellor:	And did you warn her in any way, Michael, or threaten her to keep quiet?
Michael:	I think I might have said that if she told her mummy about our secret playtime, I might have to leave the house.
Counsellor:	From your current viewpoint of Mature Michael, what do you think the effect might have been of creating an emotional separation between such a young child and her mother?
Michael:	She might have felt a bit isolated and confused, maybe.
Counsellor:	What was Suzie's reaction the first time you touched her around her vaginal area?
Michael:	Nothing. She went quiet.
Counselling:	Why do you think she may have gone quiet?

Michael:	I know, I know. At the time I told the police that she was coming onto me. I knew this was crap, even at the time, but I was desperate to say anything. She was probably scared stiff, wasn't she?
Counsellor:	And the first time you inserted your fingers into her vagina?
Michael:	(Wincing, close to tears.) Even more frightened, and it probably hurt her, didn't it?

The ripple effect

With regard to facilitating the client to engage with the consequences and harm caused to others by his sexual offending, the counsellor can suggest that it is not just the victim who is impacted by a sex offence, but significant others as well. The counsellor can draw a spiral on a piece of paper, with the offence in the middle of the spiral. The client is then asked to imagine the possible consequences, as ripples from the offence spread out to the victim, the victim's loved ones, society, the offender's family, and finally the offender himself.

The empty chair

The client can also be asked to imagine that the victim or somebody close to the victim is sitting in an empty chair in the therapy room. The client is invited to consider what he would like to say to the person about the abuse perpetrated against them. The client can also be asked to sit in the empty chair and imagine what the victim or the victim's loved ones would feel and think about the abuse, and what they would like to say to him.

Writing a letter of apology

A client can be invited to write a letter of apology to the victim and the victim's loved ones. It is important to clarify that such a letter should never be sent as this could re-traumatize the victim and significant others. Before writing the letter, the counsellor can discuss with the client what the recipient would likely want to read, using the questions below. Once the letter is written, the client can bring it to counselling to read out loud, or for the counsellor to read. The counsellor can then gently challenge any remaining cognitive distortions, minimizations, rationalizations, and blame shifting, with the client perhaps re-writing the letter. It is best if this challenging exercise is done in a strengths-focused way, using open and Socratic questions:

- I wonder what the victim would make of this?
- How would you guess that this would make the victim feel about herself?
- What are the pros and cons of saying this?
- What are you trying to achieve by saying this?

Conclusion

Working with clients to increase victim empathy takes the form of a gradual desensitizing process. Firstly, the counselling process as a whole, and the sense for the client that he is being held in a safe therapeutic relationship, act as preparation for him to confront the harm caused to others by his sexual offending. This includes facilitating the client to get in touch with his own victim experience. The next part of this gradual process is providing the client with information about the impact on and consequences of sexual abuse for victims generally. The experiences of victims can then be personalized through exploration of a fictional case study. The final stage is for the client to engage with the likely suffering he caused to the actual victim/s. This can lead on to accepting responsibility for the harm caused and expressing remorse by writing an apology letter to the victim/s, which is never sent. This can be freeing and unburdening for many clients who have sexually offended, helping them to move on.

References

Bumby, K.M. (2000) 'Empathy inhibition, intimacy deficits and attachment difficulties in sex offenders', in D.R. Laws, S.M. Hudson and T. Ward (eds.) *Remaking relapse prevention with sex offenders: A sourcebook*. Thousand Oaks, CA: Sage, pp. 143–166.

Hanson, R.K. and Bussière, M.T. (1998) 'Predicting relapse: A meta-analysis of sexual offender recidivism studies', *Journal of Consulting and Clinical Psychology*, 66 (2): pp. 348–362.

Hanson, R.K. and Morton-Bourgon, K.E. (2004) *Predictors of sexual recidivism: An updated meta-analysis* (User Report No 2004–02). Ottawa: Public Safety Canada. Available from: www.publicsafety.gc.ca/cnt/rsrcs/pblctns/2004-02-prdctrs-sxl-rcdvsm-pdtd/index-eng.aspx [22 September 2016].

Nunes, K.L., Hanson, R.K., Firestone, P., Moulden, H.M., Greenberg, D.M. and Bradford, J.M. (2007) 'Denial predicts recidivism for some sexual offenders', *Sexual Abuse: A Journal of Research and Treatment*, 19 (2): pp. 91–105.

Ward, T., Fon, C., Hudson, S.M. and McCormack, J. (1998) 'A descriptive model of dysfunctional cognition in child molesters', *Journal of Interpersonal Violence*, 13 (1): pp. 129–155.

Chapter 10

Fantasy management

Introduction

This chapter will briefly discuss whether individuals who have committed sexual offences, or who have fantasies about illegal and sexually abusive behaviour, can be termed 'sexually addicted'. An exploration of the relationship between sexual fantasy and sexual offending follows. A controversial topic is raised: whether fantasizing and masturbating about illegal sexual acts can substitute for the real thing, constituting a harm-reduction strategy. Common fantasy management techniques are discussed before a case study is presented. This features a middle-aged man who suffers significant shame about his indecent exposure (flashing) activities.

Are individuals who sexually offend sexually addicted?

Sexual addiction (Hall, 2013), in the context of this chapter, is defined as a pattern of compulsive sexual behaviour causing harm to self or others and/or at odds with a person's stable value base. Ward et al. (2004) propose a model of sexual offending involving four different pathways which can lead to a sexual offence, suggesting that different individuals have different trajectories of sexual offending, and abuse at differing rates. It should also be remembered that risk of offending is not the same as risk and level of harm. For instance, generally, individuals who expose themselves are at a heightened risk of reoffending, as they are high-frequency offenders (Abel et al., 1987; Murphy and Page, 2008). Generally, incest offenders who offend only within the family have a relatively low risk of reoffending, albeit after being caught (Hanson and Thornton, 1999). However, if an incest offender repeats the crime, the risk of serious harm being caused would probably be much higher than for an individual who commits a non-contact exposure offence.

As noted elsewhere, predicting the risk of reoffending is a complex and often contested business. Nevertheless, it is agreed by most specialists in the field, and backed up by research data, that the rate of known reoffending is significantly lower than the prevalence of actual abuse. It has been estimated that only one in eight victims of sexual abuse come to the attention of statutory authorities (Children's Commissioner's Inquiry Report, 2015).

Very deviant sex offenders who are at a high risk of reoffending do exist. Often these individuals are preoccupied with illegal sexual acts, have a history of sexual offending, display distorted thinking about sex and children, have violent or anti-social traits, or emotionally identify with children and have problems establishing satisfying relationships with adults (Cortini, 2009: 42; also see Chapter 2 for risk factors).

The picture is complex with regard to paedophiles, individuals whose main sexual arousal is towards pre-pubescent children. Goode (2009) describes various positions that paedophilic adults can adopt. Different positions can be summarized in the following ways:

- Are sexually attracted to pre-pubescent children, but desist from sex with children, believing it is harmful and morally wrong
- Basically believe that sex with children is wrong, but at times can be ambivalent about this belief and/or have difficulty in controlling sexual urges, leading to sexual abuse
- Believe sex with children is not harmful, morally wrong, or a sign of a sexual disorder, so pursue this course of action
- Do not care if sex with children is harmful or wrong, being intent on gaining sexual satisfaction in any case

Part of the complexity of risk assessment is that many individuals addicted to the pursuit of legal or illegal online sexual material will not be predominantly paedophilic and are at low risk of committing a contact offence, if they have no previous offending or anti-social history (Seto and Eke, 2005). The rate of sexual reoffending is lower than for many other crimes (Flora and Keohane, 2013: 4), despite the public perception of 'once a sex offender always a sex offender.' There are also many individuals who have committed sexual abuse against a child or an adult at one time in their lives – at a certain stage of development or in a particular context or set of circumstances – who are at relatively low risk of reoffending, and who can therefore not be classified as being addicted to sexual crime.

The link between fantasy and sexual offending

Both the influential Finkelhor cyclic model (1984), featured in Chapter 7, and the Wolf (1984) cyclic model of sexual offending link sexual fantasy to masturbation and, in turn, to sexual offending. Sexual fantasy can be seen to act as a form of operant conditioning, reinforced by masturbation and orgasm. The process can lower moral inhibitions and reinforce cognitive distortions, which also operate as permission-giving cognitions with regard to abusive sex. Fantasizing about sexual offending can also act as a dry run, as it were, with regard to grooming victims for harmful and illegal sex. The perpetrator tests out different grooming scenarios in his own mind before embarking on them, much as an individual would rehearse the normative social ritual of chatting-up a consenting adult he fancies, leading on to dating as part of the courtship and seduction process. Post-sexual offence sexual fantasy can also degrade protective barriers against further offending, such as guilt, as pleasure-seeking parts of the brain override moral constraints and consequential thinking about the impact of sexual offending for both victim and perpetrator.

Common methods used to control sexual fantasy

How can clients manage their sexual desires, if such fantasies involve the abuse of others? Firstly, as explained elsewhere, many individuals who have committed sexual offences or who are at risk of doing so, are not classic paedophiles, in that they are not predominantly aroused by pre-pubescent children. Such persons may have:

- Sexually offended against a pre-pubescent child, although remaining primarily attracted to adults
- Sexually offended against a post-pubescent, but underage teenager, with adult physical sexual characteristics (curves, breasts, pubic hair)
- Sexually offended against an adult

These individuals can be helped to focus on fantasies and masturbation involving legal sex with peer-age adults, strengthening these neural pathways, whilst weakening neural pathways connected to having sex with children or other forms of harmful sex. For these people there exists the option of developing and consolidating mutually satisfying sexual relationships with fellow adults.

However, as Goode (2009) points out, for paedophiles (individuals with an exclusive sexual attraction to children below the age of puberty), there can be no legitimate sexual contact or relationship with another human being of choice (i.e. an underage child), with this being an illegal act which would inevitably cause harm. Such individuals are faced with the choice of either having sex with children and risking prosecution and imprisonment, as well as being responsible for seriously harming a child, or choosing to desist from having sex at all, living a celibate life.

The therapeutic task is not to moralize to clients, no matter how subtly, about desisting from abusive sex. Advice giving is not the job of a counsellor, and is unlikely to be effective in bringing about change with any client group (Miller and Rollnick, 1991). A useful intervention is enabling the client to reflect on the pros and cons of choosing to offend or not offend. Useful areas of exploration include:

- The client exploring and identifying his stable value base, with regard to sex
- The client exploring the sort of pleasures and fulfilment he will have to forego if he chooses a life of celibacy or limiting sex to age-appropriate relationships
- The client exploring the consequences for self and loved ones of choosing to have illegal sex

- The client exploring the consequences for victims of choosing to have abusive sex (see Chapter 9)
- The client exploring any advantages of celibacy and self-imposed limits on sexual behaviour
- Whether the sexual drive can be non-repressively sublimated into other satisfying activities

Many individuals manage their sexual drives through fantasy and masturbation, without this leading to them acting out their fantasies in real life (Marshall and O'Brien, 2009: 167). Substituting actual sex with fantasy and masturbation might undermine a sexual relationship, as every sex and relationship therapist will tell you, although such activities in themselves by no means necessarily lead to unfaithfulness or sexual encounters. More likely, the sexual drive is simply satiated. This is also likely to be the case, in my view, with some clients with sexual offending problems, who genuinely and consistently view sexual offending as harmful and morally reprehensible, even though they might be turned on by it.

Each client will have a different pathway towards sexual abuse. For some, viewing pornography or even fantasizing about illegal or abusive imagery may satiate desire, leading to reduced risk of offending. For others the reverse could be true, with deviant sexual fantasy and masturbation constituting a definite pathway towards sexual crime. For instance, Gee et al. (2006) outline how research shows many links between deviant sexual fantasies involving the abuse of others and committing sexual crime.

Whereas a period of abstinence from fantasy and masturbation is sometimes recommended for clients with sexual offending problems, especially if the fantasies are deviant and offence related, there may be unforeseen consequences. If sexual arousal is not being periodically relieved through fantasy and masturbation, the build-up of sexual tension might become uncontrollable if, for instance, the client is in the presence of a vulnerable child and there is no supervising adult present. Johnston et al. (1997), cited by Gee et al. (2006: 224) make the point that inhibiting all fantasies through treatment might prove unrealistic, leading to paradoxical outcomes.

Managing sexual fantasies has traditionally been viewed in a relapse-prevention context, with therapist and client coming up with realistic and sustainable 'avoidance goals' (see Chapter 11 for discussion of avoidance and approach goals). This takes the form of avoiding stimuli (places, people, activities, sights, sounds, and smells) which could induce offence-permissive sexual fantasies and masturbation. Strengths-focused proponents posit that it is more effective in the long run to emphasize 'approach goals' rather than 'avoidance goals', focusing on positive enjoyable activities which can distract clients from unhelpful sexual thoughts. It is argued that human beings are more likely to consistently embrace enjoyable pro-social, positive behaviours (positive reinforcement) as a way of managing deviant arousal, than to try through gritted teeth, as it were, to deny themselves anti-social pleasures (negative reinforcement).

Dealing with risky sexual fantasies can be approached from two additional different perspectives, although they are not mutually exclusive. One is the largely cognitive-behavioural approach, where the client is encouraged to devise ways in which to escape from the problematic sexual fantasy as soon as possible by thinking or doing something else (Marshall et al., 2009). Another way is the Mindfulness approach where the client is taught through meditative techniques to be non-judgementally and compassionately present to the fantasy, fostering a state of detachment, not acting on the fantasy but waiting until a less problematic thought form eventually and inevitably takes its place. To date, there is limited research as to the effectiveness of Mindfulness with regard to sex offenders and problematic sexual fantasies, but the technique is used with a host of human problems and client groups (Dunkley and Stanton, 2013).

Yet another way of looking at fantasy management comes, again, from the strengths-focused perspective. As discussed in Chapter 1, desistance from sexual offending does not merely depend on addressing risk domains such as fantasy management, in piecemeal fashion, but is perhaps most likely to be achieved when a more profound shift in personal identity occurs. As a heterosexual man, when I was younger and part of a largely uneducated working-class peer group, I would sometimes talk with my friends about women in sexually objectifying terms. I no longer do this. I would also sometimes treat family and friends with casual rudeness and insensitivity. I now do this far less frequently. Why? I believe it is not just the case that I am older, more mature, and have better emotional regulation. My sense of myself has changed. To think and act in former ways would be at odds, would be incongruent, with my current sense of identity. Likewise, from a strengths-focused perspective, desistance from sexual offending and deviant sexual fantasies can take place through the transformative experience of a long-term therapeutic relationship, where new ways of perceiving self and others emerge – a process more essentially character changing than that of simple urge management.

Traditionally, fantasy management has involved managing 'bad' sex. However, logically, what can contribute to this area is the development of 'good sex': instead of sexual fantasy which harms and causes unhappiness, sexual practices which are harmless and lead to happiness. Sex therapists can play a key role here, adding their particular expertise to this area of practice, especially once sexual offending impulses are under control. Perceiving and experiencing sex as a mutual exchange of power and pleasure with a consenting adult, rather than sex involving non-consenting oppressive power and control in the pursuit of egocentric gratification, can be a significant rehabilitative factor.

Of course, the difficulty of working with the very private realm of the psyche is that one can never be sure what is going to work for an individual client, and it is not ever possible to be certain that what the client is saying is an accurate reflection of conscious or unconscious motivations. Even if the client genuinely seeks to impart an accurate impression of intention in the calm of the therapy room, he may behave very differently in other surroundings and when highly aroused.

Counsellors, like clients, can suffer from distorted thinking, tending towards omniscience (being sure about the mental state of the client) and omnipotence (overestimating their influence on that mental state). The subject of sexual fantasy is fraught with shame, as discussed in Chapter 1, often leading to accounts of sexual fantasy and masturbation which are sanitized and adjusted in the direction of what the client considers to be socially acceptable.

In the face of such uncertainty, the best a counsellor can do is to place the responsibility for change with the individual, increasing the client's awareness of the different forms of fantasy management, and leaving it with the client to choose appropriate strategies. The counsellor can occasionally check in with the client how and if the strategies chosen are still working, negotiating how often this checking in process should occur. Negotiating with the client in the following way, I believe, is the limit of the counsellor's (still significant) influence in this essentially private, ultimately unaccountable area of personal life:

- Exploring the client's value base when it comes to fantasy. What the client thinks are 'OK Fantasies' and 'not OK Fantasies' and the reasons for this
- Establishing the client's 'bottom line:' the boundary the client intends never to cross
- Identifying with the client what would be a relapse (crossing the 'bottom line') and a lapse, which can lead to a relapse
- Keeping a Fantasy Management Diary, which can help the client monitor and manage sexual thoughts and behaviour, and which can be used by the client to make himself transparently accountable to the counsellor, before becoming autonomously accountable to himself (see Appendix 17 for Fantasy Management Diary)
- Devising a New Life Safety Plan (see Chapter 11), incorporating the behavioural, environmental, and cognitive distraction techniques in this list (which is also available in Appendix 18):
  - Taking a shower
  - Taking physical exercise
  - Listening to calming music
  - Positive self-talk
  - Phoning a person
  - Looking at an image of a loved one
  - Looking at a list of the consequences of relapsing (the list to be kept on the person, e.g. on a smart phone)
  - Using accountability as a deterrent to relapsing. (It is important for the client to take proactive responsibility in making himself accountable, avoiding, in transactional analysis terms, a counterproductive parent–child dynamic with a therapist or partner with whom the client has this accountable relationship.)
  - If having 'not OK' fantasies, de-objectifying the individuals in the fantasies by thinking of them as complex human beings, somebody's child or

parent, a precious, fragile human being who is loved by others, with fears and hopes, experiencing joy and sadness

- Thinking of 'OK' pleasurable sexual fantasies when masturbating
- If relapsing by thinking of 'not OK' sexual fantasies when masturbating, reverting to 'OK' sexual fantasies just before climax (a particularly addictive point)
- Feeling compassion for self and others (including the fantasy figures)

Case study: Brian

Brian (58) is a businessman who goes on frequent trips abroad, including to Thailand. He has been married for 25 years to Jo, who is the chief executive of a small charity. They have twin daughters, both at university. Brian has been convicted of acts of indecent exposure. He was arrested after he flashed to a group of teenage schoolgirls, in a park close to a school, where the girls were playing hockey. The police also found many images of women in schoolgirl uniforms on his computer, although all were over the age of consent, and downloaded from legal pornographic sites. A common theme was young women dressed in school uniforms and provocatively posing in sportswear, or engaged in various sporting and gym activities. For the flashing offence Brian was given a sentence of 180 hours of community service, with the condition that he receives therapeutic help. He and his wife have moved out of the small village where they have spent most of their life and raised their two daughters, without any apparent problems. Brian's wife is not sure whether or not she wishes to continue the relationship, and wants time to see how Brian responds to counselling, saying their relationship will have to be put on a new footing. Brian decided to leave the company he was working for because of the social embarrassment of facing his colleagues, after the case was reported in the press. He intends to set up his own business, and has promised his wife that this will not involve any trips abroad or overnight stays, as when he did this previously his use of pornography on the internet increased. He maintains that he never participated in sexual activities on his previous business trips, but his wife has lost trust in him. He comes for counselling, deeply ashamed of his behaviour, and provides what the counsellor considers a sanitized account of his fantasy and masturbation habits, saying that he fantasizes only about his wife and never masturbates, as he and his wife have a regular sex life. Brian is a particularly defended client.

Therapeutic work with Brian

The counsellor considered that it was unlikely that Brian would be honest about his fantasy life and any times he may have exposed himself previously. To pressurize him to be more honest, no matter how gently such pressure was exerted, would be likely to lead to the 'confrontation-denial trap' (Miller and Rollnick, 1991). The counsellor decided, therefore, to adopt a strengths-focused approach to addressing the issue of fantasy management. The first stage of this was exploring with the client his stable value base (when he was not in a state of high arousal, whereby moral considerations might be likely to be compromised).

Counsellor:	Brian, I know you say that you only fantasize about your wife, but could I ask you to tell me what you would consider 'OK' sexual fantasies and 'not OK' sexual fantasies?
Brian:	I've never thought about it.
Counsellor:	It may be that you are telling the truth when you say that you never fantasize about other people. However, I frequently work with men who are too ashamed to talk about their sexual fantasies, including men who fantasize about teenage girls, including schoolgirls. Most people, in fact, fantasize about all sorts of things they would rather not talk about – this is just how we are as human beings. But you came for counselling on the basis that the court expected you to receive some sort of therapy that would address your offending behaviour. Part of this is me giving you options to manage any sexual fantasies which could lead to you reoffending.
Brian:	But I will never reoffend. I've lost too much.
Counsellor:	That could well be the case. But this is a sort of insurance policy that the court and the probation service, and maybe your wife and daughters, would want put in place. If we conduct the work in this session, and perhaps over the next one or two, I won't be expecting you to talk about your fantasy life. But it would be a positive sign to everybody that you take your offences seriously, if you can say that you understand the link between fantasy, masturbation, and acting out sexually, and you are aware of some ways to manage this process – although I accept that you say that you don't have any such fantasies yourself. Are you willing to engage with this work, as an indication that you are taking some responsibility?
Brian:	OK, go ahead.

In this case, Brian was willing to address the general subject of sexual fantasy, albeit on a hypothetical level, having been invited to demonstrate that he was taking his offending seriously. If a client refuses such an invitation, it is counterproductive to get into an argument about this. It is better to 'roll with the resistance' and begin to explore another seemingly fruitful area that the client is motivated to discuss.

Counsellor: Right, let's start then, Brian, with you telling me about what fantasies you would disapprove of, in some way.

Brian: Well, anything that would hurt anybody.

Counsellor: Can you nail that down, give me more details?

Brian: Violence, I suppose, doing something against a person's will.

Counsellor: How could you tell that something was against a person's will?

Brian: I guess if they looked frightened, or were saying 'stop' or giving 'no' signals.

Counsellor: I guess 'no' signals can be subtle. Can you say what these 'no' signals would be?

Brian: Looking uncomfortable, wanting to get away from you, at an extreme end if somebody was in pain. I can never understand all that sado-masochistic stuff, it's bloody weird if you ask me.

Counsellor: Yes, Brian, I can see that you wouldn't want to hurt anybody.

It is common for human beings in general to consolidate ego and combat shame by pointing out people whose behaviour we construct as worse than our own. Hence, prisoners who have sexually abused children will say 'at least I don't go around raping people.' In turn, rapists will say 'at least I don't abuse children.' This phenomenon, which Hudson (2005) describes as distancing techniques, was apparent with some of the respondents I interviewed during the research I conducted:

> *I know there are some evil bastards out there. Kids are not safe in their own bloody bath now.*
>
> (Offender 1)

> *Sometimes, I think it doesn't quite apply to me. I don't think I'm high risk of anything.*
>
> (Offender 2)

We see here the phenomenon of Brian, like the offenders quoted, taking the moral high ground about sado-masochistic behaviour, especially as part of the motivation for indecent exposure can be the gratification the offender experiences, when seeing the shock and fear on the victim's face. This distancing or displacement behaviour can prove challenging to the counsellor, especially when clients have committed serious sexual offences. One response is for the counsellor to climb onto his own moral high ground and seek to point out the hypocrisy. Such moralizing tit-for-tat is usually counterproductive, eroding the therapeutic relationship. As noted elsewhere, it can be more effective to employ what solution-focused therapists call 'selective inattention': deliberately ignoring responsibility shifting or anti-social statements, whilst complimenting and encouraging any pro-social responsibility taking discourse. The counsellor above attempts this with Brian, ignoring the hypocritical sado-masochistic comment, whilst affirming the pro-social sentiments.

Therapy also has a naturally cyclic, waxing and waning quality to it. As is apparent in previous chapters, talking about sexual offending can be particularly ego sapping.

> *I think the self-esteem during the actual therapeutic process was still fairly low; the whole sense of devastation, shame, having – you know, particularly for a person from my background and opportunity and kind of professional standing – having acted in this appalling way, was very difficult.*

(Offender 8)

Having been asked to talk for a while about psychologically threatening material, such as having deviant fantasies, the client often needs periods of relief from the strain, talking about non-threatening or ego-consolidating topics. Part of the counsellor's skill is recognizing and respecting these respite periods, whilst not colluding with avoiding difficult subject matter because of the counsellor's own issues, as discussed in Chapter 7.

Counselling:	OK Brian, you've mentioned fantasies involving force and frightening people – is it alright if we call them 'not OK' fantasies as a term we can work with?
Brian:	Yeah, fine with me.
Counselling:	So what other sexual fantasies would you consider generally 'not OK'?
Brian:	Well, I don't know about anyone else, but for me – I wouldn't fantasize about any other woman, only my wife.
Counsellor:	OK, anything else?
Brian:	I can't think.
Counsellor:	I'll give you a couple of minutes to think.
Brian:	(at the end of the two minutes). Nope, I can't think of anything else.
Counsellor:	How about sexual fantasies of schoolgirls? I say this, Brian, because images of young women in school uniform and in what some would call sexually provocative poses, many involving sporting activities, were found on your computer. Your actual offence also involved exposing yourself to schoolgirls, after watching them playing a hockey match – you can probably see the link I'm making.
Brian:	That's all behind me now. As I've said to you people [professionals in general], I have no explanation for my conduct. It was completely out of character. But I am not interested in schoolgirls, and I certainly have never had any sexual fantasies about underage girls.

The counsellor considers that Brian's account is unlikely, and hypothesizes to himself that Brian probably has a fetish for schoolgirls revolving around sporting activity that he cannot acknowledge. However, Brian is not at a motivational stage to explore such issues.

Counsellor: I acknowledge where you are at about this, Brian. However, some clients I work with come up with other 'not OK' sexual fantasies. Can I share some with you, and you can say if you agree whether they would be 'OK' or 'not OK'?

Brian: Fine.

The counsellor comes up with the following list:

* Fantasies involving an underage person, below the age of 16
* Fantasies involving a person where there is a significant age gap
* Fantasies involving any sort of offence-focused fetish (which, for Brian, would probably include voyeuristic interest in teenage girls involved in sport)
* Fantasies involving the use of pornographic materials, including internet pornography, if this is related to their offending

Brian: Yeah, forgive me. I'm being dim. Obviously all of those fantasies would be definite 'no-nos'.

Counsellor: Would they, I wonder? Some men, for instance, say that fantasizing and masturbating to pornography is a release valve, which stops them acting out their fantasies and harming other people. Other men say that fantasizing about pornography is part of a pathway towards reoffending, as it leads to them losing moral perspective and sexually objectifying children and adults.

Brian: I can see how it could work both ways. But as I say, I don't have any fantasies like that.

Counsellor: (With a good-natured smile) Alright, I'm not going to argue with you and I'm going to take you at face value. But just in case you do have sexual fantasies that you are worried about and too embarrassed to discuss, can I introduce you to a model of how 'not OK' fantasies work? Think of it as an insurance policy if you like, or so that I can be sure that I've provided you with the tools you need not to reoffend and cause more misery to yourself and others. I know you are saying that you will never offend – so humour me if you like, Brian.

Brian: (sighs) Go ahead then.

The counsellor explained that the main motivation for sexual offending tends to be sexual arousal, but other motivations also include: wanting emotional intimacy and comfort, escaping from problems and pressures, simulating power and control, feeling excited by indulging in taboo activities, and the possibility of getting caught. Often there can be a number of motivations for committing a sexual offence, with 'not OK' fantasies about sexual offending being initially triggered by negative or disinhibited mood states. Usually 'not OK' fantasies lead to masturbation and orgasm which can create an addictive or compulsive behavioural pattern, as a neural pathway is established in the brain, much the same as a desire for alcohol or tobacco is created. Part of the 'not OK' fantasy often involves behaviour and situations acting as rehearsals and planning for the real thing (e.g. flashing at underage girls in a park, or fantasizing and masturbating about them in sporty, seductive poses). Some individuals cross the line, turning fantasy into reality. During and after the offence there can be a period of great excitement, before fear of getting caught and guilt set in. Often the fear and guilt reduce over time (for some this could be hours after the offence, for others it could be years), before the cycle starts all over again as the person begins to entertain 'not OK' fantasies.

As a strengths-focused therapist I believe clients can be empowered by being provided with information to make informed choices about their lives (see Chapter 8). Hence, I often provide this information to clients when discussing fantasy management, adjusting the explanation to the intellectual capacity of the person with whom I am working. I may choose, however, not to use this psychoeducational intervention if I consider that a client would be too threatened by it, or if the main tenets are being explored in a less structured way, through the ongoing counselling process.

Returning to Brian, he was quiet and looked uncomfortable as the counsellor explained the links between sexual fantasy and offending. It was the counsellor's interpretation that, despite Brian's silence, he was relating what was being explained to his own sexual behaviour. In this way his consciousness was being raised about the links between fantasy, masturbation, and sexual offending. The counsellor expected a muted, defensive response to this threatening material, and duly got it.

Brian:	I follow all that, very interesting and all, but it doesn't really apply to me.
Counsellor:	I accept that, but let's talk hypothetically. List the main 'not OK' sexual fantasies that would be a concern if they came into your head.
Brian:	They wouldn't come into my head, but I'll give it a go. But I'm not saying that that I do have these fantasies, mind you!
Counsellor:	That's fine, Brian. Go ahead.
Brian:	Well, it's pretty obvious isn't it? I would say thinking about any teenage girls especially dressed in school informs, involved with sports, and looking at this sort of stuff on the internet.
Counsellor:	And you say you don't do this now.
Brian:	Definitely not.

Counsellor: And leading up to the offence, and when you were looking at pornographic images on the internet?
Brian: Back then, perhaps.
Counsellor: Perhaps?
Brian: OK, well sure. I can't deny it because they found it on my computer.
Counsellor: Can we call that chap back there 'Pre-Offence Brian', and you as
you are now, 'Post-Offence Brian'? There must have been many
times when Pre-Offence Brian didn't give in to the temptation to
fantasize about 'not OK' stuff. How did he manage that?

Here, the counsellor is employing two strengths-focused techniques. The first
technique (Pre-Offence Brian and Post-Offence Brian) is separating the problematic behaviour from the emerging pro-social identity of the client, allowing the
client to talk in meaningful ways about problematic behaviour, whilst not losing face. This externalizing technique is also highlighted in other chapters of the
book, and is a variation on the helpful 'Old Me, New Me' rehabilitative dichotomy
proposed by Haaven and Coleman (2000). The second technique is looking for
exceptions to the problem, utilizing the strengths the client has already shown in
previously resisting temptation. Most, although not all, individuals who sexually
offend are ambivalent about their offending behaviour, as most of us are about
our problematic habits, such as overeating or drinking too much. Part of us wants
to do it, another part of us doesn't. Looking for exceptions to problems utilizes
and builds upon previous strategies that a client may have used to make positive
choices. Utilizing strategies that are germane to the client, rather than those suggested by the counsellor, is more likely to be effective as these strategies have
worked, at least some of the time, in the past. Highlighting the existing strengths
of the client also gives credit, offsetting some of the ego-sapping stigma attached
to having committed a sexual offence, and having to talk about it.

Brian: Well Pre-Offence Brian was pretty wrapped up in himself there for
a time, but he would have thought about his wife and kids, and that
some of the girls in the pictures were younger than his daughters.
(Brian's eyes fill with tears.)
Counsellor: Anything else?
Brian: Sometimes he would go out for a walk, anything to take his mind
off it.
Counsellor: Brian, can I give you a list of sexual fantasy and masturbation techniques (see Appendix 18) to take away and consider, and suggest
that maybe next week we could discuss if any of these techniques
would have been useful to Pre-Offence Brian, at the time leading
up to his offending.

Brian came to counselling the following week and discussed the fantasy management that might have worked for Pre-Offence Brian. He subsequently typed up a
fantasy management plan based on this.

Conclusion

If the counsellor's hypothesis was correct, and Brian did have an established sporting schoolgirl fetish, much useful work could possibly have been completed, concerning Brian's feelings and thoughts (perhaps previously unacknowledged) about part of his life that had been unlived, or at least unexamined. The therapeutic goal would have been for him to come to a constructive accommodation with this part of himself. However, Brian was a particularly closed client, and this tack was not possible. The case study was deliberately presented to demonstrate interventions which can be used to possible good effect with clients too ashamed to talk openly about their sexual fantasy and masturbatory life. Many clients will not be as guarded as Brian and will be keener to collaborate in constructing a fantasy management or sexual behaviour plan that works for them. Different strategies will work for different clients. In the end the counsellor will not know if the client is being honest about his sexual thoughts and activities, and will need to be able to make friends with this uncertainty. The therapist is doing a good job if he provides the client with increased insight and options, leaving the responsibility with the client to make informed choices about the management of his own mental and relational life.

References

Abel, G.G., Becker, J.V., Mittleman, M., Cunningham-Rathner, J., Rouleau, J.L. and Murphy, W.D. (1987) 'Self-reported sex crimes of non-incarcerated paraphiliacs', *Journal of Interpersonal Violence*, 2 (1): pp. 3–25.

Children's Commissioner's Inquiry Report (2015), *Protecting children from harm: A critical assessment of child sexual abuse in the family network in England and priorities for action*. Available from: www.childrenscommissioner.gov.uk/learn-more/child-sexual-exploitation-abuse/protecting-children-harm [18 December 2015].

Cortini, F. (2009) 'Factors associated with sexual recidivism', in A.R. Beech, L.A. Craig and K.D. Browne (eds.) *Assessment and treatment of sex offenders: A handbook*. Chichester: Wiley-Blackwell, pp. 39–52.

Dunkley, C. and Stanton, M. (2013) *Teaching clients to use Mindfulness skills: A practical guide*. London and New York: Routledge.

Finkelhor, D. (1984) *Child sexual abuse: New theory and research*. New York: The Free Press.

Flora, R. and Keohane, M.L. (2013) *How to work with sex offenders: A handbook for criminal justice, human service and mental health professionals*, 2nd edition. New York and London: Routledge.

Gee, D., Ward, T., Belofastov, A. and Beech, A. (2006) 'The structural properties of sexual fantasies for sexual offenders', *Journal of Sexual Aggression*, 12 (3): pp. 213–226.

Goode, S.D. (2009) *Understanding and addressing adult sexual attraction to children: A study of paedophiles in contemporary society*. New York: Routledge.

Haaven, J.L. and Coleman, E.M. (2000) 'Treatment of the developmentally disabled sex offender', in D.R. Laws, S.M. Hudson and T. Ward (eds.) *Remaking relapse prevention with sex offenders: A sourcebook*. Thousand Oaks, CA: Sage, pp. 369–388.

Hall, P. (2013) *Understanding and treating sexual addiction: A comprehensive guide for people who struggle with sex addiction and those who want to help them.* London and New York: Routledge.

Hanson, R.K. and Thornton, D. (1999) *Static 99: Improving actuarial risk assessment for sex offenders* (User report No. 99–02). Ottawa: Public Safety Canada. Available from: www.publicsafety.gc.ca/cnt/rsrcs/pblctns/sttc-mprvng-actrl/sttc-mprvng-actrl-eng.pdf [19 September 2016].

Hudson, K. (2005) *Offending identities: Sex offenders' perspectives on their treatment and management.* Devon: Willan.

Johnston, L., Ward, T. and Hudson, S.M. (1997) 'Deviant sexual thoughts: Mental control and the treatment of sexual offenders', *Journal of Sex Research*, 34 (2): pp. 121–130.

Marshall, L.E. and O'Brien, M.D. (2009) 'Assessment of sexual addiction', in A.R. Beech, L.A. Craig and K.D. Browne (eds.) *Assessment and treatment of sex offenders: A handbook.* Chichester: Wiley-Blackwell, pp. 163–178.

Miller, W.R. and Rollnick, S. (1991) *Motivational interviewing: Helping people change.* New York: Guilford Press.

Murphy, W.D. and Page, I.J. (2008) 'Exhibitionism: Psychopathology and theory', in R.D. Laws and W.T. O'Donohue (eds.) *Sexual deviance: Theory, assessment and treatment*, 2nd edition. New York: Guilford Press, pp. 61–75.

Seto, M.C. and Eke, A.W. (2005) 'The criminal histories and later offending of child pornography offenders', *Sexual Abuse: A Journal of Research and Treatment*, 17 (2): pp. 201–210.

Ward, T., Bickley, J., Webster, S.D., Fisher, D., Beech, A. and Eldridge, H. (2004) *The self regulation model of the offence and relapse process. Vol. 1: Assessment.* Victoria, BC: Pacific Psychological Assessment Corporation–Trafford Publishing.

Wolf, S. (1984) 'A multifactor model of deviant sexuality', Paper presented at 3rd International Conference on Victimology, Lisbon, Portugal, November 1984.

Chapter 11

Applying strengths-focused interventions to safety planning

Introduction

This final chapter is about bringing all the preceding therapeutic work together in the form of a risk management plan, the New Life Safety Plan. The concept of relapse prevention will be discussed from a strengths-focused point of view, focusing on *approach goals*, but incorporating *avoidance goals* as well. Risk reduction and risk management strategies are outlined from a strengths-focused perspective. Two case studies will be referenced. The first features a newly retired man, 'Sandy', who has been convicted of a voyeuristic offence. He is a relatively low risk in terms of causing serious harm to others and committing sexual offences against loved ones, and will likely continue to live in a family setting. The second case study features a high-risk predatory paedophile who has committed very serious sexual offences against young boys. 'George' will never be allowed to live with children.

Relapse prevention and safety plans

Firstly, many counsellors do not formulate written plans with clients, believing that change occurs more through osmosis and cannot be neatly written down and wrapped up into some sort of plan to which a client will promise to abide through self-control. I have sympathy with this view. I believe personal, transformational change is a mysterious and profound process. When it seems right to end therapy, the 'juice' just seems to go out of it. I and the client appear to be going through the motions. Often it is at this point that the client seems to be in a different place. He sees life and himself differently. Previous problematic behaviour appears no longer so necessary and proves incongruent with the new identity that has emerged.

However, for some clients, charting change through written goals related to future behaviour appears to be helpful. This process for people who have sexual offending problems has traditionally been termed 'relapse prevention'. Compiling what I call a New Life Safety Plan is my strengths-focused version of this safeguarding process. Relapse prevention planning has been used in substance addiction work (Marlatt and Gordon, 1980) and in the criminal justice system when working with people who have committed sexual crimes (Laws, 1999). The concept of relapse prevention has been defined as:

- Identifying psychological triggers
- Recognizing high-risk situations
- Being aware of one's addiction cycle
- Developing a personal recovery plan
- Using alternative behaviours that lessen the risk of relapse

(Flora and Keohane, 2013: 224)

In strengths-based treatment programmes, the term 'relapse prevention plan' is often replaced with a more hopeful, positive term which embraces the holistic concept of the individual building a new life or having a fresh start. Such plans are given various names: safeguarding plans, safety plans, better life plans, positive life plans, etc. The term I use is New Life Safety Plan. It is important, however, that this positive renaming is not just a rebranding exercise. For a future plan to qualify as strengths-based, strengths-focused principles and methods, such as those illustrated throughout this book, have to have been intrinsic to the therapeutic approach leading up to and informing the plan.

Austin and Vancouver (1996) divide motivation into *avoidance goals* – connected to restriction and elimination (avoiding risks) – and *approach goals* – involving enlargement and realization (seeking out situations which provide interest and fulfilment in pro-social ways). Ward and Maruna (2007) argue that rather than merely concentrating on problem-based deficits in functioning, risk management, and relapse prevention should place more emphasis on helping individuals who have sexually offended to lead fulfilling lives. In this way, needs and desires can be met pro-socially by other means than sex offending, and individuals will be more likely to be deterred from sexual reoffending by fear of forfeiting the satisfying life they have built up for themselves. The testimony of the following individuals who have sexually offended bears witness to the transformative power of having something to live for and something to lose.

This is my life now, and I want to be free to live my life. I don't want to be banged up on prison. . . . I am not going to reoffend. I have too much to lose. I'm doing so well. . . . I'm not going to throw that away; I'm not going to throw that away.

(Offender 9)

Mostly, friends and family, and girlfriend, and thinking about the future. I mean, I've got so much to lose. Yeah, so it's working towards that; something that I don't want taken away from me.

(Offender 2)

My family stuck with me, even though my offences were connected to the family. . . . As I say I got responsibilities, and that is another thing that goes against anybody, stopping them reoffending, being responsible to someone, and thinking, you know, well these people are good. They are looking after you, and don't you dare let them down.

(Offender 4)

I don't see them [young boys] as sexual targets, if you like. I'm happy with the sex life that I have with my partner, with the life beyond sex I have. I don't want to jeopardize that at all . . . it's kind of like that I'm bisexual and accept that. Like I say I think that Damon [Matt Damon the movie star] is nice. . . . I don't think I'll ever get rid of the attraction or the thought of it. But I don't want to. The fact that it would be destructive to me, destructive to the person, destructive to my family.

(Offender 5)

A limitation of concentrating exclusively on approach goals, however, can be seen when working with individuals where the motive for sexual abuse is primarily, if not wholly, erotic: where the client's exclusive attraction is towards children. In such cases, a sexual relationship with an adult (an approach goal) may not be possible or desirable. It must be debatable whether other pleasurable or fulfilling activities can ever totally replace or sublimate the sexual urge, leaving *avoidance goals* of increasing self-control and avoiding risky cognitions and situations as significant options, if children and adults are not to be sexually harmed.

In practice, when I work with clients I negotiate with them a combination of *avoidance goals* and *approach goals* (see example New Life Safety Plan that follows and in Appendix 8). The main issue is that the New Life Safety Plan is a genuinely collaborative effort, and that the client believes and has hope in the plan, has a realistic chance of sticking to it and is not set up to fail.

As stated in Chapter 3, my preference is to make New Life Safety Plans as simple as possible. When working in the criminal justice system, first as a probation officer and then as an expert witness, I came across many complex risk management plans which look good on paper, but seem predominantly written to impress fellow professionals, rather than to have optimum utility for clients. Individuals who have offended often have trouble internalizing what is in complex plans, only remembering the basics. Hence, it is important to get the basics right.

Below is a blank format of the New Life Safety Plan that I use. A full-length copy can be found in Appendix 9.

New Life Safety Plan

Signs of positive and safer life
Signs of risk
Responses to signs of risk

As discussed in Chapter 3, the New Life Safety Plan can be used in two ways. The first way is to negotiate a basic plan with the client at the beginning of the counselling process. This can have the advantage of providing the client with useful strategies right from the start of therapy, to manage any risk of sexual reoffending, suicide, or self-harm. The plan can then evolve as the therapy progresses, and be used as a frequent reference point for useful reflection. The other way is to agree upon the plan at the end of counselling, with learning gained from the therapeutic process culminating in and incorporated into the plan.

A rough outline of a typical course of counselling I use for a person who has sexually offended is provided by the sequencing of the chapters in this book. This narrative structure is not meant to be prescriptive. When I have completed the course of counselling described, which usually takes between three to six months, I can then see clients for longer periods if required, for up to two years or potentially longer. Some clients also get back in touch after the main work is completed, in order to address specific life issues as they arise. This additional engagement usually consists of helping the client ground progress – new insights, cognitive shifts, positive self-talk, behavioural changes, risk management strategies etc. – into everyday life, as the client responds to existing and new challenges. The New Life Safety Plan can be a useful part of this ongoing reflective process, helping the client to monitor whether therapeutic gains are being sustained. Fulfilling needs and desires in pro-social rather than anti-social ways

The 'Good Lives Model' (Ward and Brown, 2004; Ward and Marshall, 2004; Ward and Stewart, 2003a, 2003b) posits that when universal 'primary goods' (i.e. happiness) are obtained through positive 'secondary goods' (i.e. mutually fulfilling relationships), rather than negative 'secondary goods' (i.e. sexual offending) this reduces the risk of reoffending. Some parallels can be drawn with James' therapeutic recipe for living a 'good life', called 'healthy mindedness' (James, 1985, first published 1902) and also with Maslow's 'hierarchy of needs', the developmental fulfilment of which lead to 'self-actualization' (1943).

However, the conceptual framework and language I adopt in my practice is the following: assisting clients to fulfil needs and desires in pro-social rather than anti-social ways. Two approaches can be used, which are not mutually exclusive. The first is for the therapist to keep this approach in mind, whilst not actually introducing the model to the client. This would be similar to many therapeutic models and ideas which inform a counsellor's practice, but are never actually talked about in the therapy. This is how I frequently use this approach.

The second way is to use this conceptual framework explicitly with clients, if I consider this of benefit and if this way of perceiving human behaviour is likely to fit with their learning style. This involves explaining that we are all the trying all of the time to fulfil needs and desires, but we find constructive or less constructive ways of going about this. I can then discuss with the clients the needs and desires, and also the values which underpin these. Through the course of the therapeutic process the needs and desires which are particularly important to the client will usually emerge naturally. Each need and desire can then be looked at in turn, with the client being encouraged to reflect upon the following:

- What needs and desires were the client trying to meet when committing the sexual offence?
- How can these needs and desires be obtained pro-socially?
- Are sufficient needs and desires being fulfilled in the client's life?
- Are there deficits?
- Is there a surfeit in some needs and desires and a deficit in others?
- Which needs and desires are most important to the client?
- Does the client want to rebalance life? (What are the pros and cons of that?)
- Does the client want to prioritize certain needs and desires? (What are the pros and cons of this?)
- What are the means (skills and resources) needed to acquire the desired mix of needs and desires in pro-social ways?
- Can needs and desires be realistically acquired; if so, how?

A scaling exercise can help with some of these reflections, with the client asked to scale the presence of needs and desires in his life from 0 to 10, with 0 denoting minimum presence and 10 maximum presence. The client can then be asked to give each need and desire an ideal number, between 0 and 10, which would be optimally satisfactory. The practitioner can further inquire whether and how this ideal can be achieved and the effect this would likely have on the client's life and the lives of others. The values underpinning any given need and desire can also be unpacked, raising the client's awareness of any anti-social values underlying preferences.

Case study: Sandy

Sandy was a 60-year-old civil engineer who had been retired for two years. He was tanned, handsome, looked younger than his age, and obviously kept himself fit. He wore casual but stylish and expensive clothes. For most of his life he had worked abroad, contracted to overseas construction projects in dangerous parts of the world, including Somalia, Iraq, and Afghanistan. He described being in dangerous situations, where colleagues and friends had lost their lives, and where he had seen much death and suffering amongst indigenous populations. He generally talked with devil-may-care abandon. At other times he was emotional, speaking with tears in his eyes about the suffering he had seen. Sandy did not seem cut off from his emotions or other people's pain. But in between discharging emotion, he talked with relentless and wearing positivity, saying how important it was to take personal responsibility, to be organized and to make the best of whatever life throws at you. There were many things to admire about Sandy. He had been married for 30 years to Pat and had an adult son, a solicitor. He described his wife as a wonderfully caring woman and 'homemaker' although she had always been a bit 'nervy'. She never accompanied him on his trips abroad, preferring to 'keep the home fires burning', as Sandy described it. He said that they had always had a satisfactory sex life, and that he had never been unfaithful to Pat. They were both churchgoers, but she was more heavily involved than him, with Sandy describing the vicar as 'a bit of a wet blanket'. Three months ago Sandy was caught going into the changing room of a trendy High Street clothes shop, and putting a mirror under the gap at the bottom of the unisex changing room partition, so he could see a 19-year-old girl undressing. She had screamed and he had been detained by security staff, until the police arrived. He said that he had done this half a dozen times previously, without getting caught. He explained he had put a lot of time into planning the offence, finding shops that had unisex changing rooms. He then looked for the changing rooms which had just the right degree of gap at the bottom of the partition to allow him to adjust the mirror at an angle where only a bit of it showed in the other cubicle (the less it showed the less chance of detection), but which allowed him to get a good view of the person on the other side. He then waited in these stores for women he found attractive to try clothes on, following them into the changing room area with an item of clothing he had already picked up in the store. He said that these women would be aged from late teens up to middle age, his choice based purely on which women he found 'sexy'. He explained that he had to go through this process a number of times, as often he would follow the woman into the changing room area only to find that the neighbouring cubicle would be occupied. He was assessed by the probation service as being at low risk of causing serious harm to the public, and was given a one-year suspended sentence. His wife and son were shocked and highly embarrassed by his behaviour. They have remained supportive to him, but insisted he should see a counsellor, which Sandy was also very keen to do, as he was ashamed and remorseful about his behaviour.

Therapeutic work with Sandy

The counsellor had worked with other clients with voyeuristic issues, previously. The main difficulty had been linked to persons feeling disempowered in some way, and enjoying the compensatory power and sense of agency of offending against unsuspecting victims. For some of these clients, it was a matter of identifying how they could obtain the need or desire for power and agency without harming others. This often involved clients learning to be assertive generally, and more intimate and transparent in personal relationships with partners, fulfilling the need or desire for relational connection. In some cases, these gains led to a more fulfilling emotional and sexual life with a partner.

With regard to Sandy, his voyeuristic behaviour started a year before he retired. Contemplating retiring had been an existential crisis. He described to the counsellor frequent thoughts about death that had never bothered him when he was at actual risk of dying in the war zones he had worked in. It transpired that, for Sandy, the thought of retirement seemed like a living death, with a desert of time to fill in before the end. Sandy reflected that he had never felt more alive than when working in trouble spots and, although he loved his wife and son, family life had always secretly bored him.

An inexperienced therapist may have considered that what Sandy needed to do was to develop a more balanced life, learning to appreciate relationships more, or to re-evaluate his faith, and discover meaning in everyday life. Whereas such a rebalancing of life and learning to tolerate the adrenalin withdrawal of working in dangerous situations would be right for some clients, the counsellor sensed that Sandy was not at a motivational stage to seriously consider these alternatives. Instead, she encouraged Sandy to speak about what he liked, and found rewarding and meaningful about risking his life. Sandy described the excitement, the challenge of planning and pulling off a job under pressure, the comradeship, and the sense of making a difference. As they spoke about the voyeuristic behaviour, Sandy came to see that many of these elements – the planning, executing a plan under pressure, making an impact, the excitement about breaking a taboo, and the danger of getting caught (as opposed to danger of death) – closely replicated his lost work experiences.

Sandy agreed that the priority at the moment was consolidating his relationship with his wife and son and reintegrating himself into the church – fulfilling need and desires for community and friendship. However, once these needs and desires were secured he would be liable to get bored and be looking for excitement again and the buzz of making an impact, to give his life meaning by pursuing needs, desires, and values ultimately more essential to his character.

Sandy explained to his wife and son that through therapy he came to see that he needed this sort of excitement in his life, and had been compensating for the lack of it. The couple eventually came to view these factors in their own Christian terms, perceiving that God had made Sandy this way, and he needed to find ways of continuing his spiritual calling. This narrative met Sandy's desire for spiritual meaning, and he started to look around for voluntary work he could do in troubled parts of the world. He also bought a powerful motorbike and joined a Christian motorbike network. There were many men of his age, and he found the comradeship that he had missed from working abroad. He had never before bought a motorbike because his wife, Pat, was worried about him having an accident, saying he took enough risks at work. However, Pat now understood that this was a risk that Sandy desired and needed at this stage in his life.

What puzzled the counsellor, however, was why Sandy seemed to act out and take sexual risks rather than climbing mountains or engaging in some other dangerous activity. Sandy stated that he had started to look at internet pornography in the latter stages of his career, when the younger workers he met abroad – including some young women soldiers and engineers – talked unashamedly about doing this. This had excited him, although he felt guilty about using pornography because of his Christian faith and not telling Pat about this habit. Using pornography had allowed him to objectify women, which had been another factor in his offending. Below is the New Life Safety Plan, finally agreed with Sandy.

New Life Safety Plan

Signs of a positive life and safety

- Sandy making a positive impact in a risky area of work
- Sandy buying a powerful motorbike
- Sandy keeping a regular time to pray and meditate every day
- Sandy doing regular exercise to burn off surplus energy
- Sandy being open with his wife about any lapses into viewing pornography online
- Sandy to imagine any women he is sexually fantasizing about as a human being rather than a sex object
- Sandy to keep in mind what it would be like for his wife to be spied on in a changing room
- Sandy to keep a photograph of his wife and son to look at in times of temptation

Signs of risk

- The above signs of safety being eroded
- Thoughts of death and meaninglessness
- Looking at pornography
- Going to clothes shops on his own
- Keeping his frame of mind secret from his wife

Responses to signs of risk

- Keep away from shops
- Talk to his wife or minister
- Contact his counsellor
- Change lifestyle habits
- Monitor boredom levels
- Report any lapses to his wife or minister

Other strengths-focused techniques for negotiating a New Life Safety Plan

Another useful way of getting clients to think about their future life is to ask the person to consider or draw two future life paths (Baim and Guthrie, 2014). One is an offending road and the other a non-offending road. Clients can draw two roads on flip chart paper: for instance a reoffending one ending in prison and a lonely bedsitter (symbolizing failure), and the other ending up in a warm family home or desired single accommodation (symbolizing hope and success). On the offending road a future is depicted where a client has lost his partner and contact with his children and reverted to 'Old Me' ways of behaving. On the non-offending road, a pro-social identity and lifestyle is illustrated, featuring 'New Me'.

I ask the client to imagine that I have a magic telescope and I am able to observe every aspect of the client's life five years from now, including the client's thought processes. I then ask him to consider the Signs of Safety I would observe in his life, asking some of the following:

- What would he be doing?
- How would he be thinking and functioning?
- How would others around him be experiencing him?
- How would he know that others felt safe and happy around him?
- What situations and sorts of people would not be in his life?
- What situations and sorts of people would be in his life?
- How would he be managing any risky thoughts or fantasies?

I then ask the client to imagine himself being on the verge of sexual offending. In this scenario, what Signs of Risk would I be likely to observe? If it helps, the client can be asked to prioritize Signs of Risk. Following is an example:

Immediate danger

- Being sexually aroused and alone with a vulnerable child
- Forming an increasingly close relationship with a vulnerable child
- Reverting to looking at online pornography

- Stopping medication
- Reverting to substance misuse
- Loss of relationship with partner

Potential danger

- Being alone with a potential victim, even though you have no intention to offend
- Perpetrating domestic abuse
- Keeping a secret from partner
- Feeling depressed
- Losing job
- Feeling disempowered or humiliated

Stop-and-think situations

- A potential victim coming into your life, even though you may have little contact with this person and have no current motivation to offend
- Becoming increasingly critical
- Becoming increasingly irritable
- Stopping exercising and doing the things you know are good for you

I finally ask the client to consider what I would be seeing through my telescope if he were putting into place appropriate responses to Signs of Risk. Some typical responses (which do not appear in Sandy's New Life Safety Plan) would be:

- Take self away from the situation
- Engage in pleasurable diverting activity
- Employ positive self-talk
- Look at New Life Safety Plan
- Talk to partner or significant other
- Talk to own counsellor/therapist or contact StopSO UK for list of specialist counsellors and therapists (Tel: 07473 299883; email: info@stopso.org.uk)
- Ring the Lucy Faithfull Foundation Stop It Now! confidential helpline for advice (Freephone: 08081000900; email: help@stopitnow.org.uk).

Final case study: George

The final case study in this book features George, a sex offender who will always be considered high risk, because of the extent and serious-ness of his previous sexual offending. Unlike many offenders presented in this book, George has been a high-risk predatory paedophile, only sexually interested in pre-pubescent boys. He will never be allowed to live in a family setting with children of either sex. He lives an isolated life in the community, but sought counselling because his mother has recently died and he is suffering from grief and loneliness. The following fictional case study raises interesting issues. Firstly, even the most serious sex offenders have non-offending issues, like the rest of us: in George's case, grief and loneliness. Secondly, by virtue of the seriousness of some people's sexual crimes, some offenders such as George are destined to live relatively isolated lives in the community.

George lived in a small, rural community with his mother until he was given a 10-year prison sentence in his late 20s for sexual offending against a 12-year-old boy, which included forcing anal sex. He was working in a children's home at the time, where the boy was a resident. When George was released from prison, he could not go back to live with his mother, because of fears for his safety, as everybody in the village knew the nature of his crime. He ended up being resettled in a rough area of a city, but kept in regular touch with his mother.

Two years after being released from prison, he sexually offended against two brothers (8 and 10), inviting them into his flat, and plying them with cigarettes and alcohol. The offending involved him getting to know the victims' family and abusing the boys over many months. He was given another long prison sentence. His mother was the only person to visit him, as she did during his first incarceration. He was released on licence but recalled when indecent images of young boys were found on his mobile phone. He had, again, been resettled into a crime-ridden area and said he had escaped into a world of fantasy to cope with his fear. When he came out of prison, for the last time, he agreed to take part in a probation service sex offender group work programme. He had refused this offer of treatment in the past. Since then, he has not reoffended. He lives in a flat in a quiet area, but has sought counselling because his mother died a month ago. He says he does not want to offend again, but says he is desperately lonely and was happier in prison where at least he had company.

Therapeutic work with George

Constructing a New Life Safety Plan with George was not going to be easy, as he had few resources. His confidence was low, given the stigma of his sexual offending. He had been in prison much of his adult life and, as a result, had little in common with non-criminals. He was also in deep grief over the death of his mother, the only person with whom he had anything like a close adult relationship. George was on the Sex Offender Register for life and, because he was considered a high risk, the police kept a relatively close eye on him, making unannounced visits to his flat every couple of months or so. Finding a job was not going to be easy, given his offending history (which he would have to declare), his poor employment record, and his underdeveloped social skills. George felt hopeless about finding employment and was consequently unmotivated to do so. He was in receipt of benefits for anxiety and depression when he came to see the counsellor.

The first phase of the counselling process took the form of contracting and goal-setting, as discussed in Chapters 2 and 3 respectively. The counsellor then did grief work with George, exploring what his mother meant to him, and providing George with space to reflect upon and express his loss, mourning the loss of his actual mother and of the ideal mother and son relationship he never had. This led to further in-depth exploration of his personal life story that did not occur on the probation group work programme he attended.

For George, the forming of a New Life Safety Plan turned out to be unnecessary. He already had a Relapse Prevention Plan from when he participated on the probation programme, which largely served the same purpose. What George required more than anything else was to be non-judgementally heard. Apart from his relationship with his mother, which turned out to be dysfunctional in many respects, he had never formed an intimate relationship with an adult. The therapeutic relationship met this developmental need, albeit in a limited way. The counsellor listened to George talking about his isolation and struggles to maintain an offence-free life, when the only human beings he found sexually attractive were pre-pubescent boys and relationships were unavailable to him if he did not want to return to prison. The difficulty was that sometimes prison seemed to him like the preferred option, as at least in prison he was part of a community.

Fortunately, as the result of his participation on the group work programme, George's consciousness had been raised about the harm caused by an adult having sex with a child. He was no longer able to deny and minimize the suffering caused to victims. This left him conflicted as his sexual and emotional attraction to boys remained. George was well aware of the cognitive and behavioural management techniques to employ in order to prevent him reoffending. These had been instilled into him.

However, sustaining long-term motivation to avoid offending was connected to George feeling a valued part of a larger moral community, beyond himself. Regular, long-term boundaried interaction with another human being (i.e. the counsellor) offered a partial reintegration back into the human family, with therapy offering an existential and transpersonal process through which George could explore what it is to live a meaningful, moral life beyond sexual gratification and drive management.

Conclusion

We leave off where we began. Therapy, including counselling males at risk of sexual offending, is not a science that can be neatly packaged. A New Life Safety Plan or a similar risk management plan called by another name is, on one level, just words on a page. It is the elements that inform the plan which are the keys: the client's motivation and capacity for change; the quality of the therapeutic relationship; whether or not there has been a significant shift towards a pro-social identity; and positive perspective on the world.

I hope that the ideas in this book have encouraged and contributed to the equipping of counsellors and other practitioners, if they feel called to work with this highly stigmatized client group: not only for the benefit of the clients themselves but also to hopefully reduce the number of potential victims harmed by sexual crime.

References

Austin, J.T. and Vancouver, J.B. (1996) 'Goal constructs in psychology: Structure, process and content', *Psychological Bulletin*, 120 (3): pp. 338–375.

Baim, C. and Guthrie, L. (2014) *Changing offending behaviour: A handbook of practical exercises and photocopiable resources for promoting positive change*. London: Jessica Kingsley Publishers.

Flora, R. and Keohane, M.L. (2013) *How to work with sex offenders: A handbook for criminal justice, human service and mental health professionals*, 2nd edition. New York and London: Routledge.

James, W. (1985) *The varieties of religious experience: A study in human nature*, new edition. Harmondsworth: Penguin Classics. First published in 1902.

Laws, D.R. (1999) 'Relapse prevention: The state of the art', *Journal of Interpersonal Violence*, 14 (3): pp. 285–302.

Marlatt, G.A. and Gordon, J.R. (1980) 'Determinants for relapse: Implications for the maintenance of behavior change', in P.O. Davidson and S.M. Davidson (eds.) *Behavioral medicine: Changing health lifestyles*. New York: Brunner/Mazel, pp. 410–445.

Maslow, A.H. (1943) 'A theory of motivation', *Psychological Review*, 50 (4): pp. 370–396.

Ward, T. and Brown, M. (2004) 'The good lives model and conceptual issues in offender rehabilitation', *Psychology, Crime and Law*, 10 (3): pp. 243–257.

Ward, T. and Marshall, W.L. (2004) 'Good lives, aetiology and the rehabilitation of sex offenders: A bridging theory', *Journal of Sexual Aggression*, 10: pp. 153–169.

Ward, T. and Maruna, S. (2007) *Rehabilitation: Beyond the risk paradigm*. London and New York: Routledge.

Ward, T. and Stewart, C.A. (2003a) 'The treatment of sex offenders: Risk management and good lives', *Professional Psychology: Research and Practice*, 34 (4): pp. 353–360.

Ward, T. and Stewart, C. (2003b) 'Good lives and the rehabilitation of sex offenders', in T. Ward, R. Laws and S.M. Hudson (eds.) *Sexual deviance: Issues and controversies*. London: Sage, pp. 21–44.

Appendix I

Counselling contract

1   My aim, as your counsellor, is to be compassionate, respectful, and genuine, endeavouring to create the therapeutic conditions for you to achieve your goals.

2   If you require, I will confirm to a third party that you have attended counselling, stating duration and what themes have been explored. However, I cannot make any comments regarding risk issues.

3   Minimal notes will be taken to help me remember significant details and for us to reflect on progress. I will keep a copy of these notes in a locked cabinet.

4   No individual or professional body will have access to these notes, unless there is a court order subpoenaing the information in the event of a court case or official investigation.

5   It is regulatory practice that I undertake regular confidential supervision with an accredited supervisor. I may discuss aspects of your case, along with others, without reference to identifying details.

6   As a member of BACP (British Association for Counselling and Psychotherapy), I adhere to their Ethical Framework for Good Practice and am aware of my primary responsibility for maintaining confidentiality between myself and the client. However, this general rule of confidentiality can be broken in the following exceptional circumstances:

    a   If you disclose information about a criminal offence or conduct that puts others or yourself at serious risk of harm. An attempt would be made to talk to you before disclosure if this does not further compromise anybody's personal safety.

    b   If you are involved with social services, probation, the police or mental health professionals, I may ask your permission to liaise with them.

7   Before the start of the first session, two copies of this agreement need to be signed, to stipulate that this policy has been read and understood. Both parties will keep a copy.

Counsellor .... Date ....

Client .... Date ....

Sample letter

To whom it concerns:

This is to confirm that X has sought counselling from me in order to address internet offending issues. So far we have had eight 1-hour sessions, but plan to have further sessions in the future, the ninth session taking place on Monday 6th July 2015. No final number of sessions has been agreed. This will be negotiated as the counselling progresses.

However, the following issues are being addressed through the therapeutic engagement:

- Historical and personality factors which may have been contributing factors to the offending in question
- Relationship issues which may have contributed to the offending
- The relationship between compulsive use of pornography and accessing illegal sexual material on the internet
- Facts and myths about child pornography and the internet
- The vulnerability of and harmful consequences to children and young people who are sexually exploited and abused, including via the internet
- The cognitive and behavioural processes that can lead to people sexually offending
- Future risk management issues
- How to meet legitimate human needs and desires in pro-social rather than anti-social ways

X has engaged well in the sessions so far, and has showed understanding of the above matters. However, as a private counsellor I do not comment on risk issues. In line with the counselling contract I have with the client, how X's counselling impacts on risk issues will have to be independently assessed by a professional qualified to make such an assessment.

Yours faithfully

Appendix 3

Risk factor check list

(factors in bold should be especially considered)

- **Client has court appearances for sexual offences.**
- **Client has been accused of sexual offending more than once.**
- **Client has sexually offended against unrelated victim (did not know the victim 24 hours before the offence).**
- **Client has committed contact sexual offence against a pre-pubescent male.**
- Client has an exclusive sexual preference for children.
- Client has a pattern of meeting social, emotional, and esteem needs predominantly through children rather than adults.
- Client is currently abnormally sexually preoccupied.
- Client has a strong sense of sexual entitlement.
- Client has a history of violence (including domestic abuse).
- Client believes that children enjoy sex and are sexually seductive.
- Client has a current pattern of grievance thinking.
- Client has a pattern of callousness.
- Client has a current pattern of lifestyle impulsiveness.
- Client has a history of chaotic/shallow attachments.
- Client has dropped out of a prison or probation group work programme.
- Client has poor cognitive problem solving.
- Client has current substance misuse problems.
- **Client is in contact with children of the same age and sex that he has shown deviant interest in.**
- **Client is an intimidating presence in the home where the child at risk resides.**
- **The child's at risk parent/s does not recognize the risk posed by the client.**

Guidelines: disclosing

- Decision was made on basis of confidentiality policy (better if written and signed)
- Client revealed criminal behaviour, or breaking child protection agreements
- Client began to have more intimate contact with children similar to the ages and sex he was aroused to
- Risk suddenly increased (see risk factors)
- Disclosure was discussed with supervisor
- Disclosure was discussed with client, and you tried to get him to report abuse himself, first (consider consequences of this in terms of risk of harm to self)

Guidelines: not disclosing

- Decision was made on basis of confidentiality policy (better if written and signed)
- Client did not reveal criminal behaviour, or breaking child protection agreements
- No indications emerged that client began to have more intimate contact with children similar to the ages and sex he was aroused to
- No evidence of increased risk (see risk factors)
- Decision not to disclose was discussed with supervisor

Indications of reduced risk

- The longer there is an absence of sexual reoffending or allegations of sexual abuse, the less child protection professionals will worry about the risk of reoffending.
- Whilst you do not have to admit to sexual offending or say you pose a risk, genuinely acknowledge that others have legitimate concerns which need to be addressed, is necessary.
- Rather than being preoccupied on why life is not as you would want it, focus on everything you can do to change the situation.
- Understand the factors (including your life history) which resulted in your current situation.
- Understand the thoughts, behaviour, and situations to avoid in order to make future sexual offending and allegations less likely.
- Understand the impact and consequences of sexual offending on victims and loved ones.
- Establish a satisfying, safe life, where you don't have to resort to destructive behaviour to meet needs and desires.
- If you remain in a relationship with a partner, develop a relationship in which you are open and transparent and accountable about your behaviour.
- If social services require your partner to monitor your risk, with regard to children, do everything you can to make this as easy as possible for her.
- Negotiate a Safety Plan, consisting of *Signs of Safety* that you are living a constructive and safe life; *Signs of Risk* that you may be going down a pathway which could cause harm to others or yourself; and agreeing upon *Responses to Emerging Signs of Risk* which could be implemented if things started to go wrong.
- Agree that this Safety Plan can be shared with significant others, in order to freely make yourself accountable, so you can be supported in living an offence-free life.

Appendix 7

Person A completely denies risk, and sees no need to undertake protective work	Person B denies, or accepts risk to some extent, but either way recognizes the concerns of others, and is willing to undertake protective work
Does not take on the concerns of others	Is willing to focus on the concerns of others
Focuses on how allegations are false, exaggerated, or how there has been a miscarriage of justice	Decides to learn all about how different sexual abuse occurs so he can make sure he does not put himself into situations where children may be at risk or another allegation could be made against him
Thinks that by repeating that there is no risk, this is enough	Is willing to discuss how safe boundaries can be maintained in the home
	Is prepared to make himself accountable to loved ones
Makes it difficult for others, including loved ones, to talk about concerns by becoming angry, upset, or showing by tone of voice, body language and facial expression that people should not mention the subject	Makes it easy for others to monitor and challenge him, giving off messages that it is OK to do so
	Is realistic about the difficulties of being challenged and monitored by a loved one and being thought of as a possible risk to children
	Accepts that a loved one might have to report him if serious risk emerges, and encourages the loved one that this would be the right thing to do
Not being open, or only giving people scraps of information about the abuse or alleged abuse	Is willing to work with professionals and child protection agreements

Example of final New Life Safety Plan

Signs of positive and safer life

Sharing emotional life with partner
Spending quality time with partner and family
Maintaining employment
Maintaining regular exercise
Seeing friends regularly
Partner knowing passwords of all internet accounts and having access to bank accounts

Signs of risk

If positive life begins to deteriorate
Being on own with children in the bedroom, bathroom, overnight, or for long periods
Play fighting and cuddling children
Forming a special relationship with a child/young person
Having secrets with a child/young person
Using the internet for sexual purposes
Drinking heavily
Feeling you want to get people back
Feeling hopeless
Becoming more resentful and angry
Cutting off from people

Responses to signs of risk

Look at this Plan when you get up in the morning and before going to bed.

If you have negative feelings associated with anxiety, boredom, or depression, or want to avoid talking about difficult issues, or are tempted to use the internet for sexual purposes or are tempted to have inappropriate contact with a child or young person, try the following:

- Do something practical: take a shower; do some exercise; go out for a walk; put some music on that puts you in a happy mood; phone somebody who's going to make you feel better about yourself; keep a photograph of your family on you to look at when you are tempted to make choices or behave in ways which could compromise your and your family's happiness in the future/

- Take five deep breaths, drawing in for five seconds and then exhaling for five seconds. Then imagine the negative thoughts and feelings are like twigs floating down a river. Don't try to resist them; just tell yourself they are no big deal and they will eventually float away downstream, out of sight. If you just observe them going by and keep on breathing deeply they will eventually fade and disappear.
- If you spend 10 minutes a day on your own meditating in this way, you will be training your brain to have more control over regulating your emotions, giving you more conscious choice over your reactions and behaviour, and leading to a greater sense of wellbeing as your neurobiological system calms down over a period of time. This is a learnt skill, just like practising to become good at sport or playing an instrument.
- Spend more quality time with your partner and family.
- Rather than avoiding difficult issues with your partner, go against your temperamental type and take initiative in talking though matters with her, tuning into your own feelings and to hers, and resisting the urge to cut the conversation short or move the subject onto a more superficial level.
- Remember OK and NOT OK sexual fantasies which correspond to the person you want to be. If the NOT OK fantasies come into your mind, try to re-focus on the OK fantasies, especially when you climax.

Most of us have a constant inner dialogue going on in our heads consisting of an unfriendly voice which is critical and accusatory, undermining our confidence and self-esteem. We can calm this voice by the breathing/meditation exercises suggested earlier. However, we also have a friendly voice, which we can encourage through positive self-talk.

Self-talk

Critical voice	Friendly voice
You have betrayed your partner's trust.	This crisis has resulted in an opportunity you to develop and enrich your life and your life with your partner and family.
Hurt yourself as punishment for what you did.	You're a good person and you try to help people.
At the end of the day it's not worth dwelling on stuff, just move on.	Facing issues will benefit you and your family in the long run.

New Life Safety Plan

Signs of a positive and safer life

Signs of risk

Responses to signs of risk

Circumstances	Feelings	Thoughts	Behaviour (grooming)
In circumstances where anything goes/ loose sexual boundaries	Feeling angry Feeling resentful Feeling aggrieved Feeling lonely Feeling depressed	S/he's leading me on Children can enjoy sex with adults	Gaining carer's trust to gain access to child Making the carer dependent, fearful
Unsatisfactory relationship, life circumstances or event	Feeling nothing Feeling everything is futile	Kids are up for it these days It won't do any harm	or responsible Make sure that the sex is good with partner, so she'll
Access to victim (including via the internet)	Feeling humiliation Feeling more comfortable	Only this once We have a special relationship nobody else	never suspect Talk about how disgusting sex offenders are
In a position of power over victim	with children Feeling sexual desire	understands It happened to me at this age,	Choose victim in most need of attention or less
Victim is vulnerable	Feeling, or wanting to feel,	and it didn't cause me any	likely to tell Make victim feel
Victim is unlikely to tell	emotionally close to victim	harm I won't get caught	special Make jokes and
Drinking and drugs masking conscience	Feeling the child victim is a peer Feeling the	Nobody will believe her/him if they tell	talk about sex to children Use cuddling and
On own with victim	excitement of the forbidden	Everyone will believe me	play-fighting to touch the child
	Feeling in control Feeling powerful Feeling sadistic pleasure in causing pain	I'm too clever, I'll never get caught My life is horrible, why should I care? You only live once	sexually Give the child cigarettes, alcohol or drugs, show pornography Committing the act or acts of sexual abuse Use guilt or fear to keep victim quiet

Appendix 11

What is sexual abuse?

- Sexual contact between an adult and a child under the age of 16 (18 via the internet)
- Unwanted sexual contact between one adult and another
- Unwanted sexual contact between an older or more powerful person and another
- Sexual abuse can take the form of: general touching in a sexual way, touching sexual parts, oral sex, vaginal sex, anal sex, talking in a sexual way, using sexual innuendo, exposing oneself, performing sexual acts in front of others, viewing sexual material in front of others, and viewing indecent images of children

Who commits sexual abuse and where does it typically occur?

- Most sexual abuse is committed by men, often fathers, stepfathers, or men who are known to the children.
- Adolescents also commit high levels of sexual abuse.
- Teenage girls, under the age of 16, are the most common victims of sexual abuse, although male and female children suffer much sexual abuse that is never reported.
- Contrary to popular fear, it is relatively rare for children to be abused by people in the street whom they don't know.
- Most sexual abuse occurs in the home. Sexual abuse commonly occurs around the following activities:

Bath time
Bedtime
Baby-sitting
Applying medicinal creams
Physical play with children
Adults being drunk and/or on drugs
Lack of sexual boundaries in the home

Why does so much sexual abuse go unreported?

- Victim was groomed to think abuse was not serious or wrong
- Didn't want parents to find out
- Didn't want friends to find out
- Didn't want authorities to find out
- Was frightened
- Didn't think s/he would be believed
- Had been threatened by the abuser
- Often there is no physical evidence
- Child and traumatized witnesses unreliable
- Details of historical abuse difficult to remember
- Adversarial system is good at undermining victims
- Victims can love their abusers (not just trauma ties) but hate the abuse

Reasons why people deny sexual abuse

The person is deeply ashamed and embarrassed about the offence.

He has too much to lose by publicly admitting guilt (e.g. job, money, status, family, friends, the opportunity to continue offending).

There may be great pressure from family members to conceal the offending for fear of the effect on them.

He may not trust the professionals with whom he is engaged, with regard to these offences.

Reasons to admit to sexual abuse

To prevent the victim suffering further through doubt being thrown on the validity of the abuse.

Admitting the abuse and apologizing can help the healing process for the victim and the family.

To enable professionals to help you understand and manage the thoughts and feelings which triggered the abuse, making it less likely that further abuse will occur.

To enable empathy with the victim's suffering. Getting in touch with the suffering caused and consequences for others of abusive actions can act as a deterrent to future abuse. If an individual is prepared to go through the pain of fully recognizing the suffering he has caused this can result in genuine remorse, and an increased determination not to cause such suffering again.

Impact of sexual abuse

> *Each individual's experience of sexual abuse is different. However, the following factors tend to be aggravating features.*

The more frightened the victim was by the abuse

If the victim felt/feels unprotected from further abuse, and is living in a state of fear

If the abuse was carried out by a trusted family member the victim relied upon for security (e.g. a parent figure)

If the abuse was particularly invasive (e.g. oral sex, intercourse)

If the victim was not believed by family members, and blamed for causing trouble

If the victim was made to feel responsible for the abuse

If the victim was particularly vulnerable, with existing emotional and welfare problems

Longer-term possible consequences of sexual abuse

Not being believed and being labelled as a troublemaker
Rejected, scapegoated by family because of reporting abuse
Guilt because of reporting abuse
Falsely believing there must be something wrong with them for attract-
    ing the abuse
Low self-esteem
Trust issues
Feeling different from others
Mental health/psychological problems
Drug/alcohol problems
Low educational and occupational achievement
Relationship problems
Promiscuity
Difficulty in forming sexual relationships
Caught in cycle of abusive relationships
Social isolation
Problems with authority figures

Appendix 17

Fantasy Management Diary

Date and time	Details of OK or not OK period of fantasy and/or masturbation	Coping technique employed or could have been employed

Fantasy management techniques

- Taking a shower
- Taking physical exercise
- Listening to calming music
- Positive self-talk
- Phoning a person
- Looking at an image of a loved one
- Looking at a list of the consequences of relapsing (the list to be kept on the person, e.g. on a smart phone)
- Using accountability as a deterrent to relapsing. (It is important for the client to take proactive responsibility in making himself accountable, avoiding, in transactional analysis terms, a counterproductive parent–child dynamic with a therapist or partner with whom the client has this accountable relationship.)
- If having 'not OK' fantasies, de-objectifying the individuals in the fantasies by thinking of them as complex human beings, somebody's child or parent, a precious, fragile human being who is loved by others, with fears and hopes, experiencing joy and sadness
- Thinking of 'OK' pleasurable sexual fantasies when masturbating
- If relapsing by thinking of 'not OK' sexual fantasies when masturbating, reverting to 'OK' sexual fantasies just before climax (a particularly addictive point)
- Feeling compassion for self and others (including the fantasy figures)

Index